Jews *of* South Florida

SOUTH FLORIDA

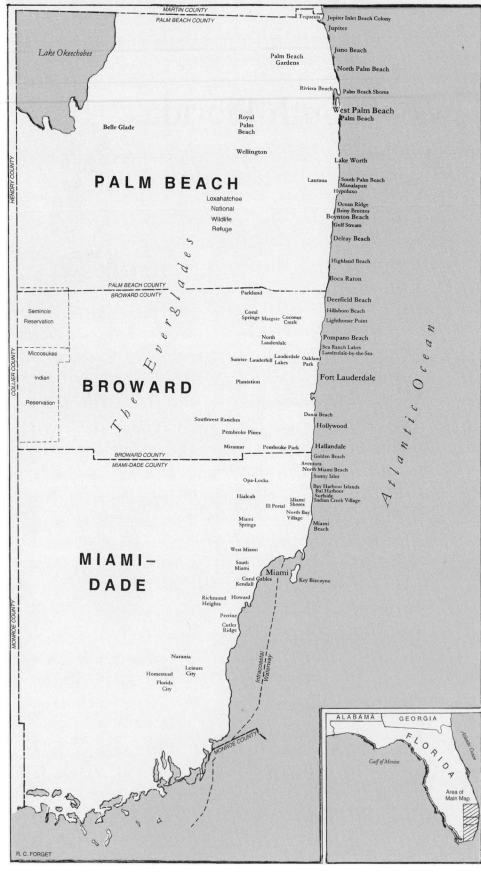

MARTIN COUNTY
PALM BEACH COUNTY

Tequesta
Jupiter Inlet Beach Colony
Jupiter

Lake Okeechobee

Juno Beach

Palm Beach
Gardens

North Palm Beach

Riviera Beach
Palm Beach Shores

West Palm Beach
Palm Beach

Royal
Palm
Beach

Belle Glade

Wellington

Lake Worth

Lantana

South Palm Beach
Manalapan
Hypoluxo

PALM BEACH

Loxahatchee

National

Wildlife

Refuge

Ocean Ridge
Briny Breezes
Boynton Beach
Gulf Stream

Delray Beach

Highland Beach

Boca Raton

PALM BEACH COUNTY
BROWARD COUNTY

Parkland

Deerfield Beach

Seminole
Reservation

Coral
Springs Margate Coconut
Creek

Hillsboro Beach

Lighthouse Point

North
Lauderdale

Pompano Beach
Sea Ranch Lakes
Lauderdale-by-the-Sea

Miccosukee

Sunrise Lauderhill Lauderdale Oakland
Lakes Park

Indian

BROWARD

Plantation

Fort Lauderdale

Reservation

The Everglades

Southwest Ranches

Dania Beach

Hollywood

Pembroke Pines

Miramar Pembroke Park

Hallandale

Golden Beach

BROWARD COUNTY
MIAMI-DADE COUNTY

Aventura
North Miami Beach
Sunny Isles

Opa-Locka

Bay Harbour Islands
Bal Harbour
Surfside
Indian Creek Village

Hialeah

El Portal

Miami
Shores

Miami
Springs

North Bay
Village

Miami
Beach

West Miami

MIAMI-
DADE

South
Miami

Miami

Coral Gables
Kendall

Key Biscayne

Richmond
Heights Howard

Perrine

Cutler
Ridge

Atlantic Ocean

Narania

Leisure
City

Homestead

Florida
City

Intracoastal Waterway

MONROE COUNTY

R. C. FORGET

ALABAMA GEORGIA

F L O R I D A

Gulf of Mexico

Atlantic Ocean

Area of
Main Map

Jews *of* South Florida

ANDREA GREENBAUM EDITOR

BRANDEIS UNIVERSITY PRESS

Waltham, Massachusetts

Published by University Press of New England

Hanover and London

Brandeis University Press
Published by University Press of New England,
One Court Street, Lebanon, NH 03766
www.upne.com
© 2005 by Brandeis University Press
Printed in the United States of America

5 4 3 2 1

Library of Congress Cataloging-in-Publication Data
Jews of south Florida / Andrea Greenbaum, editor.
     p.   cm.—(Brandeis series in American
Jewish history, culture, and life)
Includes bibliographical references and index.
ISBN 1–58465–309–4 (cloth : alk. paper)
  1. Jews—Florida—History. 2. Jews—Florida—
Social life and customs. 3. Jews—Florida—
Politics and government. 4. Florida—Ethnic
relations. I. Greenbaum, Andrea. II. Series.
F320.J5J49 2005
975.9'004924—dc22   2004028283

Seth Farber, 2003
An American Orthodox Dreamer: Rabbi Joseph B. Soloveitchik and Boston's Maimonides School

Amy L. Sales and Leonard Saxe, 2003
"How Goodly Are Thy Tents": Summer Camps as Jewish Socializing Experiences

Sylvia Barack Fishman, 2004
Double or Nothing: Jewish Families and Mixed Marriage

George M. Goodwin and Ellen Smith, editors, 2004
The Jews of Rhode Island

Shulamit Reinharz and Mark A. Raider, editors, 2004
American Jewish Women and the Zionist Enterprise

Michael E. Staub, editor, 2004
The Jewish '60s: An American Sourcebook

Andrea Greenbaum, editor, 2005
Jews of South Florida

To Those Who Carry Us,

Dorothy Lichtenstein and Irene Bernson

Evelyn and Abraham Cohen

CONTENTS

ACKNOWLEDGMENTS

An edited collection is always a collaborative endeavor, and while I've edited collections before, I have never experienced the sense of community involvement that I have with this publication. I am indebted to all the contributors, who placed their faith and passion in this project, and who lent their considerable skills as scholars, journalists, collectors, and artists.

I am deeply grateful to the Southern Jewish Historical Society for their generous grant, and Barry University's Mini-Grant Committee for financially supporting this project. I also express gratitude to the American Jewish Historical Society for allowing its article to be reprinted in this publication.

This book would have been much more difficult to assemble without the tireless effort of Marcia Kerstein Zerivitz, executive director of the Jewish Museum of Florida. Marcia not only contributed to the scholarship of this book, but also lent research assistance in the massive task of compiling the photographs for this collection. I am grateful to her associate, Matt Martinson, registrar at the Jewish Museum, who always returned my phone calls, and whose work enabled me to complete this project. Many thanks, as well, to Professor Steve Rubin, who referred me to the publisher, and to Phyllis Deutsch at the University Press of New England, who gave me the opportunity to pursue this project. I also acknowledge Rabbi Nightingale from Hollywood's Aish Ha'Torah—a very patient man. I am indebted to Evelyn Cohen, who reviewed this manuscript in its various stages, helped with the mechanics of editing, and offered insight into the culture of South Florida Jewry.

In the course of this publication, my dear colleague, friend, and fellow contributor, Professor Jack Moore, passed away. Jack was my mentor, an honorable man and an impressive scholar, who lived his life as a mensch and taught others to do the same. I miss him, but I am pleased that his writing lives on in this book.

I am blessed by my wonderfully supportive family: Ari, who I know will grow up to be a great man, as he is already a great kid; Yarden, whose wit and intellect far exceeds her eleven years; and Ellie, my fortieth birthday present. Finally, to Neil, the funniest person I know.

May peace dwell in Jerusalem.

INTRODUCTION

One need only watch late-night television to know that South Florida has become the new California: admiringly quirky, hedonistic, paradoxical (chic, club-hopping youth culture intermingled with retired, golf-playing elderly) — and dangerous. A sun-drenched paradise where, the talk-show hosts joked, voters were so dazzled by the heat and sun that they were simply too weak to punch the voter ballots all the way through. Rarely has a state acquired such humorous renown, but that's to be expected when you're accused of screwing up a national election. While South Florida's ethos of paradise (figure 1) still prevails, it is also where the terrorists of September 11 hung their hats while they perfected their flying lessons. It is where anti-Semitism persisted well into the second half of the twentieth century, and where anti-Israel protestors staged a loud rally outside the Holocaust Memorial on Yom Ha'shoah in 2001, unintentionally punctuating the point of Zionism. If the Devil lives in California, he most certainly vacations on Miami Beach.

Several features distinguish South Florida Jews from other Jewish communities in the United States. Many South Florida Jews are migrants to the region. The Jewish community of South Florida comprises tens of thousands of retirees, mainly from the Atlantic seaboard, but also from other cold climates throughout the United States. These "snowbirds" are often part-time residents, live in "gated communities" like Century Village located in Boca Raton and Pembroke Pines, and maintain strong ties with the communities they left behind. Their roots in, and allegiance to, a Jewish South Florida culture may be compromised by these conditions. But as Joel Saxe's essay on South Beach Jews shows, these snowbirds once brought their own special brand of *Yiddishkeit* to the warm shores of the Atlantic.

South Florida is also home to nearly eighteen thousand Holocaust survivors and their children, who reside in Broward, South Palm Beach, Miami-Dade and West Palm (figure 2). My own encounter with the Holocaust survivor population began several years ago when I started research on this book and spoke with several survivors who volunteered their time at the Miami Holocaust Memorial. Their memories and sensibilities are another component of Jewish South Florida.

In addition, South Florida Judaism has a distinctive Latin flavor. Beginning with the post-Castro migration of Cubans, Hispanic Jews have moved to South Florida from Colombia, Peru, Puerto Rico, and Argentina. These Jews brought with them a distinct culture that often separated them from the (mainly) Ashkenazim (Jews from Eastern Europe) who had settled in South Florida. Writing in this volume about the bicultural identity of Cuban Jews, Stephen Benz reveals that while Jewish organizations often used their resources in support of Soviet Jewry, they neglected Cuban Jews. According to Benz, there was likely some "anti-Latin sentiment" among the Ashkenazim to Jews not just from Cuba, but from countries such as

FIGURE 2. *Holocaust survivor. Like many Holocaust survivors in South Florida, who speak openly about their experience, Gerhard Maschkowsky shows his tattooed number on his arm. Photograph by Miami News Staff member Michael O'Brien. Courtesy of Historical Museum of Southern Florida.*

Morocco, Turkey, Greece, Spain, Algeria, Iran, and Iraq. Contributor Annette B. Fromm offers a comprehensive history of Sephardic Jews (Jews originally from the Iberian Peninsula) in South Florida. Both Sephardic and Cuban Jews created an array of religious and cultural organizations, and have carved unique Jewish identities for themselves in South Florida.

More recent Jewish immigrants from Arab nations, the Soviet Union, and Israel have added to the diversity of Jews and Jewish life. Hence, historical, geographical, and political developments have created a special environment for South Florida Jews, and provided challenges as well. How does a disparate Jewish community, with a strong component of older part-time retirees and a large number of relatively recent Spanish-speaking immigrants, create a viable and recognizable Jewish community in a sun-drenched setting that can convey the transience of a vacation, a summer thunderstorm, or a rerun of *Miami Vice*? Although the essays in this volume showcase difference and variety, taken together they demonstrate how the efforts and contributions of very diverse groups of Jews have made South Florida a distinctive Jewish place.

Jews have lived in South Florida since the end of the nineteenth century, but their numbers grew exponentially after World War II. At present, South Florida, which comprises Miami-Dade, Broward, and Palm Beach Counties, is home to ten percent of American Jews (see geographer Ira Sheskin's essay in this volume). It houses the third largest Jewish concentration in the United States, following New York and southern California. Following World War II and until the 1980s, the vast majority of these Jews lived in Miami-Dade County. In recent decades, however, Jews (particularly those who migrated to South Florida for retirement) have moved up the southeast coast to Broward and Palm Beach Counties. Sheskin says that in the 1980s, Broward County was the fastest growing Jewish community in the country. This distinction shifted to Palm Beach County in the 1990s. At present, almost twice as many Jews live in Broward and Palm Beach Counties as in Miami-Dade. Sheskin counts 113,000 Jews in Miami-Dade County; 234,000 in Broward County; and 218,000 in Palm Beach County.

As Marcia Kerstein Zerivitz's historical essay shows, the growth of a Jewish community in South Florida is closely tied to the overall development of the state. Until the nineteenth century, settlements in Florida were largely confined to the northern and central regions, with the exception of Key West (which was a commercial port for the Caribbean). Heat, swamp, mosquitoes, and hostile natives kept most white settlers well north of Lake Okeechobee. Nonetheless, Sephardic Jew Moses Elias Levy (perhaps the most famous early Jewish settler) moved to Florida from Saint Thomas in the Virgin Islands, in 1819. With the fortune he had made in the lumber business, he created Pilgrimage Plantation in Micanopy (near what is today Gainesville) as a haven for persecuted Jews. Pilgrimage Plantation lasted from 1822 to 1835, when Seminoles destroyed it. Moses Levy's more lasting legacy was his son David, who played an important role in the drafting of Florida's constitution. In 1845, he was elected the first Jewish U.S. Senator from Florida, arguing for Florida statehood, which was granted that same year (Florida's Levy County honors this family). In the spirit of American assimilation, David Levy changed his name to Yulee, married a Christian, and joined a Presbyterian church. Despite David's effort to blend in, John Quincy Adams, in his diary in the 1840s, described Yulee as "the Jew delegate from Florida," the "alien Jew delegate from Florida," and "The Squeaky Jew delegate from Florida" (Jaher, *Scapegoat*, 190).

In the mid-nineteenth century and through the Civil War, a handful of Jews appeared, usually as peddlers or the owners of small retail stores, in towns in northern and central Florida such as Jacksonville, Pensacola, Orlando, Live Oak, and Sanford (figure 3). Although Jews were by this time a strong presence in southern cities such as Atlanta and Charleston, Jewish communities in Florida remained very small. As Zerivitz notes, the first Jewish cemetery in Florida was not built until 1857 (in Jacksonville); Florida's first synagogue was not constructed until 1876 (in Pensacola). By the turn of the century, settlement throughout Florida was accelerated with the completion of Henry M. Flagler's railroad, which connected Jacksonville with points farther south. The railroad reached Miami in April 1896. Three months later the city of Miami was incorporated.

From the early 1880s until World War I, the Jewish population in the United States grew from 250,000 to one million, due largely to the immigration of tens of thousands of Jews from eastern Europe. In reaction to this influx of Jews, anti-Semitism grew nationwide. Henry Abramson's essay describes manifestations of anti-Semitism in Florida. Railroad magnate and real estate developer Henry M.

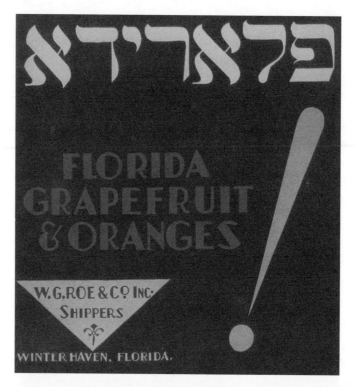

Flagler attached restricted covenants to his land sales, as did Miami Beach entrepreneur Carl Fisher. Yet, with Flagler's railroad branching south to Palm Beach and Miami, South Florida became increasingly attractive to settlers (figure 4). By the 1920s, Miami boasted a small, but discernable Jewish presence.

During the 1920s, improved transportation and an elaborate and overly optimistic advertising campaign aimed at land developers and tourists inspired a surge of northerners (including people from northern Florida) to move down the coast. A massive landgrab ensued, halted only by the twofold punch of a major hurricane (1926) and the Great Depression. But the tropical climate and hundreds of thousands of acres of undeveloped land still beckoned, and by the mid-1930s, Miami was recovering.

World War II changed the face of Miami-Dade County. The growth of the entire South Florida population blossomed after World War II, in large part because the Army Air Forces Technical Training Command decided to station its forces on Miami Beach. According to Deborah Dash Moore, the army gradually "took over 85 percent of the Miami Beach hotels. Twenty-five percent of the Air Force officer candidates and 20 percent of the enlisted men trained at Miami Beach" (Dash Moore, *To the Golden Cities*, 25). Having experienced the climate of Miami Beach, many soldiers, both Gentile and Jewish, got "sand in their shoes," and returned to Florida after the war. With the advent of air-conditioning and mosquito control, Miami became a desirable location. As this land of milk and honey (and roadside citrus and year-round swimming) opened up, Jews, looking for economic opportunities moved in large numbers to South Florida (figures 5 and 6). By 1950, there were fifty-five thousand Jews in Miami-Dade County.

Jewish life on Miami Beach was particularly vital in the postwar period, with numerous Jewish hoteliers buying and running hotels south of 5th street, an area

FIGURE 5. *Florida East Coast Railway. Shot by the company photographer of the Florida East Coast Railway, Henry M. Wolfe, in the winter of 1935–36. Many Jews first entered the state through that station. Photograph by Harry M. Wolfe, Collection of Myrna and Seth Bramson.*

FIGURE 6. *"Swim All Winter."*
Advertising the joys of South
Florida living, circa 1921. Courtesy
Jewish Museum of Florida.

free from anti-Jewish restrictive covenants. Hotels catered to Jewish snowbirds, offered kosher meals, and brought in entertainment that appealed to their clientele. As land was transferred from hand to hand, it was difficult to prohibit Jews buying real estate north of 5th street, and gradually Jewish settlement spread north to Lincoln Road and beyond. Jewish-owned hotels and small apartments became, by the 1960s, home for hundreds of thousands of Jewish retirees, including thousands of Holocaust survivors. As early as 1960, 80 percent of Miami Beach's population was Jewish.

Essayist Stephen J. Whitfield notes that as Miami Beach became a mecca for retirees, it also became famous for housing the parents of literary celebrities like Judy Blume, Herman Wouk, J. D. Salinger, Norman Mailer, Bernard Malamud, Sidney Sheldon, Chaim Potok, and Harold Robbins. Celebrities like Sophie Tucker and Jackie Gleason performed in nightclubs and hotels, and the streets of Miami Beach were filled with kosher butchers, synagogues, and delis. Literary luminary Isaac Bashevis Singer lived on Miami Beach. Of his neighbors, many of whom were Holocaust survivors, he wrote: "It was remarkable: Jewishness had survived every atrocity of Hitler and his Nazis against the Jews. Here the sound of the Old World was as alive as ever. What I learned is that many peoples from the shtetlach, which I knew so well, came here, and some of them continued their love affair" (Nagler, *My Love Affair with Miami Beach*, vii). Contributor Joel Saxe conveys the vitality of this Yiddish-rich culture in his prose, and photographer Gary Monroe captures it in his photographs in this volume.

Meyer Lansky was another aging Jew who chose Miami Beach as his final home. Lansky, fictionalized in the media, was perhaps less notorious than his reputation. But, as Jack Moore's biographic essay makes clear, Lansky chose South Florida as his center for overseeing the mob's gambling operations in Havana and Miami from the 1940s through the 1960s. A devout Zionist, he attempted to make aliyah to Israel in the 1970s, but was rejected by the Israeli government. Lansky spent his last years on Miami Beach, doing what all old Jews did: schmoozing, playing gin rummy, and eating at Wolfie's.

Lansky's death on January 15, 1983, is in some ways symbolic: it marked the beginning of the end for an entire generation of elderly Jews who had made Miami Beach their home. By the late 1980s, many of these old Jews had died. Miami Beach gentrified and its population became richer, younger, and more Hispanic. Contributor Gary Monroe provides dramatic photographic evidence of a Jewish culture, he argues, that faced diaspora twice: first from the European shtetls and then from the transformation of South Beach. Zev Beitchman's photographs commemorate a similar decline with synagogues as they appeared in the 1970s and 1980s and as they are today—lofts, dance clubs, and restaurants.

As Jews in Miami-Dade County assumed critical mass, they entered more fully in dialogue with non-Jewish neighbors. Following the 1958 bombing of Temple Beth El, one of Miami's oldest synagogues, Miami Jews began forming alliances with black organizations, specifically the National Association for the Advancement of Colored People (NAACP), in a joint effort to prevent racism and improve civil rights. Nonetheless, Raymond Mohl suggests, "Jews in South Florida were often divided about how far and how fast to push on civil rights and whether they should push at all" ("South of the South," 9).

Despite the bold efforts of individuals like Rabbi Leon Kronish, who inaugurated a civil rights program as part of Miami Beach congregation Beth Sholom's mission, Jewish work with black organizations remained lukewarm in this period owing to Jewish fear of anti-Semitic repercussions. In the early 1960s, McCarthyism spread to Florida (long after it had dissipated from the national scene), and both the state and Miami-Dade County legislatures "established witch-hunting anti-communist investigations that slowed civil rights and progressive reform generally. These investigations targeted particularly Miami's small left-wing Jewish community and the Miami NAACP" (Mohl, "South of the South," 10). Further, "Jewish observers attending Klan rallies noted that really large rounds of applause came when speakers lambasted the Jews. Jews were seen as the brains—and the money—behind black attacks on segregation" (Deborah Dash Moore, *Golden Cities*, 177). Although Miami's early civil rights movement involved an alliance between Jews and the NAACP, Jewish support was often contingent on fears of igniting racist actions directed against the Jewish community.

Jews also set about firming up their own foothold as South Florida citizens by establishing religious and cultural institutions and professional organizations catering to Jewish needs. Rabbi Leon Kronish, whose contributions to South Florida Jewish life are chronicled here by Henry A. Green, was a prominent figure in the region from the 1940s to the 1980s. From his post as rabbi of Temple Beth Sholom on Miami Beach, one of the largest Jewish congregations in the southeastern United States, Rabbi Kronish promoted a liberal variant of Reform Judaism that embraced the social challenges of the day. A strong advocate of civil rights, the peace and disarmament movements, and close ties to Israel, Rabbi Kronish's vision of a socially responsible Judaism affected Jewish worship and practice in South Florida and beyond.

Once permanent Jewish residences were established in South Florida in the 1940s, Jews began to develop specifically Jewish educational centers for children, adolescents, and adults, Setting her work in national developments over the past half century, Susan Neimand's essay offers an overview of the creation of South Florida Jewish day schools, synagogue schools, and other institutions catering to Jewish learning. Similarly, Joanie Glickstein chronicles the hundred-year history of the Greater Miami Chapter of the National Council of Jewish Women, the oldest Jewish women's volunteer organization in the United States. Founded in 1918 by twelve women, the GMC adopted the mission of the parent organization: to serve social justice and "tikkum olam" (repairing the world). For more than a century, the GMC has been involved in social issues ranging from children's needs to poverty, civil rights, women's equality, reproductive rights, gun control, and domestic violence.

South Florida Jewry have always been politically active, but were particularly so in the 1970s, when Meir Kahane's Brooklyn-based Jewish Defense League, a largely working-class organization, originally created to protect Jews living in crime-ridden neighborhoods, reached out to South Florida (figures 7 and 8). From

FIGURE 7. *Jewish Defense League Protest. The 1970s saw the rise of Rabbi Meir Kahane's Jewish militant organization, the Jewish Defense League. Much of their efforts were directed at freeing Soviet Jewry and creating Zionist activism. This photo shows a protest at North Miami Beach City Hall, circa 1979. Courtesy Historical Museum of Southern Florida.*

FIGURE 8. *JDL Weapons' Training Class. A boy identified as Brett Birnbaum, 13, of Miami Beach is taught how to fire a .22. The JDL's slogan was "A .22 for Every Jew," circa 1978. Photograph by Charles Trainor, Jr. Courtesy of the Historical Museum of Southern Florida.*

its post in South Florida, the JDL advocated and succeeded in its attempt to liberate Soviet Jewry. Jewish activism is still a priority and, while it has taken a less militant form, it exists largely through efforts like the aforementioned National Council of Jewish Women, American Israel Public Affairs Committee (AIPAC), and Jewish Federation.

The decline in population of Miami-Dade County does not spell the end of Jewish South Florida. To the contrary, both Broward and Palm Beach Counties have experienced a dramatic demographic shift as Miami-Dade Jews moved north, joined by snowbirds and other migrant Jews. Zerivitz's photo essay conveys the gradual development of the Broward Jewish community, and Linda Brockman offers a bird's-eye view of Jewish Boca Raton. Natives and snowbirds in these locations continue to invest heavily in its Jewish residents; there are new synagogues, Hebrew day schools, Jewish community centers and adult educational outreach programs like those sponsored by Aish Ha'Torah, which strives to educate Jews about their culture and religion. And Jewish cultural revival is taking place in Miami as well. David Weintraub's essay on the Dora Teitelboim Center for Yiddish Culture describes the center's efforts to invigorate the nearly vanished Yiddish culture that once thrived on South Beach.

South Florida Jews comprise a diverse population of Jewish culture. Elderly Eastern European Jews, Jews from Latin American nations, Jews from the Soviet Union, Israel, and elsewhere, have created a vibrant and unique South Florida Jewish culture. South Florida Jews, in all their variety, have worked to carve out identities that preserve the traditions of their heritage.

Although the Golden Age of *Yiddishkeit* on Miami Beach has come and gone, South Florida Jewry continues to be a strong presence in American Jewish culture and life. The Jewish community itself retains strong ties to Israel, is committed to Jewish education and organizations, and is host to one of the largest remaining residences of Holocaust survivors in the world. It is my hope that this book reflects the spirit, the *ruach*, of this unique culture.

REFERENCES

Cobb, Charles E., Jr. "Miami." *National Geographic* 181, no. 1 (January 1992): 87–113.

Cohen, Rich. *Tough Jews: Fathers, Sons, and Gangster Dreams.* New York: Simon & Schuster, 1998.

Jaher, Frederic Cople. *A Scapegoat in the New Wilderness: The Origins and Rise of Anti-Semitism in America.* Cambridge, Mass.: Harvard University Press, 1994.

Mohl, Raymond. "'South of the South': Jews, Blacks, and the Civil Rights Movement in Miami, 1945–1960." *Journal of American Ethnic History* (Winter 1999): 3–36.

Moore, Deborah Dash. *To the Golden Cities: Pursuing the American Jewish Dream in Miami and L.A.* New York: Free Press, 1994.

Nagler, Richard, photographer. *My Love Affair with Miami Beach* ("Introduction" and "Commentary" by Isaac Bashevis Singer). New York: Simon & Schuster, 1991.

Sheskin, Ira. *The Jewish Community Study of Broward County.* Fort Lauderdale, Fla.: Jewish Federation of Broward County, 1997.

———. *The Jewish Community Study of Palm Beach County.* West Palm Beach, Fla.: Jewish Federation of Palm Beach County, 1999.

———. *Jewish Demographic Study of South Palm Beach County.* Boca Raton, Fla.: South Palm Beach Country Jewish Federation, 1996.

———. *The 1994 Jewish Demographic Study of Dade County.* Miami, Fla.: Greater Miami Jewish Federation, 1995.

PART I Culture & Communities

Ira Sheskin

Ten Percent of American Jews

According to the preliminary results of the 2000–2001 National Jewish Population Survey, approximately 5,200,000 Jews live in the United States. This number is subject to dispute for two reasons. First, difficulty exists in defining who is Jewish and, thus, whom to count. Second, different research methodologies yield different estimates of the number of Jews. The 2002 *American Jewish Year Book*, which collates local estimates of the number of Jews provided by Jewish Federations and synagogues, reports a total of 6,155,000 Jews in the United States in 2001.

What is not in dispute is that the three-county South Florida area (Miami-Dade County, Broward County, and Palm Beach County) is home to 565,000 Jews, representing about 10 percent of American Jews. The South Florida Jewish community has the third-largest concentration of Jews (after New York and southern California) in the country. In Miami-Dade County there are 131,000 Jews; Broward County has 234,000; and Palm Beach County has 218,000 (table 1). Seven percent of the Miami-Dade County population resides in Jewish households, as does 16 percent of the Broward County population and 20 percent of the Palm Beach County population. Twelve percent of the South Florida population as a whole resides in Jewish households, creating a Jewish milieu in many areas of South Florida. Only the New York metropolitan area may have a larger percentage if Jewish households than South Florida. The influence of the Jewish population is felt significantly in the cultural, political, and economic arenas of South Florida.

The first section of this chapter examines the demographic history of the Jewish community of South Florida, tracing the growth of this community and its migration to and within South Florida. The second section presents a profile of the Jewish community, examining spatial variations in key indicators of demography, geography, and "Jewishness," comparing South Florida Jewish communities with one another and with other American Jewish communities.

A Demographic History of the Jewish Community of South Florida

The growth of the Jewish community of South Florida should be viewed within the context of the major locational shift of American Jewry that has occurred over the past sixty years. During this period, Jews migrated from the Northeast and the Midwest to the South and the West. In 1940, the United States contained about 4.7 million Jews, with 69 percent living in the Northeast, 19 percent living in the Midwest, 7 percent living in the South, and 5 percent living in the West. By 2001, the United States contained about 6.1 million Jews, with 46 percent living in the Northeast, 11 percent living in the Midwest, 21 percent living in the South, and 22 percent living in the West. The Jewish population of Florida increased from 21,000 in 1940 to almost 650,000 in 2001, accounting for a large portion of the increase of Jews in the South.

Table 2 shows the growth in the number of persons in Jewish households in South Florida, by county, from 1940 to 2000. The seven thousand persons in Jewish households in Miami-Dade County in 1940 were located in South Beach and in the Shenandoah area (just to the south of the Miami Central Business District). By 1950, as the number of persons in Jewish households increased to 47,000, the Jewish population of the Shenandoah area spread west to Westchester and the Jewish population of South Beach increased and spread to the middle Beach area. By 1960, as the number of persons in Jewish households increased to 119,000, the Jewish population of Shenandoah/Westchester began to decrease (being replaced by Cuban refugees), and the Jewish population of North Miami-Dade and the Kendall area of South Miami-Dade began to increase. During the 1960s, thou-

TABLE 1: Jewish Communities in South Florida

Community	Number of Jews in Full-Year Households	Number of Jews in Part-Year and Full-Year Households	Number of Persons[a] in Part-Year and Full-Year Jewish Households
Miami-Dade County (2004)	107,000	113,300	121,300
Broward County (1999)	213,000	234,000	261,000
South Palm Beach (1999) (Boca Raton/Delray Beach)	92,300	123,000	128,000
West Palm Beach (1999) (Boynton Beach to Jupiter)	74,000	95,000	102,000
Total Palm Beach County	166,300	218,000	230,000
Total South Florida	486,300	565,300	612,300

Notes: (1) Full-year households reside in Florida for 8–12 months of the year; (2) Part-year households reside in Florida for 3–7 months of the year; (3) Dates in parentheses indicate the date of the most recent scientific community study; (4) Palm Beach County contains two Jewish communities served by two Jewish Federations: the Jewish Federation of South Palm Beach County and the Jewish Federation of Palm Beach County.

[a]This chapter distinguishes between the number of Jews and the number of persons in Jewish households. Persons in Jewish households are any persons (both Jewish and non-Jewish) living in a household containing one or more self-defined Jews.

Year	Miami-Dade County	Broward County	Palm Beach County	South Florida
Number of Persons in Jewish Households				
1940	7,000	1,000	1,000	9,000
1950	47,000	2,000	3,000	52,000
1960	119,000	10,000	5,000	134,000
1970	198,000	39,000	10,000	247,000
1980	230,000	174,000	92,000	496,000
1990	169,000	275,000	174,000	618,000
2000	121,000	261,000	230,000	612,000
Percentage of Persons in Jewish Households				
1940	77.8%	11.1%	11.1%	100.0%
1950	90.4%	3.8%	5.8%	100.0%
1960	88.8%	7.5%	3.7%	100.0%
1970	80.2%	15.8%	4.0%	100.0%
1980	46.4%	35.1%	18.5%	100.0%
1990	27.3%	44.5%	28.2%	100.0%
2000	19.8%	42.6%	37.6%	100.0%

Source: Author. For further information on the methodology used in
the development of these data, see Ira M. Sheskin, "A Methodology
for Examining the Changing Size and Spatial Distribution of a Jewish
Population: A Miami Case Study," in *Shofar, Special Issue: Studies in
Jewish Geography* (Neil G. Jacobs, Special Guest Editor), vol. 17, no. 1
(fall 1998): 97–116.

Note: Data include persons in both part-year and full-year households.

sands of Cuban Jews entered the United States, settling mostly in Miami Beach.
The increase in the Jewish population from 1940 to 1970 was composed of both
families (with fathers who had been stationed in South Florida during World War
II) and retirees. Retirees continued to swell the ranks of the Miami-Dade County
Jewish community until the early 1970s, when the number of persons in Jewish
households reached 198,000. By 1970, the original Shenandoah core area all but
disappeared as a center of Miami-Dade Jewish life. The two core areas were now
The Beaches (Miami Beach, Surfside, Bay Harbor Islands, Bal Harbor, and Indian
Creek Village, with 54 percent of persons in Jewish households) and North Miami-
Dade (with 20 percent). By 1980, the number of persons in Jewish households in
Miami-Dade County peaked at 230,000, with the proportion on The Beaches de-
creasing to 38 percent of the Jewish population and North Miami-Dade increasing
to 37 percent. After 1980, as the mortality among the retirees who had migrated in
earlier decades reached significant proportions and new retirees were increasingly

choosing to live in Broward and Palm Beach Counties, the number of persons in Jewish households in Miami-Dade County began to decrease. Hence, there were 169,000 persons in Jewish households in 1990 and 121,000 in 2004. By 2004, some 47 percent of persons in Jewish households in Miami-Dade County lived in North Miami-Dade, 36 percent lived in South Miami-Dade, and only 17 percent lived in The Beaches.

The number of persons in Jewish households in Broward County increased from only one thousand in 1940 and two thousand in 1950 to ten thousand in 1960. During the 1960s, retirees began to arrive in Broward County (mostly in South Broward) in large numbers, bringing the number of persons in Jewish households to thirty-nine thousand in 1970. The 1970s and 1980s saw explosive growth throughout Broward County. The number of persons in Jewish households increased to 174,000 in 1980 and 275,000 in 1990. During these two decades, Broward County was the fastest-growing Jewish community in the country. From 1980 to 1987, significant growth occurred in all geographic areas of Broward County except Southeast Broward (Hollywood and Hallandale). The percentage growth from 1980 to 1987 was greatest in Northwest Broward (Coral Springs and Parkland), North Central Broward (Palm Aire, Century Village Deerfield, Margate, Coconut Creek, and Wynmoor Village) and Southwest Broward (Pembroke Pines, Cooper City, and Davie), while the greatest growth in absolute numbers occurred in West Central Broward (Plantation, North Lauderdale, Tamarac, Lauderdale Lakes, and Sunrise—an increase of 27,000 persons in Jewish households) and North Central Broward (an increase of 22,600). Starting in 1990, similar to Miami-Dade, as the mortality among the retirees who had migrated in earlier decades reached significant proportions and new retirees were increasingly choosing to live in Palm Beach County, the number of persons in Jewish households in Broward County decreased from a high of 275,000 in 1990, to 261,000 in 2000. From 1987 to 1999, the most significant growth occurred in Southwest Broward (an increase of 34,000 persons in Jewish households) and Northwest Broward (an increase of 22,000) and a significant decrease occurred in Southeast Broward (a decrease of 10,000).

The number of persons in Jewish households in Palm Beach County increased slowly, from only one thousand in 1940 to ten thousand in 1970. Starting in the 1970s, retirees arrived in large numbers, bringing the number of persons in Jewish households to 92,000 in 1980, then 174,000 in 1990, and 230,000 in 2000. During the 1990s, Palm Beach County was the fastest-growing Jewish community in the country. From 1970 to 1980, the number of persons in Jewish households in South Palm Beach (Boca Raton/Delray Beach) increased from 1,000 to 37,000, while the number of persons in Jewish households in West Palm Beach (from Boynton Beach to Jupiter) increased from 9,000 to 55,000. From 1980 to 2000, the number of persons in Jewish households in South Palm Beach increased from 37,000 to 129,000, with Boca Raton increasing faster than Delray Beach. From 1987 to 2000, the number of persons in Jewish households in Boynton Beach increased from 9,000 to 37,000 (making it the leading growth area of the Jewish population in South Florida) and the number of persons in Jewish households in the North (Jupiter, North Palm Beach, and Palm Beach Gardens) increased from 6,000 to 14,000. From 1987 to 2000, the West (Wellington, Royal Palm Beach, and Golden Lakes), Lake Worth, and the City of Palm Beach had stable Jewish populations and the Central (the City of West Palm Beach and Century Village (West Palm Beach)) decreased from 25,000 persons in Jewish households to 13,000 persons.

Thus, the Jewish community of South Florida as a whole increased from an insignificant outpost of 9,000 persons in Jewish households in 1940 to almost a half million in 1980. More than 100,000 persons were added to this population in the 1980s, but the Jewish population of South Florida leveled off during the 1990s, showing a 1 percent decrease, to 612,000 in 2000.

The bottom half of table 2 shows that a significant geographic shift in the location of the Jewish population within the three-county South Florida area occurred over the past sixty years. Prior to 1980, some 80 to 90 percent of the South Florida Jewish population lived in Miami-Dade County. This percentage decreased from 80 percent in 1970 to 46 percent in 1980, 27 percent in 1990, and 20 percent in 2000. The percentage of the South Florida Jewish population living in Broward County increased from 8 percent in 1960 to 45 percent in 1990 and then decreased to 43 percent in 2000. The percentage of the South Florida Jewish population living in Palm Beach County increased from 4 percent in 1970 to 19 percent in 1980; 28 percent in 1990; and 38 percent in 2000.

In summary, a major internal shift occurred in the location of the Jewish population of South Florida, away from Miami-Dade County to Broward and Palm Beach Counties. As of 2000, the Jewish population of Miami-Dade County continued to decrease, Broward County's Jewish population leveled off, and the Jewish population of Palm Beach County continued to increase. Overall, then, we see that the Jewish population has spread continuously "up the coast" from Miami-Dade. One implication of this locational shift is that the geographic center of the three-county Jewish community is now in central Broward County. Quite clearly, although Miami-Dade will remain the "heart" of the South Florida Jewish community for many reasons, Jewish organizations looking to service South Florida from one main office will increasingly look to Broward County, which is geographically central and contains more Jews than either Miami-Dade or Palm Beach Counties.

Three major reasons may be cited for the shift of the Jewish population of South Florida from Miami-Dade County to Broward and Palm Beach Counties: (1) the mortality of Jews in Miami-Dade County; (2) the migration of Jews from the Northeast and Midwest directly to Broward and Palm Beach Counties; and (3) the migration of Jews from Miami-Dade County to Broward and Palm Beach Counties.

Mortality in Miami-Dade County. The decrease in the number of Jews in Miami-Dade County is due in large part to mortality in the two areas that contained about 75 percent of Miami-Dade's Jewish population in 1980: The Beaches and North Miami-Dade. From 1982 to 2004, the number of persons in Jewish households in The Beaches decreased from 72,000 to 21,000 and in North Miami-Dade, from 81,000 to 58,000. In 1982, the median age of persons in Jewish households in The Beaches was sixty-seven and in North Miami-Dade, fifty-seven. In 1982, some

42 percent of Jewish households in The Beaches and 27 percent of Jewish households in North Miami-Dade contained a widow. Thus, it is not surprising that this population decreased significantly from 1982 to 2004.

Migration from the Northeast. Most of the growth in Broward and Palm Beach Counties lies in the clear preference of new Jewish migrants to South Florida to select these counties as destinations. Sometime in the 1970s, Broward and Palm Beach Counties reached a "threshold" number of Jews and a chain migration process developed. In such a process, potential migrants from the Northeast visit friends or relatives in their South Florida homes. They soon migrate to South Florida, with their friends/relatives assisting in their adaptation to their new environment. Evidence of the importance of this process is seen in Palm Beach County, where 27 percent of the respondents to the 1987 Jewish community study *volunteered* the response that the major reason they chose to live in their current housing development was that their friends/relatives from "back home" were already living there.

This chain migration process had, of course, worked to favor Miami-Dade County as a migration destination for years. By 1970, however, low-rise retirement complexes were being developed in Broward and Palm Beach Counties—retirement complexes that looked more suburban, more like the lifestyle these second-generation (born in the United States of European parents), middle-class Jews had left behind in the Northeast, combining somewhat familiar housing styles with a country club atmosphere. In contrast, much of the migration of retirees into Miami-Dade County in the 1950s and 1960s was of first-generation Jews (born in Europe), of somewhat lower socioeconomic status, who were accustomed to living in high-rise buildings and moved into the same in The Beaches and North Miami-Dade. Also, Broward and Palm Beach Counties offered lower-cost housing and an overall lower cost of living.

Migration from Miami-Dade County. As of 1997, some 50,000 persons in Jewish households in Broward County had moved to Broward County from Miami-Dade County, while only 4,000 persons in Jewish households in Miami-Dade County had moved to Miami-Dade County from Broward County. As of 1997, some 15,000 persons in Jewish households in Palm Beach County had moved to Palm Beach County from Miami-Dade County.

It is clear that *some* Jews and other "Anglos" have departed Miami-Dade County in the wake of a Hispanic population that has increased from 5 percent in 1960 to 57 percent in 2000 and a black population that has increased from 15 percent to 20 percent in the same period. In addition, Miami-Dade County has taken on many of the attributes of a large metropolitan area, including crime, crowding, and traffic congestion, all of which have made it less attractive as a migration destination, particularly for retirees. Finally, there is little question that much of the negative publicity about Miami-Dade County in the early 1980s, profiling crime, drugs, illegal immigrants, and riots, helped to dissuade potential South Florida migrants (of all ethnic groups) from moving into Miami-Dade County.

Both the direct migration of Jews from the Northeast and Midwest and the migration of Jews from Miami-Dade County to Broward and Palm Beach Counties are based upon the phenomenon of the "Century Village–type" development, which caters to the reality that Jews continue to show a significant desire to live in areas that maintain a Jewish milieu. At least 80 percent of most of the Century Village–type developments are Jewish. In fact, when the first Century Village was opened in West Palm Beach (in the late 1960s), sales were sluggish until advertisements were placed in the Anglo-Jewish press in New York. Some housing developments, which originated as mostly Jewish, eventually became almost uniformly Jewish as the non-Jewish population departs and is replaced almost exclusively by Jews (gentile flight?). On the other hand, as housing developments become twenty years old and the original Jewish retirees die, Jews are sometimes replaced with younger Haitian and Hispanic immigrants.

Demographic and Religious Profile of the Jewish Community of South Florida

The demography of persons in Jewish households in South Florida is atypical of American Jewish communities, because of the age- and income-selective migration process that brought the Jewish community of South Florida from the Northeast and the Midwest. In addition, within South Florida, significant spatial variation exists in demographic characteristics, partly as a result of the different types of housing developed in different areas and partly as a result of the different time periods when various geographic areas were settled. This section examines several demographic and geographic indicators (age distribution, household size, marital status, level of secular education, household income, length of residence, place of birth, and "snowbird" status) (table 3) and "Jewishness" indicators (Jewish identification, intermarriage, synagogue attendance, synagogue membership, Jewish Community Center (JCC) membership, familiarity with the local Jewish Federation, mezuzah on the front door, participation in a Passover Seder, lighting Sabbath candles, and donations to Jewish charities) (table 4) and compares South Florida with other American Jewish communities.[1]

Age Distribution (Table 3). The age distribution in South Florida reflects the large number of retirees. Fifty percent of persons in Jewish households in South Florida are age sixty-five and over, compared to the median of 18 percent for all American Jewish communities. South Palm Beach (69 percent) and West Palm Beach (63 percent) are considerably older than Broward County (46 percent) and Miami-Dade County (30 percent). Of all persons in Palm Beach County (both Jewish and non-Jewish), 23 percent are age sixty-five and over, compared to 16 percent of all persons in Broward County and 13 percent of all persons in Miami-Dade County. Thus, persons in Jewish households are older than South Floridians as a whole.

The major concern raised by this unbalanced age distribution is that the retiree population, which migrates to South Florida as early as age fifty-five, may very well reside in South Florida for thirty or more years. While the migration of persons age fifty-five often brings economic and other benefits to an area, eventually many elderly outlive their economic means and/or become frail and vulnerable. The large number of elderly will require the diversion of resources that might otherwise be spent on others in the community. Where the elderly live in a geographically clustered fashion, the provision of social service programs by Jewish and governmental agencies is facilitated, but where the elderly live in single-family homes in a more geographically dispersed manner, agencies are at a disadvantage in providing social services.

Consistent with the high percentage of persons age sixty-five and over is the fact that only 13 percent of persons in Jewish households in South Florida are age seventeen and under (children), compared to the median of 23 percent for all American Jewish communities. Miami-Dade County (18 percent) and Broward County (15 percent) contain higher percentages of children than do West Palm Beach (7 percent) and South Palm Beach (6 percent). Of all persons in Palm Beach County (both Jewish and non-Jewish), 21 percent are age seventeen and under, compared to 24 percent of all persons in Broward County and 25 percent of all persons in Miami-Dade County.

TABLE 3: Demographic and Geographic Indicators in South Florida

Indicator	Miami-Dade County	Broward County	South Palm Beach	West Palm Beach	Total South Florida	U.S. Median[a]
Demographic Indicators						
Age 65 and over	30%	46%	69%	63%	50%	18%
Age 0–17	18%	15%	6%	7%	13%	23%
Average household size	2.24	2.02	1.89	1.92	2.02	2.50
Currently married	62%	65%	80%	76%	70%	69%
Currently widowed	13%	19%	13%	15%	16%	7%
Four-year college degree or higher	60%	34%	40%	46%	41%	60%
Median household income (2002 dollars)	$64,100	$46,000	$51,500	$64,800	$53,500	$66,600
Geographic Indicators						
In residence 20+ years	62%	31%	5%	19%	29%	44%
Locally born	13%	2%	0%	1%	4%	20%
Part-year households	7%	9%	25%	22%	14%	NA

Sources: Jewish community studies completed by the author for the Jewish Federations in Miami (2004), South Palm Beach (1995), Broward (1997), and West Palm Beach (1999). Each of these studies is based upon 1,000– 1,800 fifteen- to twenty-minute random digit–dialed telephone surveys. See the References for full information.

[a]The median value for about 35–50 Jewish communities that have completed random digit–dialing telephone surveys of their community. This value should not be interpreted as an "average" or median value for all American Jews. The data from the 1990 National Jewish Population Survey are not comparable to the results from local Jewish community studies. The 2000 National Jewish Population Survey was not public at the time of this writing.

The low percentage of children in South Florida is reflected in the low percentage of adults who attend synagogue services once per month or more and in the low synagogue and JCC membership rates discussed below. All Jewish organizations and synagogues in South Florida should recognize that they must market their services and programs to households without children, more so than most American Jewish communities.

Household Size.   Reflecting the unbalanced age distribution is the fact that the average Jewish household size in South Florida is only 2.0 persons, compared to the median of 2.5 persons for all American Jewish communities. Reflecting the geographic variations in age, the average Jewish household size is slightly higher in Miami-Dade County (2.2) and Broward County (2.0) than in Palm Beach County (1.9). For all households in Miami-Dade County (both Jewish and non-Jewish), the average household size is 2.8 persons, compared to 2.5 persons for all households in Broward County and 2.3 persons for all households in Palm Beach County. Thus, the average Jewish household size is significantly lower than the average household size for all South Florida households. A lower household size often implies a smaller internal support system in a household. Clearly, elderly persons living alone will need social services, medical care, and institutionalization sooner than those living as married couples or in other household types. As elderly persons live longer, we can only expect that the percentage living alone will increase. Most of these persons will be female, as life expectancy for U.S. females is now seven years longer than for males.

Marital Status.   Seventy percent of adults in Jewish households in South Florida are currently married, about the same as the median of 69 percent for all American Jewish communities. The percentage of those currently married is higher in areas of recent settlement (80 percent in South Palm Beach and 76 percent in West Palm Beach) than in areas of longer-term settlement (62 percent in Miami-Dade County and 65 percent in Broward County). Much of the settlement in Palm Beach County, as discussed above, is of recent origin and most of the settlers are young elderly who are married without children rather than widowed. By way of comparison, Broward County's elderly retirees include larger numbers of "old, old," and 19 percent of adults are widowed. Most retirees move to South Florida as married couples, but within ten to fifteen years, a female living alone usually remains. Eighteen percent of Broward County Jewish households contain single females living alone age seventy-five and over.

Level of Secular Education.   The low percentage of adults in Jewish households in South Florida with a four-year college degree or higher reflects the relatively low levels of educational attainment of elderly Jewish women. Forty-one percent of persons in Jewish households in South Florida have a four-year college degree or higher, compared to the median of 60 percent for all American Jewish communities. The percentages of adults in Jewish households with a four-year college degree or higher are higher in Miami-Dade County (60 percent) and West Palm

Beach (46 percent) than in South Palm Beach (40 percent) and Broward County (34 percent).

Household Income.   Reflecting the unbalanced age distribution is the fact that median Jewish household income in South Florida is only $53,500, compared to a median household income of $66,600 for all American Jewish communities. Median Jewish household income is higher in West Palm Beach ($64,000) and Miami-Dade County ($64,100) than in South Palm Beach ($51,500) and Broward County ($46,000). For all households in Palm Beach County (both Jewish and non-Jewish), the median household income is $49,000, compared to $45,000 for all households in Broward County, and $39,000 for all households in Miami-Dade County. Thus, Jewish household income is significantly higher than the household income of all households in both Miami-Dade and Palm Beach Counties.

In Residence for Twenty or More Years.   Reflecting the historic order of settlement of Jews within South Florida discussed above, 62 percent of Jewish households in Miami-Dade County are in residence for twenty or more years, compared to 31 percent of Jewish households in Broward County, 19 percent in West Palm Beach, and 5 percent in South Palm Beach. For South Florida as a whole, 29 percent of households are in residence for 20 or more years, compared to a median of 44 percent for all American Jewish communities.

Locally Born and Part-Year Households.   Four percent of adults in Jewish households in South Florida are locally born, compared to the median of 20 percent for all American Jewish communities. Reflecting the differences in recent settlement in South Florida, the percentage locally born is higher in Miami-Dade County (13 percent) than in Broward County (2 percent), West Palm Beach (1 percent), and South Palm Beach (0 percent).

Part-year households are defined as households in residence in South Florida for three to seven months of the year. The percentage of Jewish households that are part-year households is higher in South Palm Beach (25 percent) and West Palm Beach (22 percent) than in Broward County (9 percent) and Miami-Dade County (7 percent).

The implication of these data is that to many South Florida Jews, "home" is elsewhere. Significant ties still exist with friends and relatives and even with institutions—including synagogues, sports teams, organizations, and retail outlets—in other cities. This situation presents particular difficulties in the development of "community" in South Florida. Although Jews are overrepresented in community and governmental affairs throughout the area, many Jews (particularly recent migrants) have not developed an overall feeling of community or a feeling that South Florida is their home. This situation reflects itself in the lack of support for local institutions, both Jewish and general, in comparison with the levels of support shown in many northeastern Jewish communities. It may also manifest itself in a lack of support for local Jewish Federation and United Way campaigns, as well as in a lack of support for local sports teams. There is little feeling of "I grew up in this synagogue (city), my children are now members (residents), and my grandchildren will be members (residents) in the future." While this problem is endemic in our highly mobile society, it is probably more evident in recently settled Sunbelt communities.

An interesting facet of the development of a "sense of place" about South Florida is that many residents, particularly those who reside in the larger low-rise condominium complexes of Broward and Palm Beach Counties and the high-rise condominiums of North Miami-Dade, do develop a "loyalty" to their housing complex. As discussed above, many persons have friends or relatives from "back home" already living in their housing complexes when they move in. In addition, the close living quarters and activities at the clubhouse serve to develop a sense of community. People join condo boards and become active in condo-oriented clubs. Thus, much of the "community" that does develop in South Florida does so at a geographic micro-scale, at the level of housing development, rather than at a metropolitan-area level.

Jewish Identification (Table 4).   Five percent of Jewish households in South Florida identify as Orthodox, compared to the median of 4 percent for all American Jewish communities. Reflecting the high percentage of persons age sixty-five and over, South Florida has a higher percentage of Conservative Jews (37 percent, compared to a median of 31 percent for all American Jewish communities) and a lower percentage of Reform Jews (27 percent, compared to a median of 37 percent for all American Jewish communities). The percentage of Just Jewish in South Florida (30 percent) does not differ significantly from the median for all American Jewish communities (28 percent).

Orthodox Jews constitute a higher percentage of the Jewish population in Miami-Dade County (9 percent), reaching 17 percent of households in The Beaches. Thirty-two percent of households in Miami-Dade County identify as Conservative, compared to 37 percent to 40 percent in the other geographic areas. Thirty-four percent of households in West Palm Beach identify as Reform, compared to 24 percent to 28 percent in the other geographic areas. About one-third of the households in Miami-Dade and Broward Counties identify as Just Jewish, compared to about one-quarter in Palm Beach County.

Intermarriage Rate.   Fourteen percent of married couples in Jewish households in South Florida are intermarried, compared to the median of 28 percent for all American Jewish communities. The intermarriage rate decreases from 18 percent of married couples in Broward County to 16 percent in Miami-Dade County, 11 percent in West Palm Beach, and 6 percent in South Palm Beach.

The low rates of intermarriage in South Florida are clearly related to the high percentage of married couples age sixty-five and over, among whom intermarriage, in general, is very low. The lower intermarriage rate in Miami-Dade County reflects the higher percentage of Orthodox Jews in Miami-Dade County and a stronger Jewish institutional structure (kosher facilities, Jewish day schools, established synagogues, and so forth), which has attracted Jewish migrants who are more committed to Jewish practice than those who migrate to Broward County.

Synagogue Attendance. Twenty percent of Jewish adults in South Florida attend synagogue services once a month or more, compared to the median of 25 percent for all American Jewish communities. Twenty-six percent of Jewish adults in Miami-Dade County and 22 percent in South Palm Beach attend once a month or more, compared to 18 percent in West Palm Beach and 17 percent in Broward County. The low levels of synagogue attendance reflect the low percentage of households with children and the low percentage of synagogue membership discussed below.

Synagogue Membership. Thirty-three percent of Jewish households in South Florida are synagogue members, compared to the median of 46 percent for all American Jewish communities. Only 27 percent of Jewish households in Broward

TABLE 4: Jewishness Indicators in South Florida

Indicator	Miami-Dade County	Broward County	South Palm Beach	West Palm Beach	Total South Florida	U.S. Median[a]
Orthodox	9%	4%	6%	2%	5%	4%
Conservative	32%	37%	40%	38%	37%	31%
Reform	27%	24%	28%	34%	27%	37%
Just Jewish	31%	34%	25%	25%	30%	28%
Couples intermarriage rate	16%	18%	6%	11%	14%	28%
Attend synagogue services once a month or more	26%	17%	22%	18%	20%	25%
Synagogue membership[b]	39%	27%	36%	37%	33%	46%
JCC membership[c]	13%	4%	6%	9%	7%	15%
Very familiar with the local Jewish Federation	30%	12%	11%	18%	16%	26%
Have a Mezuzah on the front door	82%	79%	84%	81%	81%	64%
Always or usually participate in a Passover seder	79%	75%	79%	79%	77%	75%
Always or usually light Sabbath candles	34%	21%	23%	17%	23%	21%
Donated to a Jewish charity in the past year	69%	67%	82%	70%	71%	66%

Source: See table 3.

[a]See note a, table 3.

[b]Includes memberships in South Florida synagogues and memberships in synagogues in other communities.

[c]Includes memberships in South Florida JCCs only.

County are synagogue members, compared to 36 percent to 39 percent in the other geographic areas. The lower rate of synagogue membership in Broward County may well reflect the lower median household income and the higher intermarriage rate in that county.

The low percentage of synagogue membership in South Florida reflects the high percentage of persons age sixty-five and over, small household size, short lengths of residence, and the low percentage of locally born persons discussed above. Although the problem of having little emotional attachment to local institutions is endemic to our highly mobile society, it is more evident in recently settled Sunbelt communities. The vast majority of synagogue nonmember households were members of synagogues before migrating to South Florida. A number of studies have pointed out that many Jewish communal ties are broken upon migration. Another reason for this low rate of synagogue membership is that Jews who live in mostly Jewish condominium communities need not join Jewish institutions to reinforce their Jewish identity or to develop Jewish friendships. Jewish cultural and social activities are often offered in condominium clubhouses.

Jewish Community Center (JCC) Membership.   Seven percent of Jewish households in South Florida are JCC members, compared to the median of 15 percent for all American Jewish communities. JCC membership ranges from 4 percent of Jewish households in Broward County to 13 percent in Miami-Dade.

The reasons for these low rates of JCC membership are similar to the reasons for the low rates of synagogue membership. One additional reason may be posited: large percentages of South Florida Jewish households derive from the New York metropolitan area where JCCs do not play the same role that they play in many small and medium-size Jewish communities. There is little tradition among New York Jews of belonging to a JCC and this experience translates to low membership rates in South Florida. In fact, many South Florida Jews do not understand the difference between a synagogue and a JCC.

Familiarity with the Local Jewish Federation.   Sixteen percent of respondents in Jewish households in South Florida are very familiar with their local Jewish Federation, compared to the median of 26 percent for all American Jewish communities. Thirty percent of respondents in Miami-Dade County are very familiar with the local Jewish Federation, compared to 18 percent in West Palm Beach, 12 percent in Broward County, and 11 percent in South Palm Beach.

The reasons for the low levels of familiarity of adults in South Florida with the local Jewish Federation are similar to some of the reasons for the low levels of synagogue and JCC membership discussed above. The higher percentage of respondents very familiar in Miami-Dade County is clearly related to the higher percentage of locally born persons and the much higher percentage of households in residence for twenty or more years in this county.

Mezuzah on the Front Door.   Eighty-one percent of Jewish households in South Florida have a mezuzah on their front door, which is significantly higher than the median of 64 percent for all American Jewish communities. The percentage ranges from 76 percent of Jewish households in Miami-Dade County to 84 percent in South Palm Beach. The higher percentages for this home religious practice, as compared to the median for all American Jewish communities, are in contrast to the results discussed above for synagogue attendance, synagogue membership, JCC membership, and familiarity with the local Jewish Federation. In general, home religious practices do not require "reconnecting" to a new Jewish community and thus survive migration.

Passover Seder.   Seventy-seven percent of Jewish households in South Florida always or usually participate in a Passover Seder, which is about the same as the median of 75 percent for all American Jewish communities. No significant difference is seen among the geographic areas for this home religious practice. As with the results for having a mezuzah on the front door, this home religious practice does not require reconnecting to a new Jewish community and thus survives migration. Many households in South Florida attend Seders in the north or at the homes of relatives and friends who have also migrated to South Florida.

Sabbath Candles.   Twenty-three percent of Jewish households in South Florida always or usually light Sabbath candles, which is about the same as the median of 21 percent for all American Jewish communities. Thirty-four percent of Jewish households in Miami-Dade County always/usually light Sabbath candles, compared to 23 percent in South Palm Beach, 21 percent in Broward County, and 17 percent in West Palm Beach. The higher percentage for Miami-Dade County reflects the higher percentage of Orthodox in that county. Again, this home religious practice does not require reconnecting to a new Jewish community and thus survives migration.

Donated to a Jewish Charity.   Seventy-one percent of Jewish households in South Florida donated to a Jewish charity in the past year, which is higher than the median of 66 percent for all American Jewish communities. Eighty-two percent of Jewish households in South Palm Beach donated to a Jewish charity in the past year, compared to 67 percent to 76 percent in the other geographic areas. Like home religious practices, donating to Jewish charities does not require reconnecting to a new Jewish community and thus survives migration.

Summary and Conclusions

Over the past sixty years, the American Jewish community has undergone major changes in its geographical distribution, resulting in the creation of a South Florida Jewish community unlike any other Jewish community in history. This community of 612,000 persons in Jewish households increased from a mere 9,000 persons in 1940. During the development of this third-largest Jewish community in the United States, significant geographic changes occurred within the community as well. Most initial settlement was in Miami-Dade County. By the 1970s, Broward County became the focus of Jewish households moving to South

Florida: by the 1990s, however, that focus shifted to Palm Beach County. This shift occurred as a result of the high mortality rates in retirement communities in Miami-Dade County, direct migration of Jewish households from the Northeast and the Midwest to Broward County and then Palm Beach County, and the migration of Jewish households from Miami-Dade County to Broward County and Palm Beach Counties.

The migration to South Florida from the Northeast and the Midwest has been age-selective, with South Florida attracting large numbers of Jewish retirees. This has led to a South Florida Jewish community that, compared to other Jewish communities, is significantly older, has a lower average household size, a much higher percentage of widowed persons, lower levels of secular education, and a lower median household income. The recent migration and the existence of part-year households lessen the emotional attachment of Jews to the South Florida area.

This chapter has also examined selected indicators of Jewishness. Intermarriage in South Florida is relatively low because of the age distribution. Jewish connections that are dependent upon attachments to the local Jewish community (synagogue attendance, synagogue membership, JCC membership, and familiarity with the local Jewish Federation) are lower in South Florida than in other Jewish communities, these connections having been severed in northern communities and not reestablished in South Florida. Jewish behaviors (having a mezuzah on the front door, participation in a Passover Seder, lighting Sabbath candles, and donations to Jewish charities) that are not place-dependent continue at high levels among the Jewish population of South Florida.

The significant challenge to the organized Jewish community in South Florida remains as it has been for the past sixty years: to develop methods for "reinvolving" migrant households into Jewish life.

NOTES

1. About fifty American Jewish communities had completed Jewish community studies by 2002. The "medians for all American Jewish communities" referenced in the text is the median value of these studies. This value should not be interpreted as an average or a median value for all American Jews.

REFERENCES

Millon, Adrienne. 1989. "The Changing Size and Distribution of the Jewish Population of South Florida." Master's thesis, University of Miami, Coral Gables, Florida.

Moore, Deborah Dash. 1994. *To the Golden Cities: Pursuing the American Jewish Dream in Miami and L.A.* New York: Free Press.

Sheskin, Ira M. 2005. *The 2004 Jewish Demographic Study of Dade County*. Miami: Greater Miami Jewish Federation.

———. 2001a. "Florida's Jewish Elderly," *Florida Geographer* 32: 74–85.

———. 2001b. *How Jewish Communities Differ: Variations in the Findings of Local Jewish Demographic Studies*. New York: City University of New York, North American Jewish Data Bank.

———. 2000a. "American Jews." In *Ethnicity in Contemporary America, A Geographic Appraisal*, ed. Jesse O. McKee. Lanham, Md.: Rowman & Littlefield, 227–62.

———. 2000b. "The Dixie Diaspora: The 'Loss' of the Small Southern Jewish Community." *Southeastern Geographer* 40, no. 1: 52–74.

———. 1999. *The Jewish Community Study of Palm Beach County.* West Palm Beach, Fla.: Jewish Federation of Palm Beach County.

———. 1998. "The Changing Spatial Distribution of American Jews." In *Land and Community: Geography in Jewish Studies,* ed. Harold Brodsky. Bethesda, Md.: University Press of Maryland, 185–221.

———. 1997. *The Jewish Community Study of Broward County.* Fort Lauderdale, Fla.: Jewish Federation of Broward County.

———. 1996. *Jewish Demographic Study of South Palm Beach County.* Boca Raton, Fla.: South Palm Beach County Jewish Federation.

———. 1995. *The 1994 Jewish Demographic Study of Dade County.* Miami, Fla.: Greater Miami Jewish Federation.

———. 1993. "Jewish Ethnic Homelands in the United States." *Journal of Cultural Geography* 13, no. 2: 119–32.

———. 1987. *The Jewish Federation of Palm Beach County Demographic Study.* West Palm Beach, Fla.: Jewish Federation of Palm Beach County.

———. 1982. *Population Study of the Greater Miami Jewish Community.* Miami, Fla.: Greater Miami Jewish Federation.

Marcia Kerstein Zerivitz

Alligators and Matzo Balls

Eighty-one years before the First Zionist Congress in Basel, Switzerland (1897), Sephardic Jew Moses Elias Levy embarked on his own "Zion" plan to resettle oppressed European Jews in Florida. Born in Morocco in 1782, Moses Levy was descended from one of the many Jewish families who, having been expelled from the Iberian Peninsula at the end of the fifteenth century, found refuge in northern Africa. Raised in Gibraltar, Levy made his way to Saint Thomas, in the Virgin Islands, in 1800. There he worked in the lumber business, accumulating a considerable fortune. He became interested in Florida and, in 1819, purchased 92,000 acres Micanopy, in the north central region (near what is currently Gainesville).

Envisioning a haven for persecuted Jews, Levy called his settlement Pilgrimage Plantation. He hired Frederick Warburg, a member of the noted German Jewish banking family, to help him recruit Jewish settlers. Young Warburg, along with at least five other German Jewish families, lived on the plantation. Included among them was Levy's son David, who became Florida's first U.S. Senator. Levy built a plantation house and houses for the settlers' families, as well as a blacksmith shop, stable, sugar mill, sawmill, and cornhouse. He brought in sugar cane, fruit trees, and seeds. In an effort to create a utopian Jewish settlement, Levy included among his projects a plan for the abolition of slavery, public schools, and a Jewish school.

The one thousand–acre Pilgrimage Plantation lasted from 1822 to 1835, when it was burned down by the Seminoles at the outbreak of the Second Seminole Indian War. Sustaining the plantation had been a challenge; in early nineteenth-century Florida, it was virtually in the middle of nowhere. And the urban backgrounds of most of the Jewish settlers made adaptation to a rural outback difficult. As Levy said, "It is not easy to transform old clothes men into practical farmers."

Pioneer Floridian Jews

Levy was not the first Jewish landowner in Florida. Florida, "discovered" by Spain in 1513 (a mere twenty-one years after the Spanish Inquisition) was off-limits to Jews until the mid-eighteenth century. The Treaty of Paris (1762), which concluded the French and Indian War, gave Florida to the British and Louisiana to the Spanish. Jews living in Louisiana had to move. In 1763, three Sephardic Jews came from New Orleans to Pensacola: Samuel Israel, Joseph de Palacios, and Alexander Salomon. (Alexander Salomon may have been related to Haym Salomon, who helped finance the American Revolution).

Although Florida was returned to Spain following the American Revolution (1783), the Spanish needed settlers in the territory; thus a tiny Jewish presence was tolerated. From the mid-eighteenth century until Florida achieved statehood

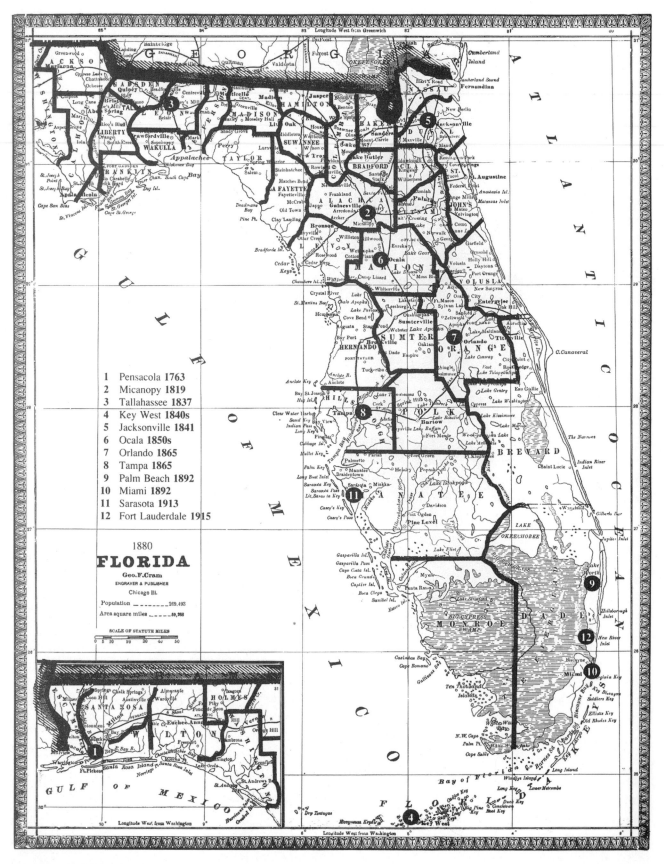

1 Pensacola **1763**
2 Micanopy **1819**
3 Tallahassee **1837**
4 Key West **1840s**
5 Jacksonville **1841**
6 Ocala **1850s**
7 Orlando **1865**
8 Tampa **1865**
9 Palm Beach **1892**
10 Miami **1892**
11 Sarasota **1913**
12 Fort Lauderdale **1915**

1880
FLORIDA
Geo.F.Cram
ENGRAVER & PUBLISHER
Chicago III.

Population _ _ _ _ _ _ _ _ 269,493
Area square miles _ _ _ _ _ 59,268

SCALE OF STATUTE MILES

FIGURE I. *Jewish immigration
into Florida from 1763 (map)*

in 1845, Jews continued to trickle into northern Florida. And the "architect of state-hood" was a Jew, David Levy Yulee, a son of pioneer Moses Levy.

Despite the failure of Moses Levy's utopian dream during the pre-statehood period, he left Florida a lasting legacy. He had brought with him to Florida two of his four children, Elias and David. Elias was sent to Harvard; David boarded with the Moses Meyer family in Norfolk to get his Jewish education, and then came to Florida by 1827 to manage some of his father's properties. He pursued the law and was admitted to the Florida bar in 1832. David Levy became extremely active in politics. He helped draft Florida's constitution and eventually was sent to the U.S. Congress as the representative of the Territory of Florida (1841), where he argued for statehood. Being the first Jew to serve in the U.s. Congress, Levy faced discrimination when John Quincy Adams referred to him as the "alien Jew delegate."

With fewer than one hundred Jews in the state, David Levy was elected to the U.S. Senate when Florida became a state in 1845. He oficially added the name of his father's Sephardic ancestry, Yulee. David Levy Yulee's political contributions to the state's development were amplified when he built the first railroad across the state, "The Florida Railway." Levy County and the town of Yulee are named after him.

Until 1822, Jews who lived in Florida came from somewhere else. The earliest-known Jewish births are a girl (Virginia Myers) in Pensacola in 1822 and a boy (George Dzialynski) in Jacksonville in 1857. In that same year (1857), also in Jacksonville, Jews built the first Jewish cemetery in Florida. In in 1874 B'nai B'rith had a chapter in Pensacola.

FIGURE 2. *David Levy Yulee, Florida's first U.S. Senator and the first Jew to serve in the U.S. Senate. 1845. Courtesy Collection of Jewish Museum of Florida.*

FIGURE 3. *West Point graduate and Quartermaster Colonel Abraham Charles Myers serving in the Seminole Indian War, circa 1836. The Florida city of Fort Myers is named for him. Courtesy Collection of Jewish Museum of Florida.*

FIGURE 4. *Second synagogue for Temple Beth El, Pensacola, the first Jewish congregation to receive a charter in Florida in 1876. The first synagogue was destroyed by fire in 1895. Courtesy Collection of Jewish Museum of Florida.*

FIGURE 5. *Florida's only Jewish governor: The state's twenty-sixth governor, David Sholtz, shown at Bayfront Park in Miami with U.S. President-elect Franklin D. Roosevelt and Chicago's Mayor Anton Cermak. This February 15, 1933, photo was taken just prior to an assassination attempt on Roosevelt when Cermak was shot by mistake and killed. The murderer was executed in thirty-two days. Courtesy Collection of Jewish Museum of Florida.*

By the end of the nineteenth century, there were six Jewish congregations and five Jewish cemeteries in Florida. Floridian Jews served on both sides during the Civil War. Following the Civil War, Jews began migrating south, settling in Tampa, Orlando, Ocala, and even Key West. The west coast city of Fort Myers, founded in 1886, was named for a Jew: Abraham C. Myers, a West Point graduate and a descnedant of the first rabbi of Charleston, South Carolina. Myers had served as quartermaster during the Second Seminole Indian War.

The first synagogue was constructed in Pensacola (1876). In 1879, German Jew Henry Brash was elected mayor of Marianna in north Florida, the first of more than one hundred Jews to serve their communities in this capacity. David Sholtz, a Russian Jew, became Florida's governor in 1933. Miami's Richard Stone became the state's second Jewish U.S. senator in 1974. Scores of Jews have served both in Congress and in the state legislature. More than 250 Jews have served as judges in Florida.

At the turn of the twentieth century, the Hebrew Immigrant Aid Society (HIAS) directed some Jewish immigrants to Florida. Among them were ardent Zionists Henry and Louis Seitlin. The Seitlin brothers left Russia and arrived in New York in 1910. Seeking placement in a Zionist collective farm, they ended up in Homestead, Florida. This experiment was not successful so the brothers moved to the new city of Miami, where they became successful businessmen and brought their families over from Russia.

In 1915 Jacksonville Jew Ben Chepenik wrote his relatives in Massachusetts, "Sell everything; come quickly to Florida, the land of milk and honey; you can walk down the streets and pick citrus." And many did come. For Jews, Florida offered a variety of occupational opportunities. Some transferred their traditional dry goods businesses to Florida; others used the state's resources to develop or expand new

FIGURE 6. *Saul Snyder, a Russian immigrant who helped found the Florida Cattlemen's Association, Saint Augustine, 1950. Courtesy Collection of Jewish Museum of Florida.*

ideas. In Florida, Jews became ranchers, farmers, cigar makers, architects, developers, hoteliers, artists, writers, scientists, retailers, educators, doctors, lawyers, civic leaders and more. Jews owned the largest shade tobacco-packing factory in Quincy, near Tallahassee. Saul Snyder, a Russian Jew who immigrated to Saint Augustine in 1904, founded the Florida Cattlemen's Association. The first Miss Florida was Jewish (1885). Much more recently, Marshall Nirenberg of Orlando was awarded the Nobel Prize in Medicine and Physiology for breaking the genetic code (1968) and four Jews have served on the Supreme Court of Florida, including as Chief Justice.

FIGURE 7. *Mena Williams,
second-generation Floridian Jew,
as the first Miss Florida, presenting
the flag at Governor Edward
Perry's inauguration, Tallahasse,
1885. Courtesy Collection of Jewish
Museum of Florida.*

Prior to the twentieth century, most Jewish settlement in Florida was in the north or Key West (Key West was a port of entry for some European immigrants). But the development of railroads made southern regions accessible, and Jews headed south. Jewish migration throughout the state increased, but numbers increased exponentially after World War II, especially in Miami-Dade County.

In the 1890s the Florida Jewish population was about 2,500; by the 1950s, the population grew to 70,000; today it is nearly 850,000 and still growing. Jews came to escape persecution in Europe, for economic opportunity, to join family members, to enjoy the climate, for their health, and to retire.

South Florida: Palm Beach County

The first South Florida community to host Jews was probably West Palm Beach, where Jews settled in 1892. Growth was slow at first; as late as 1940, the Jewish population in Palm Beach County was only one thousand. Today, the Jewish population in Palm Beach County is the second largest in the state at about 220,000; the Boca Raton metropolitan area is more than 50 percent Jewish.

Harry and Florence Brown from Saint Louis were the first Jews to settle in Boca Raton in 1931—a time when it was still possible to sit in the middle of Old Dixie Highway and play cards! In 1936, Harry's sister, Nettie, arrived with her husband Max Hutkin, a Polish immigrant. They opened Hutkin's Food Market, and Max was the founding president of Temple Beth El (1967), the first Jewish congregation in Boca Raton. Today, with a membership of two thousand families, it is one of the largest Reform congregations in the nation.

The first Jews in West Palm Beach (1890s) owned retail stores on Narcissus and Clematis Streets, which were close to the ferry that brought shoppers from Palm Beach. They formed Temple Israel in 1923. Among the founders of the congregation was Joseph Mandel, who served as mayor of West Palm Beach in 1923–24. Another founder was Max Serkin, a produce farmer who had arrived in 1896. His daughter is thought to be the first Jewish child born in Palm Beach County.

Of course, shopping malls, air-conditioning, and fax machines have changed the shape of local businesses. More recent entrepreneurs include Irwin Levy, Robert Rapaport, and Aaron Schecter, who began developing Century Village in 1967. Century Village drew large numbers of retired garment workers and teachers, often from New York and other northeastern states, to the area. These "cities within cities" provide a wide range of educational, recreational, and entertainment activities. In the 1970s and 1980s, other retirement and golf communities were developed in Delray Beach and its environs, and the "rush" of Jewish settlement accelerated.

Miami

Many of the Jews who first settled in West Palm Beach were among the earliest settlers of Miami. Founded in 1896, Miami was difficult to reach until Henry Flagler extended his railroad southward. By the mid-1890s, however, the railroad rendered Miami and sites south accessible, and Jews migrated accordingly. The first Jew to arrive in Miami in 1895 was either Sam Singer or Jake Schneidman. The earliest permanent Jewish settler was Isidor Cohen, who was a signatory of the city's charter and helped found many Jewish and civic organizations. It is believed Jews owned about twelve of Miami's first sixteen retail stores.

These early Jews (about two dozen people) held religious services in homes. A great fire in 1896, however, followed by a yellow fever epidemic in 1899 reduced Miami's population significantly. Jewish population declined by 1900 to three people. Miami remained a hostile environment for would-be settlers. Nonetheless, aided by the railroad and a fledgling tourist industry, Miami didn't give up. By 1910 the general population had reached 5,500. The census counted five Jewish families. By 1912 other Jews were settling in Miami, mostly from Tampa and Key West.

FIGURE 8. *Miami pioneers (from left): Sam Schneidman, Isidor Cohen, Marcus Frank, circa 1898. Courtesy Collection of Jewish Museum of Florida.*

The death of a Jewish tourist in 1913 forced the small Jewish community to gather to discuss creating an organization and a cemetery. Meeting at the home of Mendel Rippa, a group of thirty-five Jews established the first congregation in Miami. They called it B'nai Zion, in tribute to its first president, Morris Zion. Later, the name was changed to Beth David. By 1915, there were fifty-five Jews in Miami. That same year, Carl Fisher created the Dixie Highway, making Miami even more accessible. By the 1920s, tremendous advertising combined with abundant land, new roads and availability of the automobile and commercial aviation, created a tourist and real estate boom. A population of 30,000 (including 100 Jewish families) exploded to more than 130,000 by 1925—of which Jews constituted some thirty-five hundred.

FIGURE 9. *Abe Aronowitz, first (and still only) Jewish mayor of Miami, 1953. Courtesy Collection of Jewish Museum of Florida.*

Downtown Miami gradually lost its rustic, small-town appearance. As the city grew richer, bank deposits increased 48 percent. Jews founded Temple Israel, the first reform congregation, in 1922, and were among those who chartered the University of Miami in 1925. The hurricane that swept Miami just as Kol Nidre services on Yom Kipuur ended on September 18, 1926, brought the real estate boom to an abrupt halt. From 1926 to 1931, the city suffered a boom and bust, two hurricanes, the failure of five banks and finally the stock market crash. Headlines screamed, "Miami is Wiped Out."

But the headlines were wrong. by the mid-1930s, Miami began a gradual recovery. New residents arrived by air, train and the Mallory Steamship Line. Streetcars were introduced in the city. Tourists were lured to boating, fishing, and tropical gardens attractions. And Miami began to gain a reputation as the "gateway to Latin America"—a reputation that would increase dramatically as the century wore on. During the 1930s, approximately 4,500 Jews lived among a Miami population of more than 110,000. Satellite communities emerged. The hotel, building, and banking industries escalated with greater participation by Jews. The perilous situation of European Jews evoked a response in Miami's small but active Jewish community, which founded the Greater Miami Jewish Federation in 1938.

When the Japanese bombed Pearl Harbor, Miami was recovering from the Depression. Local leaders, seeking to expand business and visibility, convinced the government that Miami was the ideal location for training military personnel. As a result, funding and soldiers poured into the area, particularly Miami Beach. Many

of these soldiers were Jews. After the war, South Florida's image as a year-round resort reemerged. The tourist industry was revitalized with the widespread use of air-
conditioning, mosquito control, the development of Miami International Airport,
and Israeli businessman Ted Arison's expansion of the cruise ship business. The
postwar economic boom brought additional tourists and settlers to Miami. New
residents included ex-servicemen, retirees, and people of diverse religious and ethnic backgrounds. Many were Jews, attracted by new jobs created from tourism.

In 1950, Dade county had a population of 495,000 people, of which 55,000
were Jewish. For the next five years, approximately 650 Jews arrived each month.
A new house was built every seven minutes during this period—and many of the
builders were Jews. In 1952 Abe Aronovitz became the first (and to date, the only)
Jewish mayor of Miami, the main city in Dade County.

Many Jews, horrified by news of the Holocaust, began to challenge anti-Semitism
at home. The Miami branch of the Anti-Defamation League had been founded in
1940. During the McCarthy era, the Ku Klux Klan, John Birch Society, White Citizens Council, and Florida States Rights Council all contributed to a climate that
resulted in the bombings and desecration of area synagogues. Although people
were generally optimistic about Miami's resurgence, growing racial tensions, the
fear of communism, and the threat of the cold war were destabilizing factors.

Following Fidel Castro's successful communist takeover of Cuba in 1959, ten
to twelve thousand Cuban Jews immediately fled the country, finding refuge in
Miami and its environs. In Miami, the presence of middle-class Cubans with
business acumen helped revitalize the city. In the postwar period until the mid-
1960s, most jobs were related to the tourist and building industries or real estate
and the savings and loan associations that served them. Most Jews were involved
in the services and retail trades; by the 1906s, however, many were moving into
medical and legal professions. In 1963, the first two Jews from South Florida were
elected to the state legislature: Murray Dubbin and Louis Wolfson II. Jews began
to move to North Miami and North Miami Beach. Cuban Jews started their own
congregations.

The 1973 Arab oil embargo plunged Miami into the worst recession since the
1930s. Yet Jewish Miami continued to grow. By 1980, the Greater Miami Jewish
population reached its all-time peak of 230,000, with a full array of Jewish organizations. In the 1980s, Miami became the new Ellis Island for people fleeing
troubled countries like Haiti and the Dominican Republic. The influx of Caribbean
immigrants, as well as the growing Spanish-speaking Cuban population, alienated
some people, and many Jews moved north to Broward and Palm Beach counties.
By 1985 the Jewish population had declined to 209,000. Also, many of the old
Jews, who had lived on Miami Beach, had died. But the greater Miami Jewish community has been reinvigorated by the arrival of Jews from Latin America, Russia,
and Israel.

Miami Beach and Antisemitism

From the early twentieth century, people visited the southern tip of Florida to
picnic on its sandy beaches or bathe in the warm waters of the Atlantic Ocean. In

1913 the Collins Bridge opened, joining the beach to the mainland. That same year, Joe and Jenny Weiss, and their son Jesse, relocated to Miami Beach. Joe and Jennie operated a snack bar at a popular bathing spot at the tip of the beach. (Carl Fisher, developer of Miami Beach, had restricted Jews to this area.) Several years later, the Weiss family opened Joe's Stone Crab Restaurant in a small, wooden-frame house, which they continued to expand and which today remains the site of this world-famous restaurant. It is still run by descendants of the Weiss family.

Carl Fisher, a flamboyant millionaire from Indianapolis, and other developers placed restrictive covenants in their land deeds that prohibited the sale of Miami Beach lots to Jews: "No lot shall be sold, conveyed, leased to anyone not a member of the Caucasian race, nor to anyone having more than one quarter Hebrew or Syrian blood." Fisher also remarked in a letter, written in 1920, "We don't want Miami Beach to ever become a Jewish outfit—it would not only ruin the Hotel [a reference to his beautiful Flamingo Hotel on Biscayne Bay at Fifteenth Street] but ruin the property." Such discrimination was not new and was driven by a strong tradition that barred Jews, along with many other immigrants, from gaining entry to the most fashionable hotels. Carl Fisher and John Collins, another key developme of Beach properties, were following a common real estate practice of that era. Nonetheless, Carl Fisher was not reticent to sell property to the "right kind of Jews"—that is, rich ones.

Not all developers, however, restricted Jewish purchase. The Lummus properties, at the southern end of Miami Beach, did not bar Jews from ownership. These properties were named for two enterprising businessmen and civic leaders, J. N. and J. E. Lummus, who came to Miami from Georgia in 1896. They had dealt with Jews before, and were comfortable doing business with them. Accordingly, several modest Jewish-owned hotels and apartments arose on property sold to Jews south of Fifth Street. These early Beach Jews owned and lived in apartments for several practical reasons. There were few freestanding houses on the Beach at the time; furthermore, many of the early Jewish settlers could not afford the cost of a home. Jews lived in the apartment buildings and rented units to others. This was their chief source of income.

Sam Magid and Joseph and Harry Goodkowsky were successful kosher-hotel managers in New England. They moved to Miami Beach and in 1921 built the Nemo Hotel on Collins Avenue and First Street. The Nemo was the first hotel to cater to kosher Jewish winter tourists. Shortly thereafter, the Seabreeze Hotel, also kosher, opened nearby at Collins and Second Street. Rose and Jeremiah Weiss and their children lived near the Seabreeze. The Weisses, Russian Jews, emigrated first to New York and then moved to Miami Beach in 1919 because of Rose's health problems. The bought the Royal Apartments, which had dwellings for fifteen families. Rose Weiss, a deeply compassionate woman and one of the community's most popular residents, was known as "the Mother of Miami Beach." Rose Weiss attended every city commission meeting for nearly forty years; she also created the city's flag.

In the mid-1920s, the Jacobs family, lured to Miami Beach primarily because of its sun and warmth, opened the first of three hotels. The Blackstone opened in

FIGURE 10. *Original and current site of Joe's Stone Crab Restaurant, Miami Beach, circa 1917. Original proprietors Joe and Jennie Weiss were the first Jews to settle on Miami Beach in 1913; the family still owns and runs the restaurant. Courtesy Collection of Jewish Museum of Florida.*

FIGURE 11. *Photocopy of a letter sent by Miami Beach real estate magnate Carl Fisher to another hotelier advising him to be discreet about refusing Jewish patronage, especially those who are "high class" and might be offended, October 10, 1921. Courtesy Collection of Jewish Museum of Florida.*

October 10th, 1921.

Mr. Eugene C. Stahl,
    121 Northeast First Street,
    Miami - Florida.

Dear Sir :

     I have your letter of October 6th and copy of the booklet.
I don't think it is necessary for you to enclose a card which states
"Hebrew Patronage is not Solicited". You can usually tell by the
names of the people applying for apartments and their occupation
whether they are desirable or not - and I would advise if you
haven't sent these cards out with the booklets that you omit them.
There are some Hebrews who are very high class people, and it does
seem a shame to injure their feelings unnecessarily if it can be
avoided. The average run of Hebrew trade at a Hotel is not desirable,
particularly at a resort hotel, and it is quite a question of knowing
just how to handle the undesirable ones best.

     I think you have made one serious mistake in showing on the
back cover the location of the Helene as being on the Ocean front. You
might find this very serious if some of your guests arrive expecting to
be on the Ocean front and find they are several blocks away from the
Ocean. I think it would have been better to have had a picture of
the Casino and Bath-House on the back cover with a memorandum that its
only a few blocks distant to the Beach. However, it is probably too
late now for you to make any change, but in your correspondence I
would particularly call attention to the fact that the apartments
are not located right on the Beach.

     Yours very truly,

CGF:R

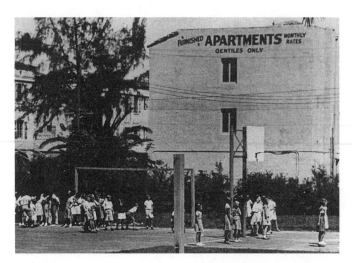

FIGURE 12. *"For Gentiles Only."*
Many apartments and hotels on
Miami Beach advertised that the
clientele was restricted, circa 1935.
Courtesy Collection of Jewish
Museum of Florida.

1929 on Washington Avenue and Eighth Street. Built by Nathan Stone, the grandfather of future United States Senator Richard Stone, this multistoried hostelry became one of South Beach's most imposing buildings, as well as a haven for Jewish visitors. (George Gershwin reportedly wrote portions of *Porgy and Bess* while reposing in the hotel's rooftop solarium).

Despite this activity, the Jewish population of Miami Beach grew slowly in the first half of the 1920s. It was confined to an area from Fifth Street south to the tip of the peninsula. Malvina Weiss Gutschmidt, the daughter of Rosie Weiss, noted that there were no Jewish residences north of Fifth Street until 1925. From 1925 until the end of the decade, however, a rapidly growing Jewish neighborhood moved north all the way to Lincoln Road at 16th Street. A fantastic real estate boom that overtook all of south Florida and much of the rest of the state in the mid-1920s prompted this growth. The boom led to the creation of hundreds of new subdivisions and communities in Greater Miami and to a sharp increase in the area's population.

This speculative era lured many young Jews, such as Leonard Abess, Max Orovitz, and Baron de Hirsch Meyer, to the Miami area. Especially active was Henri Levy, a French-born Jew who migrated with his family to Miami Beach, an area he characterized as "a lush tropical paradise." In 1922, Levy developed the smart boom-era communities of Normandy Isle and Normandy Beach North, which later became Surfside.

The boom collapsed in 1926, when a hurricane smashed into South Beach and other parts of Dade County. But many "boomers," whose ranks included a considerable number of Jews, remained in the area. In the 1930s, Miami Beach's Jewish population grew significantly, reaching at least several thousand (out of an overall population for Miami Beach of 28,012) by decade's end, as Miami-Dade County, formerly called Greater Miami, replaced Jacksonville as the center of Florida Jewry.

Many of the new arrivals to Miami Beach came initially as tourists. Most came from the northeast United States. While many hotels continued to exhibit "Gentile Only" signs, a few maintained no restrictions against Jews. Moreover, Jewish builders erected many of the finest hotels on South Beach in this decade. Many bore the

Streamline or Nautical Modern style of architecture designed by Henry Hohauser, a New York Jew who moved, along with his wife, to Miami Beach in 1936. For the next ten years, this brilliant architect was responsible for the design of more than one hundred hotels, apartments, and buildings on Miami Beach. Hohauser designed the Miami Beach Orthodox synagogue, which became the Jewish Museum of Florida. The Art Deco buildings of the 1930s and 1940s on Miami Beach are architectural treasures known throughout the world. The square-mile district is bounded by Fifth Street to Twenty-third Street, Lenox Avenue to Ocean Drive. In the 1980s, Barbara Baer Capitman, a Jew, launched the campaign that established the Art Deco District, the largest collection of 1930s Art Deco and Art Moderne buildings in the nation.

Jewish hoteliers operated many of the hostelries designed by Hohauser, L. Murray Dixon, and other gifted architects. The 1930s also marked the dismantling of restrictive barriers to Jewish ownership of real estate throughout the Beach, as large numbers of Jews purchased commercial properties from debt-ridden owners only too happy to sell them. Jews also began buying residential lots whose restrictive covenants proved impossible to enforce after the property had changed owners a couple of times. While discrimination had by no means vanished, conditions were improving.

Jews continued to migrate to the sunny shores of Miami Beach. The Jewish retail, institutional, and residential presence was most strongly felt at the southern portion of the island, especially along Washington and Collins Avenue and Ocean Drive, stretching from the tip more than one mile north to, and even beyond, Lincoln Road. Small Jewish businesses dotted Miami Beach streets and Jewish tenants filled apartments. In 1925, Jews began meeting for services in apartments. Several very observant Canadian Jewish visitors lobbied for a synagogue. As a result of their efforts, Beth Jacob Congregation was organized in 1927. In the 1930s, as the Jewish population moved into areas north of Fifth Street, many members of Beth Jacob broke away and organized a conservative congregation. Jacob Joseph of Miami Beach subsequently became the Miami Beach Community Center in the 1940s and, finally, in 1954, Temple Emmanu-El. As the Jewish population continued to move north, and many Jewish soldiers poured into the area for wartime training, Jews founded the Beth Sholom Center in a storefront on Forty-First Street in 1942 (it was renamed Temple Beth Sholom in 1945).

Commensurate with their increase in numbers, Jews began to play increasingly more important civic roles. Baron de Hirsch Meyer, who came to the area during the boom after earning a law degree from Harvard, served as president of numerous Jewish organizations and was the first Jew to sit on the Miami Beach City Council (1934). Mitchell Wolfson, who migrated to Miami with his family around 1915 from Key West, became Miami Beach's second Jewish councilman. Like de Hirsch Meyer, Wolfson was a stellar businessman, civic leader, and visionary. In 1943, the electorate elevated him to the office of mayor. Wolfson was the first of fifteen Jews who have served as mayor of Miami Beach (as of 2004).

Mitchell Wolfson was very important to business in Miami. With his brother-in-law Sidney Meyer, Wolfson formed WOMETCO (Wolfson Meyer Theater Company) in 1949. WOMETCO became the first television station in Florida, WTVJ. Wolfson also built the Seaquarium and left an endowment to create the Wolfson campus of Miami-Dade College. By the mid-1940s, the Greater Miami Jewish Federation placed the number of Jews in Dade County at 29,325 in a county nearing 400,000 in population. Nearly one-half of these Jews lived on Miami Beach.

Less civic-minded Jews also embraced Miami Beach. Most prominent of these was Meyer Lansky, the reputed boss of South Florida crime in the middle decades of the twentieth century. Less "prominent" than Lansky nationally but quite active on the Beach was the S&G Syndicate, founded and operated by five Jews. From its office on Washington Avenue, the S&G controlled bookmaking in about two hundred hotels on Miami Beach and elsewhere in the area in the 1940s, grossing millions of dollars annually. A United States Senate crime-investigating committee, chaired by Estes Kefauver, put the syndicate out of business in the early 1950s.

The tragedy of the Holocaust caused many Jews to turn to Zionism. In 1944, more than eight thousand persons gathered in Miami's Bayfront Park to hear Dr. Stephen S. Wise, a renowned scholar and leader, present the case for the Jewish people and for a homeland in Palestine. Some South Florida Jews, led by Shepard Broad, helped outfit boats to transport Jews from Displaced Persons (DPs) camps in Europe to Palestine. Inspired by firsthand experience in financing boatloads of Holocaust survivors and DPs to arrive in Palestine, Max Orovitz formed "the Miami Group" with fellow Jewish businessmen and created the Dan Hotel chain in Israel following statehood. Following World War II, Jewish doctors could not get staff privileges at any area hospitals. In response, Jewish leaders in the community founded Mount Sinai Hospital on Miami Beach. Today, the fifty-five–acre hospital, the largest employer in that city, is renowned for its leadership in medicine, especially cardiac care.

As the social and cultural fabric of Miami Beach changed following the end of World War II, so did the Beach's physical appearance. Hotels were built rapidly to satiate the desire of tourists for fancy new hotels. The hotel industry was greatly bolstered by Jews, including Ben Novack who, with Harry Mufson, built the Fontainebleau Hotel (1954). Designed by Morris Lapidus, the elegant hotel quickly became a trademark property. A year later, Mufson commissioned Lapidus to design the equally grandisoe Eden Roc Hotel next door.

The entertainment industry and the arts community have benefited greatly from Jews on Miami Beach. Sophie Tucker belted her songs in Yiddish during the 1950s and 1960s in Miami Beach hotels. Jews have taken the initiative in organizing cultural institutions on Miami Beach, including the three museums: Bass Museum of Art; Jewish Museum of Florida, and Wolfsonian-Florida International University. Jews are also key founders of the New World Symphony, Miami City Ballet, and the Concert Association.

Broward County

Since the early 1980s, the Jewish population of the Miami Beach has declined as elderly Jewish residents died and more recent retirees moved north. At present, Broward County, not Miami-Dade, has the largest percentage of Jews. One in six people in Broward County is Jewish.

FIGURES 13 and 14. *Program for Sophie Tucker's performance at the Beachcomber, Miami Beach, 1950. In the late 1940s and into the early 1950s, Miami Beach was everything that Las Vegas would become, with celebrities regularly appearing at hotels and nightclubs. Courtesy Collection of Myrna and Seth Bramson.*

In 1893 when the Bay Stage Line linked Lake Worth (in Palm Beach County) with Lemon City (Miami), passengers on the two-day stagecoach trip stopped at New River to camp overnight. This campsite became Fort Lauderdale after Florida's Governor Napoleon Bonaparte Broward drained the swamps (1909–11). Around the same time, a Jew, Dave Sokolow built a house in Dania, the first community to be incorporated in the future Broward County. With his brother-in-law Louis Brown, Sokolow had three department stores in Dania, Pompano, and Hollywood. In 1916, Max and Rose Lehrman moved to Fort Lauderdale from Miami and opened a dry goods store. Their eldest daughter Nell was the first Jewish girl born in Dade County (1914) and her sister and brother were the first Jewish children born in Broward County. There were seven Jewish families in Fort Lauderdale when Moe Katz settled in 1923 to sell real estate.

The first religious service was held September 17, 1926, on the eve of the big hurricane. In 1935, the community purchased burial plots in Evergreen Cemetery, Fort Lauderdale's first cemetery, and created a Jewish section in the northern portion of the scenic graveyard. Fort Lauderdale Hebrew Congregation, organized in 1931, later became Temple Emanu-el. The synagogue was built in 1937. Founding families included those of Mack and Moe Katz, Abe Newman, Archie Robbins, Louis Sandler, David Blume, and Dr. Albert Shapira, and Charles and Samuel Lerner (of Lerner Stores).

The most important commercial Jewish presence was that of Samuel Horvitz and his Hollywood Inc. In the mid-1920s, Horvitz acquired the vast landholdings of the bankrupted J. W. young companies, which were responsible for the early development of Hollywood. By 1937, with better times arriving, Hollywood Inc. was buying and selling single family homes in Hollywood. By 1940 there were one thousand Jews in Broward County and the dozen or so Jewish families in Hollywood began to have services. During World War II, airfields were converted to traninig facilities. After the war thousands of servicemen recalled the good life in Broward and returned with the families. Many others came and the boom was on.

Jews have contributed to the growth of the county in every sector: retail and wholesale, real estate and development, military and science, education and health, law and medicine, citrus, cattle and poultry, insurance and banking, the arts and government. For example, Wolfie Cohen of "Wolfie's" restaurant owned a chicken ranch in Cooper City, a city created by Morris Cooper of Arrow Shirt Company. Abe Mailman helped develop Hollywood and created the town of Miramar in 1952. Bill Horvitz and Herman Goodman founded Temple Sinai of Hollywood in 1956. Hollywood Beach Hotel owner Ben Tonin donated the Hillcrest country Club; it became Temple Beth El.

At the height of the Six-Day War in Israel (1967), funds were raised and the Jewish Federation began. By 1970, there were 40,000 Jews in Broward County. For the next two decades, this county was the nation's fastest-growing Jewish community; it was home to about 275,000 Jews by 1990. At least twenty Jewish men and women have served as mayors, eleven as judges, and twelve as state or federal legislators from Broward.

Today, with increasing mortality of the elderly and the influx of more Jews to Palm Beach County, the Jewish population has declined to 250,000 withmore than fifty congregations in Broward County. Jews have been an intimate part of the South Florida landscape for more than one hundred years. They have contributed in multiple ways to the development of the region, striving to maintain Jewish culture and institutions even as they've adjusted to the special nature of the place.

AUTHOR'S NOTE
The history reflected here is part of a continuing research project that began in the 1980s in preparation for the traveling exhibit "MOSAIC: Jewish Life in Florida." This project evolved into the Jewish Museum of Florida in 1995. The museum, accredited by the American Association of Museums, is housed in a restored historic former Orthodox synagogue at 301 Washington Avenue, Miami Beach, Florida. The museum features a core exhibit depicting Jewish life in Florida since 1763 as well as temporary exhibits that expand on the core themes and change three times each year with a schedule of complementary public programs and films. Other features include the Collections and Research Center, and the museum store. See www.jewishmuseum.com.

Stephen J. Whitfield

Blood and Sand

Modern Judaism requires a critical mass; it needs enough adherents to breathe, or it will expire. Consider the formulation of Maurice Samuel, who insisted that "Judaism is not only an ethos. Judaism is an outlook on life, which is associated and interwoven ideologically with the history of a people." "Let me put it in a simple way," this master of *haute vulgarisation* continued: "If, somewhere in China today, an individual were to work out for himself all the ethical and theological principles of Judaism, and live up to them, would that make him a Jew? My answer is no. He would be as good a person as any Jew, and better than most Jews; but he would not be a Jew until he had associated himself with the fellowship, and had accepted the responsibilities and instrumentalities of that fellowship."[1]

Jewish identity is impossible without a community to sustain it, without a sense of peoplehood that springs from the imperatives of a continuous religious tradition. Demography is not destiny, but it does impose limits upon potentiality. Those possibilities have been historically shackled in the South, where religious minorities have been marginal and where the ideal of pluralism has not been compelling enough to delegitimize the hegemonic ideology of Protestantism. The Sunbelt was once the Bible Belt and, to some extent, still is. The prototypical American evangelist has spoken with a Southern accent: from Billy Graham (b. North Carolina) to Jerry Falwell (b. Virginia) and Jimmy Lee Swaggart (b. Louisiana). And some of the most bizarre sites of contemporary Protestantism can be found there: from the Heritage USA that Jim and Tammy Baker had constructed in South Carolina to the seven-stories-high Christ of the Ozarks of Gerald L. K. Smith in Arkansas. However bifurcated by race, the South has worshiped at the old rugged cross of a faith that blacks and whites have shared, and remains the most homogeneously Protestant area in the Western hemisphere. When V. S. Naipaul found himself among the believers in Nashville, he counted in the Yellow Pages of the phone directory twelve pages of church listings.[2]

In so God-intoxicated a setting, vulnerable and fragile Jewish communities have generally been more sensitive to the goodwill of Gentiles than to the preservation and reinvigoration of Judaic culture. In cities like Charleston, New Orleans, Richmond, and Atlanta, Jewish life has sustained itself, though often by siphoning off the restless and the ambitious from the surrounding hamlets, and by luring Jews from metropolitan areas in the North and Midwest and even abroad. For all the valiant efforts of many individuals and families, however, the vibrancy and resilience of such places in sustaining Jewish life should not be exaggerated or romanticized. The matrix of *Yiddishkeit* in all the largest cities of the former Confederacy has generally been too thin to replenish itself, and the pressures from the general environment have been too corrosive to nurture Jewish creativity and revitalization. That is why Judaism takes such strange forms among those who took their stand to live and die in Dixie. When Rabbi Michael Matuson led the V'awhavtah prayer in Shreveport and came to the passage, "and they shall be for frontlets before thine eyes," which in Hebrew begins with *vahayu*, he claims that his congregants instinctively respond: "Fine, *hayu?*" When a New Orleans realtor, born and raised in Savannah, mourns for her deceased black maid, Janet Cohen Koppel suspected an intimacy that tends to be less genuine in the North. Her maid was especially indispensable for the Sabbath dinners that were prepared virtually every week—of shrimp rémoulade.[3] From the perspective of communal survival, such instances may be more exotic and charming than indicative of triumph over assimilation. Southern Jewry has largely been out of the loop that begins in, say, Boston and drops down to Washington, D.C., and that represents much of what is most impressive about an ancient people's adaptation to America.

Despite the hemorrhaging of the populace from the Northeast and Midwest to the Sunbelt, the proportion of Jews in most of the former Confederacy has remained a fraction of one percent. More Jews are still packed into Brooklyn than live in the combined total of ten of the eleven states that once seceded from the Union. Far fewer than one American Jew in ten has lived in those ten once rebellious states.[4] But in the southernmost part of the southernmost state in the country, some features of Jewish life in the North have been replanted. An astonishing demographic transformation has occurred in the first state of the union ever to be settled by whites, and this "blood transfusion" is fraught with consequences for communal life in the South and elsewhere. This essay is intended to explore the significance of such numbers and the circumstances within which a special pattern has emerged. I cannot pretend, however, to have examined the inner dynamic or the organizational texture of this community, much less to exhaust the subject of its distinctiveness—only to propose a hypothesis that may stimulate the research and the revision of others.

At least it can be generalized with some confidence that South Florida not only harbors lots of Jews, but also that their migration has given a jolting jump start to the ethnic vitality and pluralism of the Gold Coast, a pluralism perhaps comparable only to that of New York. In an era when local history is *histoire totale* or it is nothing, the examination of the heritage of particular communities yields no correlation between the size and importance of the community (except for New York) and the quality of the historiography that it has inspired. But nowhere is that gap more glaring—or the imbalance more in need of rectification—than in Miami, which should have benefited from the fashionable interest in ethnicity. Yet the Jews of South Florida are understudied. Even Deborah Dash Moore's important *To the Golden Cities* (1994) is a comparative study of Sunbelt communities, treating Miami not as inherently worthy of scrutiny, but in relation to Los Angeles.

Part of the explanation for scholarly indifference is, of course, the sheer velocity of the change, as though the New World Symphony suddenly became a Surprise Symphony. When the third and greatest wave of Jewish immigrants came to the United States little more than a century ago, Miami and its surrounding communities were no more extant than was the automobile or the airplane. And "overnight, or so it must have seemed . . . Miami Beach became first a Jewish city and then a Jewish joke," David Rieff has written of the community across the causeways. "Very much like the Cubans across the bay in Miami proper ten years later, the Jews did not so much adapt to their new surroundings as overrule, or even erase, them. Even today, Wolfie's Delicatessen on Collins Avenue is all but indistinguishable from its counterparts in Manhattan or in Beverly Hills." Jews find "something both vaguely embarrassing and vaguely comic even about the name of the place; it sounds odd."[5] And because Miami Beach has far more commonly been the butt of Jewish jokes than a subject for Jewish scholarship, it too risks becoming a punch line unless its devotees can come to grips with south Florida—the second most populous Jewish community in the largest Jewish community in history. The brevity of this saga and the paucity of documentation mean that oral tradition is about as important to the local historian as were the Mandingo griots to novelist Alex Haley, in trying to retrace his ancestry in *Roots* (1976).

The outlines of the transformation of modern Florida are nevertheless clear, and can be briefly recounted here. A little like the story of the Garden of Eden, modern Florida is about real estate. Unlike paradise, however, settlers had to be persuaded to find it attractive. If the southern part of the state has become a unique niche among Jews in the region, it was despite the odds against them, which the major developers of the area lengthened. Indeed Carl Fisher, who created Miami Beach virtually ex nihilo, intended it to be off-limits to Jews. The owners of famous hotels like the Roney Plaza and the Flamingo drew a line in the sand against "Hebrew" clientele. In 1913 both Fisher and John Collins did the normal thing by putting restrictive covenants ("gentlemen's agreements") in all their property deeds, which they continued through the 1920s and 1930s. To his credit Fisher was not consistently anti-Semitic: Chicagoans like John D. Hertz, the founder of Yellow Cabs, and advertising executive Albert Lasker, of Lord & Thomas, were wealthy enough to pass through the eye of the needle.[6] But the incredible boom of the 1920s, with land selling "by the gallon," was intended to be primarily for Gentiles. The materialistic mantra would remain familiar: "Keep Florida Green—Bring Cash!"

Miami would be transformed within a rural and even "redneck" state, in the deepest part of the Deep South. Carl Fisher had wanted visitors and vacationers and settlers to ignore mortality itself, and so he prohibited cemeteries within the city limits of Miami Beach.[7] But the actuarial tables pressed their inexorable claims; and the Jews, a people that could recollect an earlier exodus to the Promised Land, were almost as unstoppable. Before the interstate highway system was built, they would drive through impoverished, primitive Georgia counties like McIntosh; along Route 17, next to the All-U-Can-Eat catfish restaurants, locals put up announcements for "Kosher Sandwiches!" because, according to one observer, "*Kosher* was simply a word that, when added to a sign, mysteriously caused lots of Yankees to pull over."[8] What had enabled Jews to settle at their destination were the terrifying destructiveness of the hurricane of 1926, which struck on Kol Nidre and ruined many of the Tropical Deco homes, and the subsequent real estate bust, plus the even more powerful cataclysm of the Great Depression. Even along the

great oceanfront estates, the choice was between taking in Jewish millionaires or somehow making do with no millionaires at all.

Though restrictions remained through the 1940s, the trend toward greater social acceptance was nevertheless unmistakable, as the Schine family even took over the sacrosanct Roney Plaza. "The very process that [Carl] Fisher had unleashed on that sandbar guaranteed that his dream of a *Judenfrei* paradise would never come true," journalist T. D. Allman concluded. "Fisher's WASP Republican playground was on the way to becoming one of the first majority-Jewish cities in the United States." Already in 1939 the vacationing Harry Truman was writing to his wife from the Hotel Everglades in Miami that the area "is as flat as a pancake and the principal product seems to be hotels, filling stations, Hebrews and cabins." Exclusivity had virtually collapsed. Indeed the Broad Causeway that connects Miami Beach with the rest of Dade County refers not to its width but to the founder of Bay Harbor Islands, Shepard Broad,[9] a Jewish attorney who helped build Beth Shalom Synagogue on the site of the polo grounds of Fisher's restricted Nautilus

Club. Though "vengeance is mine, saith the Lord," it was no longer the monopoly of the Deity.

In defying Fisher's residential designs, the descendants of Abraham could have discerned a star-spangled realization of the divine promise made to the patriarch after he had offered to sacrifice his son. It is reread every Rosh Hashanah: "Thy seed shall possess the gate of his enemies" (Gen. 22:17). Jews arrived in the United States "with far less than black people now have in resources[,] and they met all kinds of prejudices," Jim Brown, a professional running back and an amateur comparative historian, later explained. "But they worked together; they used their brains and the law and money and business acumen, and by now you can't find any ethnic group in America commanding more respect. *Commanding* it! Do you know that once Jews weren't wanted in Miami? So they bought it." Brown added: "I rarely give a speech today without suggesting the Jews as a model of what black people need to do with themselves economically." It still took a court case that dragged on for seven years before the Florida Supreme Court ruled in 1959 that the Fourteenth Amendment applied to B. J. Harris, a wealthy building contractor and Kentucky banker. He had purchased land on Sunset Islands in 1952 in defiance of the Sunset Island Property Owners, Inc., which sold real estate only according to covenants that were restricted to whites, Christians, and nonfelons. Having won his case and proved his point, Harris preferred to live elsewhere.[10]

Nearly all other Jews who came to the Magic City stayed around, searching for fresh opportunities as though recapitulating the plucky, go-for-broke experience of America itself. Before the city would cater to the nation's dope fiends, it would attract hope fiends, optimists, and high rollers yearning for a big score. Writers like Allman have rhapsodized that Miami "was built on the bedrock of illusion—the dream that if only people pushed far enough, fast enough, into the uncharted vastness, they could escape the cold and corruption of the past, and build for themselves a sunny and virtuous New World." California novelist Joan Didion added that "Miami seemed not a city at all but a tale, a romance of the tropics, a kind of waking dream in which any possibility could and would be accommodated." Such a city "was and is an invented vision, a fantasy of ideal living," where "you go to leave your troubles behind." It was a setting that implied that problems could be finessed, not addressed. It seemed a place of evasion, not encounter. No wonder that Jules Verne's *De la terre à la lune* (1865), which evokes the dream of escape from the earth itself, anticipates moon travel launched from Florida. "Miami started as a resort; it has always dealt in illusion," wrote David Rieff. He added: "Its self-image has always been based on marketing, on the construction of new, improved realities. Miami invented itself, sold itself not once but several times, remade itself to please its customers. The restricted hotels of Carl Fisher gave way to the Jewish *shtetl* of South Beach, the Jewish *shtetl* to the Venezuelan tourist and the Cuban entrepreneur."[11] The atmosphere in Florida encouraged the talents of hucksters who, if I may inject some business lingo, could sell a hatrack to a moose.

Their promotional efforts helped make Florida into the fourth most populous state in the Union (behind California, New York, and Texas).[12] In part because of the influx of Jews and Cubans, the region is now tipped at the bottom with what

MIAMI BEACH, FLORIDA

Eden Roc

HOTEL, YACHT & CABANA CLUB
Oceanfront 45th St., Miami Beach, Florida 33140

*For Those Who Demand
The Very Best...*

FIGURE 2. *Eden Roc Hotel brochure, circa 1969. Built by the late Harry Mufson (former associate of Ben Novack, who opened the Fountainebleau without him after several years of partnership), the Eden Rock opened in 1955. Courtesy Collection of Myrna and Seth Bramson.*

the Census Bureau terms the Miami–Fort Lauderdale Standard Consolidated Statistical Area, which became the nation's tenth largest metropolitan area. If Miami were independent, the city would have a gross national product greater than any Latin American nation other than the behemoths of Brazil and Argentina.[13] It took Greater Boston three centuries to attract the same-size general population that Greater Miami achieved in three decades. Unlike Boston, however, with its history of nearby manufacturing (textiles, shoes) and its suburban high-tech honeycomb, Miami "produces" nothing (except pleasure). The city is postindustrial—though not quite in the sense that sociologist Daniel Bell intended. As T. D. Allman observed in 1987: "Florida doesn't have a single nationally dominant industry—not even a service-sector industry like health care or a high-tech industry like computers. It has no natural resources in the conventional sense of the word: even

its electricity has to be generated farther north." Instead of oil, generators of the
Florida Power and Light Company have sometimes used confiscated marijuana. The state was slow to promote even the semblance of a Silicon Valley, and as late as 1960 had built no university south of Gainesville. Even today Florida lacks an eminent institution of higher learning, and has "almost no corporate headquarters of the Fortune 500."[14]

What south Florida has offered instead was a smooth exit from the discontents and anxieties of the North, a feelin'-groovy fantasy of life devoted to leisure and to comfort, a distorted version of the early and radiant promise of Jefferson's test of civilization: "the pursuit of happiness." (In contrast Freud believed, with typical Central European *Kulturpessimismus*, that civilization is incompatible with happiness.) The individualistic and pleasure-oriented ethos that has vibrated through the region is not obviously reconcilable with authentic Jewishness, however;[15] and this atmosphere risks undermining the communal potential that demographic concentration now permits. While Micah's obligatory norm to "do justice, love mercy, walk humbly with thy God" could hardly be said to have pervaded any society, it has made little headway as the ideal that south Floridians might wish to realize. Such marks a dramatic revision in the way that Jewish experience has partly been considered. The individualistic hedonism of the Magic City and its environs may have contributed to a certain disintegration of Judaic values, especially in its assurance that responsibility (religious, moral) was not something to be met but something to be ducked. After all, the motto that "Mr. Miami Beach," a flack named Hank Meyer, bestowed upon the city—"Sun and Fun Capital of the World"[16]—could have been devised for the skywriting above Sodom and Gomorrah.

The widespread violation of the dietary laws that were once an impenetrable barrier between Christians and Jews is an index of that historic discontinuity. It may not be coincidental that the oldest business in continuous operation on Miami Beach is Joe's Stone Crab, which serves crustaceans to an average horde of fourteen hundred famished customers a night. (Full disclosure: the author has been among them.) Joe's Stone Crab is open for business—even on the High Holy Days. Or take the most flamboyantly famous hotel on Miami Beach; a building that has needed no nameplate and that is as ambitiously curved as Einstein's universe. The Fontainebleau, which opened in late December 1954, was the creation of Ben Novack (born in The Bronx) and Morris Lapidus (born in czarist Russia). Even though its clientele has been emphatically Jewish, the guests at the Fontainebleau annually consume a whopping 41,600 pounds of bacon. (Eventually Novack and his partner Harry Mufson split with such cosmic bitterness that Mufson retaliated with the even more awesome Eden Roc Hotel, to which Novack responded with the looming North Tower that inflicted upon the Eden Roc a daily eclipse of the sun, a nasty two o'clock shadow.)[17]

The eclipse of some intellectual vitality and ideals may be taken as another challenge to the security of Judaism in south Florida. The gnomic passage in the Talmud *Baba batra*, 25b—"He who desires to become wise should turn to the south, and he who desires to become rich should turn to the north"—has been reversed, as David Rieff complained, "in the brilliant sunshine of Florida, [where] books look odd, almost out of place." Climate cannot be the excuse for the think-or-swim dichotomy: southern California harbors distinguished institutions of learning like UCLA, plus seminaries that are training Reform, Conservative, and Orthodox rabbis. An earlier generation of European Jewish refugee artists and writers like Arnold Schoenberg, Jascha Heifetz, Artur Rubinstein, Franz Werfel, and Emil Ludwig ended up in southern California. So did giants like Stravinsky, Mann, and Brecht. But none of the important refugee intellectuals went to southern Florida. Comedian Mort Sahl drew upon the unserious reputation of the University of Miami in disparaging the school as "a rationale for surfing." Despite the abundance of senior citizens, it occurred to no one in Miami to make it the headquarters of Elderhostel; Boston is. Young Rieff reported several curious encounters in "mentally flaccid" Miami, whose inhabitants "would ask where I 'found' the time to read, as if, somehow, it was unfair that the whole thing actually required time." Perhaps South Florida Jewry yielded to some of the mental torpor associated—at least in legend—with other parts of the South. No major library of Judaica, no Jewish institution of higher learning, served this community of half a million—a situation of scholarly lacunae that is probably without precedent in the history of the Diaspora outside of the Soviet Union.[18]

So equivocal a connection to belles-lettres is one way to read Gordon Lish's savage short story, "For Jerome—with Love and Kisses," in which retiree Sol Salinger implores his reclusive and distant son up in area code 603 to act normal and make him proud. The son is J. D. Salinger; and the father's idea of *naches* would be for his *boychik* to do bookchat with Merv Griffin, the TV ringmaster for the children of other residents of the Seavue Spa Oceanfront Garden Arms and Apartments. In that one building on the beach live all the doting parents of all the successful children who have hawked their wares in the literary marketplace. Like a cruise director on an endless guilt trip, Sol Salinger shrieks at his elusive, intensely private son, his "Jerrychik," his "Jaydeezie darling": "Other children listen, Jerome. The Allen kid, Woody, *he* listens. *Philip* listens, *Saul* listens—and for your information, so does *Bernard!* Believe me, Jerome, everybody in here, they got a kid which they can count on to listen—the Krantzes do and the Plains do, and so do the Sheldons and the Friedmans and the Elkins and the Wallaces and the Segals. . . . And notice that I am not even mentioning the Robbins family and their Harold, and the Potoks and their Chaim. You think the Wouks don't have a Herman which listens? The Mailer people, their Norman *listens*."[19] And so on and on, unctuously and crudely. There on Lish's beach live none of the celebrated writers themselves, only parents who have no comprehension of the subtle standards of literary excellence.

It is therefore paradoxical that more Nobel laureates in literature made their home in Miami Beach than in, say, Chicago or Los Angeles. Until his death in 1991, Isaac Bashevis Singer lived for several months every winter in North Miami Beach and eventually all year round, in a condominium on Collins Avenue that he had purchased in 1973. But in so unliterary a town as Surfside, he was no big deal. Ninety-fifth Street was renamed in his honor near his condo, but the laureate kvetched: "Ach, it's nothing but a back alley. You can't even find it!"[20]

Such sun-kissed surroundings exerted little impact upon Singer's own celebrated

FIGURE 3. *Isaac Bashevis Singer lecturing at the University of Miami. No date. Courtesy Jewish Museum of Florida.*

narrations. To be sure the salience of place can easily be exaggerated; novelists as diverse as Kipling and Solzhenitsyn, for instance, wrote books in Vermont. But though Singer enjoyed the large terrace where he could stand and gaze upon the skyline of high-rises to the north, plus the expanse of beach and the ocean below, his tales occupy the dimension of time, not of space.

Another famous Miami resident was Meyer Lansky, who made himself into the most famous (or notorious) of Jewish gangsters, the very incarnation of the *kosher nostra*. Reputed to be the brainiest of mobsters, Lansky was even a member of the Book-of-the-Month Club (though he was not exactly a bookworm). Lansky actually wanted to *live* in Israel (not just to visit or to be buried in the Holy Land). He had tried to make *aliyah* in 1970 but, because FBI surveillance was so uncomfortably tight, he was denied citizenship and was sent back to Miami Beach a year later. Eviction soured the prospective *oleh*: "We raised money in our casinos for the United Jewish Appeal, for one thing. The first fund-raising in Miami for the state of Israel was organized and initiated in my casino in the Colonial Inn. That was a great evening, with over a thousand people partying and pledging money for Israel."

Dining in his twilight years at the Embers Restaurant (where a table was always available), this rather unusual member of the American Association of Retired Persons (AARP) recalled "in 1967, during the Six-Day War, I went myself to speak to some of the boys in Miami who were not known as generous when it came to making contributions. I told them this was the time for them to open their pockets, and open them wide. . . . So you can understand why I'm angry at the Israeli government."[21] Though Lansky may never have quite been the head comptroller of the underworld, he did personify the "Zionist hoodlums" whom the actress Vanessa Redgrave had denounced, in a different context (the Oscar ceremonies), in 1978.

His career is one proof of the generalization that, due to the velocity of accultura-
tion, certain activities are not "Jewish" merely because Jews perform them. Modern
times have narrowed the historic difference between Jew and Gentile, which the
testimony of Maurice Samuel can again be summoned to clarify. He argued, for
example, that the ancient Hebrews as well as the impoverished immigrants of his
own Manchester, England, took no notice of sports. "The language that my parents
and my *Rebbi* spoke," Samuel recalled, "was altogether free from the sporting ex-
pressions that were so thickly distributed, in strategic ideological areas, throughout
English. . . . If you read the Bible and . . . the Mishnah and Talmud, and ignored the
references to Gentile nations and customs, you would likewise never suspect that
the world of antiquity had been as addicted to sports as is the modern world."[22]

That historic distinction between Jacob and Esau got blurred in Miami, however.
The city produced the preeminent Jewish major leaguer in the era between Hank
Greenberg (the Detroit Tigers' first baseman whose fifty-eight home runs in the
1938 season rubbed against Babe Ruth's record) and Sandy Koufax (the Dodgers'
pitcher who was so good that, in Bugs Baer's immortal phrase, he "could throw a
lamb-chop past a wolf"). Though born in Spartanburg, South Carolina (in 1925),
Al Rosen was raised in Miami and went on to the University of Florida and then
the University of Miami, from which he graduated. Playing with the Cleveland
Indians from 1947 until 1956, the third baseman led the American League with
thirty-seven homers in 1950, and was selected Most Valuable Player—it was
unanimous for the first time in the history of the awards—in 1953, when he led
the league with forty-three home runs and 145 runs batted in. With his .336 batting
average, Rosen missed winning the batting title on the last day of the season by
.001. He had refused to play baseball on the Jewish High Holy days. As a sports
historian has wistfully noted, Rosen "might have won the batting title [in 1953,] had
he played those days and gotten a few hits." He also played in the 1952–55 All-Star
games, and later helped run the New York Yankees, the Houston Astros, and the
Indians.[23] Although the translation of Genesis 1:1 might be pronounced as "In
the big inning," Rosen's national prominence nevertheless suggested the Jewish
discontinuity of Miami, where an Orthodox rabbi, Solomon Schiff, has delivered
the gridiron invocation for the Dolphins.

In such a community, "Jews, like Cubans later, underwent metamorphoses
every bit as zany as Presbyterians ever had: bleached-blond beehive hairdos and
suntanned face-lifts on the daughters of Orthodox cantors; graduates of yeshivas
wearing gold chains and sports shirts that showed their nipples; synagogues that
doubled as booking centers for nightclub acts."[24] Religious life did not flourish
in such a setting. Indeed the very brevity of Florida history has upended some
familiar patterns. It is post-Orthodox, in that—unlike as in the more settled states
of the union—no Orthodox synagogues had been established in the nineteenth
century.[25] Even though the first congregation in Miami (Temple Beth David, formerly B'nai Zion) was founded by World War I (the second was built in 1922), and
even though a synagogue (Beth Jacob) was built on Miami Beach in 1929 when
the city was still highly restricted, and even though the formidable chief rabbi of
Roumania, Dr. Moses Rosen, wintered on the beach there,[26] Miami has been filled

FIGURE 4. *Blackstone Hotel brochure, circa 1940s. Courtesy Collection of Myrna and Seth Bramson.*

with H$_2$O Jews—the nickname for those who attend services on two holidays only (Rosh Hashanah and Yom Kippur). More than 4,500 have agglomerated to welcome the New Year and atone for their sins at the oldest Reform synagogue, for example, requiring Temple Israel to use the Miami Beach Convention Hall.[27] Such congregants commonly expected rabbis to be good mixers, not necessarily good scholars. They had uprooted themselves to live in south Florida well after the impact of Americanization had been registered, long after the acids of modernization had corroded the integral *Yiddishkeit* of their ancestors.

The most macabre puberty rite in Jewish history was conducted on a site, rented in 1978 that symbolized the reversal of the traditional disregard for spectator sports. Following the ritual in a Conservative shul in which Harvey Cohen became a bar mitzvah, the celebrants took over the Orange Bowl. While the scoreboard flashed "Happy Birthday, Harvey," a 64-piece high school marching band entertained the two hundred guests, who were served by waiters dressed as referees and by waitresses dressed as cheerleaders. One of the city's leading rabbis, Dr. Irving

Lehrman of Temple Emanu-El, complained that "in this case there is more bar than mitzvah"; and indeed the compliant City Commission had been persuaded to pass a special ordinance allowing liquor to be served in the stadium. Standing on the fifty-yard line after watching young Harvey say the *motzi* over bread and light the candles, grandfather Robert Cohen assured an interviewer that "it doesn't matter, I guess, where a bar mitzvah party is held, as long as there is love and family and joy."[28]

That glorification of joy became a South Florida specialty. Of course hedonism is no monopoly of Miami Jews, nor of Floridians generally. In the genealogy of morals, neither the ethos of felicity nor the quest for self-satisfaction was invented in Miami. The Hebrews were worshiping the golden calf even as the Torah was being transmitted to Moses; in Jewish history ancient revels coincided with revelation. Perhaps the fun and games at the very foot of Mount Sinai can be seen as an early version of Club Mediterranee, which a French Jew named Gilbert Trigano founded in 1954. With Miami as one terminus, much of American social history could be told in terms of the repudiation of Puritanism, recounting the transformation of the "land of the Pilgrims' pride" into a landscape littered with credit cards and enticing advertisements designed to reinforce the relentless quest for self-gratification through mass consumption. But a lavish commitment to the pursuit of happiness should at least be recognized as a rupture of Judaic tradition.

When Abraham left Ur of the Chaldees to inaugurate the singular drama of Jewish history (and the experience of wandering), he could scarcely have imagined that the Jewish corporate personality would include representative developments like Century Village. Such communities are historically unprecedented in confining membership exclusively to the old. An Israeli visitor was especially struck by the absence of children: "no toddlers, no teenagers, and except for the staff, barely anyone under sixty." The Century Villagers form "a new breed" who are "bronzed, vigorous, dedicated to a happy ending." Theirs is "life without limits, Century Village style; a life without family or the friendships and obligations of a snow-filled lifetime." Ze'ev Chafets soon discovered that "Century Village has a number of rules, but only one commandment: NO CHILDREN IN THE CLUBHOUSE. . . . Sometimes grandchildren do visit, of course; but they are second-class citizens. Considering the traditional Jewish obsession with children[,] it is an astonishing policy."[29] Nobody should expect such retirees to resemble ancestors who are depicted so quaintly in medieval woodcuts, but their one commandment contradicts the ideals of family cohesiveness and loyalty, the philoprogenitive heritage of the Jews, that a baffled Tacitus had mentioned in his Roman *Histories* (V, iv, v). Such clubhouse rules are also an ironic rebuke to the most popular, sensitive, and empathic writer of novels aimed at adolescent girls, Judy Sussman Blume, whose New Jersey family had wintered so extensively on Miami Beach in the 1940s that she attended elementary school there, later fictionalizing the experience in *Starring Sally J. Freedman as Herself* (1977).[30]

South Florida has exemplified another kind of last hurrah. Jews are the nation's most geriatric ethnic group. Of elderly Jews who move, 60 percent have moved to Florida. So skewed an aging pattern has meant that Miami Beach lifeguards devote more time to aiding victims of heart attacks than to rescuing swimmers floundering in the surf, turning leisure world into "seizure world."[31]

Such Jews lived in an ambience that was as defined by age as by ethnicity. "They have the memories of immigrants' children and these memories matter," Chafets concluded, "but the real influence on their lives has been America—its language and rhythms, culture and ethos. They are charter members of the first Jewish generation taught . . . 'to do its own thing.' And here, in Florida, in the twilight of their lives, who can blame them if that thing has turned out to be mixed doubles, early bird dining, and the fox-trot."[32] Religion is not, of course, about doing your own thing; it means doing the *right* thing. And in such communities, the moralistic and even messianic fervor that has historically impressed observers of the Jewish people seems to have dissipated in an atmosphere of humidity and hedonism.

Because Judaism has customarily been about adherence to a set of legal codes and ethical ideals, their enfeeblement under the influence of individualism is as worthy of attention as the demographic opportunity for cohesive survival that the Miami experience suggests. South Florida manifestly has the numbers for Jewish life to prevail; it is the caliber of that life that is problematic. "North Miami Beach is still intensely Jewish," according to one observer, "but . . . the ambience of the place is Jewish only in that secular, Americanized way whose substance seems to consist of little more than a few shared tastes in food, a sprinkle of vivid Yiddish expletives, and a rather desperate, reflexive passion for the state of Israel. And South Miami Beach, once the last Jewish *shtetl* of Czarist Russia, is dying, if it has not died already."[33] Where the vessels of Judaic culture are broken, the chances of Jewish continuity and consanguinity are imperiled, which is why—from the standpoint of meaningful Jewish identity—more is to be feared from the *am ha-aretz* (ignoramus) than the *apikoros* (unbeliever) or even the rare *meshumad* (apostate). This is the challenge that Jewry faces in South Florida, where the influence of grandparents is reduced because the rest of the family may be living somewhere else, and where the rates of synagogue affiliation and community center membership, as well as the per capita contributions to UJA/Federation campaigns, are among the lowest in the United States.[34] Some of the valuables have been left unattended.

It would nevertheless be defeatist to underestimate the resources that South Florida Jewry can yet summon to help another generation to discover for itself the buried treasure of its heritage; the communal record also includes such innovative programs as High School in Israel, named for Alexander Muss, whose son Stephen owned the Fontainebleau. A final word should therefore be granted to the quotable Maurice Samuel: "The endurance of the Jewish people is a continuous exertion of the will in the face of adversity, of creative ingenuity in the midst of change."[35] In South Florida that change has been accelerated; and the endurance of its huge Jewish population will be tested not against adversity, but under circumstances so benign that the seamlessness of Jewish history itself may be threatened. For the last two millennia, that experience has been punctuated by estrangement and exile, cruelty and precariousness. Such were the familiar penalties of the dispersion. The derogatory Amharic term for the Jewish minority in Ethiopia—*falasha*, which means "stranger" or "landless one"—was once applicable to *all* Jews, a stigma that helps to account for the gratitude and exultation with which they have embraced America, where Jewish history has been put out of its misery. In the United States the carapace of self-consciousness is much lighter. All Jews are free to exercise the option to disappear into the general population, with no burdens to be borne and little guilt to be assuaged, with few fears of anti-Semitism to be faced or social uncertainties to be calibrated. Not only those who have converted to Judaism, but also those born and raised within its precincts, must therefore be considered Jews by choice. Their tsuris can no longer be ascribed to the Jewish condition itself, which is why the thirst to fulfill the lovely fantasies at the nation's lowest geographic tip may mark a caesura in the annals of the Diaspora.

ACKNOWLEDGMENTS

I am very grateful to the Mazer Fund for Faculty Research of Brandeis University for supporting this project, to Professor Henry A. Green for sharing his expertise and files with me, to Mrs. Joan S. Whitfield, Mr. Donald Altschiller, Professors Jack E. Davis and Gary R. Mormino for their clipping services, to Dr. Martin and Sharon Rothberg for their hospitality, and to Professor Marc Lee Raphael for his cogent and helpful criticisms of an earlier draft of this article. The opportunity to present a version of it at the 1990 conference of the Florida Historical Society is also appreciated.

NOTES

This essay is a revised and shortened version of an article that originally appeared in *American Jewish History* 82, nos. 1–4 (1994): 73–96, and that is reprinted with permission from the American Jewish Historical Society.

1. Maurice Samuel, *The Professor and the Fossil: Some Observations on Arnold J. Toynbee's* A Study of History (New York, 1956), 175.

2. V. S. Naipaul, *A Turn in the South* (New York, 1989), 233.

3. Interview with Janet C. Koppel, New Orleans, January 10, 1990.

4. Abraham D. Lavender, ed., introduction to *A Coat of Many Colors: Jewish Subcommunities in the United States* (Westport, Conn., 1977), 9; Barry Kosmin and Jeffrey Scheckner, "Jewish Population in the United States, 1990," in *American Jewish Year Book 1991*, ed. David Singer (Philadelphia, 1991), 207–8 and 216.

5. Robert Sherrill, "Can Miami Save Itself?" *New York Times Sunday Magazine*, July 19, 1987, 18; David Rieff, *Going to Miami: Exiles, Tourists and Refugees in the New America* (Boston, 1987), 188.

6. Harold Mehling, *The Most of Everything: The Story of Miami Beach* (New York, 1960), 131–33, reprinted in "Is Miami Beach Jewish?" in Lavender, ed., *Coat of Many Colors*, 120–23; Harry Simonhoff, *Under Strange Skies* (New York, 1953), 292–94.

7. John Rothchild, *Up for Grabs: A Trip through Time and Space in the Sunshine State* (New York, 1985), 35, 38–43, 76–77, and 209.

8. Melissa Faye Greene, *Praying for Sheetrock* (Reading, Mass., 1991), 58; Simonhoff, *Under Strange Skies*, 283–90; Malvina W. Liebman and Seymour B. Liebman, *Jewish Frontiersmen: Historical Highlights of Early South Florida, Jewish Communities* (Miami Beach, Fla., n.d.), 39–41.

9. Judith Nelson Drucker, quoted in Howard Simons, *Jewish Times: Voices of the American Jewish Experience* (Boston, 1988), pp. 140–42; T. D. Allman, *Miami: City of the Future* (New York, 1987), 228–29, and 234; Robert H. Ferrell, ed., *Dear Bess: The Letters from*

Harry to Bess Truman, 1910–1959 (New York, 1983), 436; Bernard Postal and Lionel Koppman, *A Jewish Tourist's Guide to the U.S.* (Philadelphia, 1954), 117 and 121.

10. Alex Haley, "Playboy Interview: Jim Brown," *Playboy* 15 (February 1968), 64; Polly Redford, *Billion-Dollar Sandbar: A Biography of Miami Beach* (New York: Dutton, 1970), 274; Benjamin R. Epstein and Arnold Forster, *Some of My Best Friends . . .* (New York, 1962), 131–33.

11. Allman, *Miami*, 16 and 244; Joan Didion, *Miami* (New York, 1987), 33; Rieff, *Going to Miami*, 12, 25, and 26; Jules Verne, *From the Earth to the Moon and Round the Moon* (New York, n.d.), 62, 70, 141–46, and passim.

12. Raymond Arsenault and Gary R. Mormino, "From Dixie to Dreamland," in *Shades of the Sunbelt: Essays on Ethnicity, Race, and the Urban South*, ed. Randall M. Miller and George E. Pozzetta (Westport, Conn., 1988), 180.

13. T. D. Allman, "The City of the Future," *Esquire* 99 (February 1983), 42 and 44.

14. Allman, *Miami*, 245–46; "Trouble in Paradise," *Time* 118 (November 23, 1981), 29.

15. Simonhoff, *Under Strange Skies*, 326.

16. Redford, *Billion-Dollar Sandbar*, 283–84.

17. Ibid., 211, 212, and 287; "More Tiles and Tales . . . ," *Tiles: The Newsletter of MOSAIC* 3 (Spring 1990), 7; interview with JoAnne Bass [1992], in *Mosaic* (on videocassette, JFTV, Miami); Allman, *Miami*, 112–16, 253, and 256–57; Mehling, *The Most of Everything*, 86–88.

18. Rieff, *Going to Miami*, 52 and 72; John Gunther, *Inside U.S.A.* (New York, 1947), 7; Herb Tobin, "The Myth of Community in the Sunbelt," *Journal of Jewish Communal Service* 61 (Fall 1984), 48–49.

19. Gordon Lish, "For Jerome—with Love and Kisses," in *What I Know So Far* (New York, 1986), 128.

20. Quoted in Dorothea Straus, *Under the Canopy* (New York, 1982), 131–32; Richard Nagler and Isaac Bashevis Singer, *My Love Affair with Miami Beach* (New York, 1991), vii–ix.

21. Quoted in Dennis Eisenberg, Uri Dan, and Eli Landau, *Meyer Lansky: Mogul of the Mob* (New York, 1979), 319–20; Hank Messick, *Lansky* (New York, 1971), 13–15, 254, and 272–77; Robert Lacey, *Little Man: Meyer Lansky and the Gangster Life* (New York, 1991), 3–4 and 7.

22. Maurice Samuel, *The Gentleman and the Jew* (New York, 1950), 103–5.

23. Quoted in Red Smith, *To Absent Friends* (New York, 1982), 207; Robert Slater, *Great Jews in Sports* (Middle Village, N.Y., 1983), 172–74; Peter Levine, *Ellis Island to Ebbets Field: Sport and the American Jewish Experience* (New York, 1992), 128–29.

24. Allman, *Miami*, 235.

25. Henry A. Green, "Mosaic: Jewish Life in Florida," *Florida Jewish Demography* 3 (December 1, 1989), n.p.

26. Interview with Chief Rabbi Moses Rosen, Bucharest, Roumania, March 27, 1989.

27. Charlton W. Tebeau, *Synagogue in the Central City: Temple Israel of Greater Miami, 1922–1972* (Coral Gables, Fla., 1972), 71–73 and 101–2.

28. "Dubious Achievement Awards," *Esquire* 91 (January 2–16, 1979), 33; Jon Nordheimer, "Miami Bar Mitzvah Has 'Love and Family and Joy'—and Cheerleaders," *New York Times*, May 15, 1978, D10.

29. Frances FitzGerald, *Cities on a Hill: A Journey Through Contemporary American Cultures* (New York, 1986), 212; Ze'ev Chafets, *Members of the Tribe: On the Road in Jewish America* (New York, 1988), 234 and 236–37; Edward S. Shapiro, *A Time for Healing: American Jewry Since World War II* (Baltimore, Md., 1992), 139; Ira M. Sheskin, "Implications of

the Geographic Shift in the Jewish Population," *Florida Jewish Demography* 3 (December 1, 1989), n.p.

30. Milton Himmelfarb, *The Jews of Modernity* (New York, 1973), 137; Betsy Lee, *Judy Blume's Story* (Minneapolis, Minn., 1981), 23–31, and 43.

31. Deborah Dash Moore, "Jewish Migration to the Sunbelt," in *Shades of the Sunbelt*, 46–47; Allen Glicksman, *The New Jewish Elderly: A Literature Review* (New York, 1991), 11; "Ebb Tide at Miami Beach," *Time* 110 (December 19, 1977), 83.

32. Chafets, *Members of the Tribe*, 239.

33. Rieff, *Going to Miami*, 189.

34. Sheskin, "Implications of the Geographic Shift in the Jewish Population," n.p.; Tobin, "Myth of Community," *Journal of Jewish Communal Service*, 45–47 and 49; Melvyn Bloom, "The Missing $500,000,000," *Moment* 6 (January–February, 1981), 31–34.

35. Samuel, *The Professor and the Fossil*, 182.

Henry Abramson

Anti-Semitism in Florida Culture

Floridians know that in this state, north is south and south is very much north. That is, northern Florida is really southern Georgia, and southern Florida—especially the Gold Coast, from Miami up to West Palm Beach—is the southern extension of Long Island, New York. The Panhandle and cities like Jacksonville, Gainesville, and Pensacola are part of the cultural orbit of the old South, whereas the great post-war immigration centers of the Gold Coast gave way to the northeastern seaboard as easily as jalousie windows gave way to central air-conditioning. Such is certainly true for the Jewish communities of this state, and it is also true of the Floridian variety of anti-Semitism. Prejudice against Jews in the north is more likely to conform to the version of the antipathy evidenced in the American South, a form that dominated the earlier part of the twentieth century. To the south, however, a more virulent strain of anti-Jewish sentiment is in evidence, often conveying themes that are far more commonly found in the urban northeast.[1]

In large part, this distinction is true because Floridian anti-Semitism is very much subordinated to the far larger dynamic of racial tensions in this state, and in the country as a whole. Jews in the Old South experienced some discrimination, to be sure, but their experience must be placed within the context of the discrimination directed against African-Americans, which was far more pervasive and deep-seated. Southern Jews were "whitened" by virtue of the presence of blacks, and this was a status that they wished to preserve.[2] Protected in some measure by their skin color, however, the Jews of north Florida were nevertheless targeted by anti-black groups such as the Ku Klux Klan, and therefore experienced a form of anti-Semitism that ultimately linked them to the struggle for civil rights. The Jews of South Florida—by and large, later migrants to the Sunshine State—were subjected to a form of anti-Semitism that was heavily influenced by movements more commonly found in the northern parts of the country, with a strong strain of European anti-Semitism during the Depression years. Ultimately, the homogenizing factor of hate on the Internet (a medium pioneered by Floridians) would diminish the ideological elements native to the state.

Early Jewish migration to Florida was limited by the fact that the territory, under Spanish colonization, was officially *Judenrein*. The first recorded Jewish settlers were a group of Jews from Louisiana in 1763, who were joined by several others from the Caribbean and centered in Pensacola. The community grew in fits and starts, adapting to the shifting policies of the ruling powers, until Florida became an American territory in 1821. Although small in number, Jews were prominent in the early political life of the state, including the first Jewish senator, David Levy Yulee.[3] Migration to the southern reaches of the state began in earnest when Isidor Cohen arrived in 1896 to establish a steadily increasing flow of Jewish entrepreneurs.[4]

Nineteenth-century anti-Semitism in Florida was heavily influenced by the intense social pressures attendant to the emancipation of blacks. It is instructive that John Quincy Adams once disparaged Yulee as having "a dash of African blood in him."[5] This is all the more ironic, given Yulee's position supporting slavery. More commonly, Jews were apt to view blacks as employable—sometimes in an exploitative fashion—and could cross white sensibilities, often with dangerous results. For example, in 1869, Samuel Fleishman of Marianna, Florida, was ordered by local residents to leave town by sundown, as he had employed and extended credit to newly freed slaves. Abandoning his business, he sought protection in Tallahassee without success, and decided to return. His body was found on the outskirts of town, and local rumor held that it was the work of the newly founded Ku Klux Klan.[6]

The Klan exerted a strong influence on Floridian anti-Semitism to the 1930s, the peak of its popularity (see figure 1). The organization was originally founded in the wake of the Civil War, a clandestine group that engaged in subversive, anti-Northern activity by harassing newly freed slaves, burning and occasionally lynching while hiding under hoods and cloaks. Publication in 1905 of Thomas Dixon's *The Clansman* and its adaptation to the screen in *Birth of a Nation* (1917) increased the popularity of the KKK, whose influence spread over most of the southern states. Jews did not figure prominently in the agenda of the early Klan, which was just as likely to oppose "Papism" as Judaism. Nevertheless, as more Jews began to arrive from the northern states through the twentieth century, the appearance of the Klan in public spaces was certainly a cause for alarm, as was the case with their 1993 rally in Hollywood, Florida (see figure 2).

FIGURE 1. *Klansmen and Klanswomen in the Fourth of July parade, Miami, Florida, 1927. Courtesy Romer Collection, Miami-Dade Public Library System. Reprinted from* The Art of Hatred: Images of Intolerance in Florida Culture. *Courtesy the Jewish Museum of Florida.*

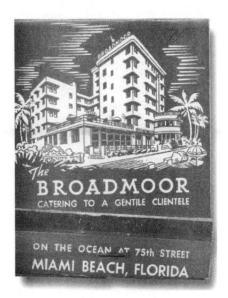

Perhaps the most significant aspect of early Floridian anti-Semitism was the exclusionist attitude, inspired perhaps by Klan activity. Blacks were of course segregated as elsewhere in the South, but Jews were somewhat more difficult to isolate. Until the late 1940s, when films like *Gentleman's Agreement* (Elia Kazan, 1947) made exclusionist policies at recreational sites less fashionable, it was standard for hotels and resorts in the burgeoning tourist economy to prohibit Jews from enjoying their facilities. Slogans like "restricted clientele" or "exclusive" clientele hinted at what others stated outright: "gentile clientele only" (see figures 3 and 4). In a remarkably revealing document, the mayor of Saint Louis, Victor Miller, wrote

FIGURE 4. *Hotel brochure, circa 1960. Courtesy Collection of Myrna and Seth Bramson.*

FIGURE 5. *Detail of Broadsheet, circa 1937.* Nationalist Youth Gazette, *published in Chicago, distributed in Florida. Reprinted from* The Art of Hatred: Images of Intolerance in Florida Culture. *Courtesy the Jewish Museum of Florida, gift of Mr. Burnett Roth.*

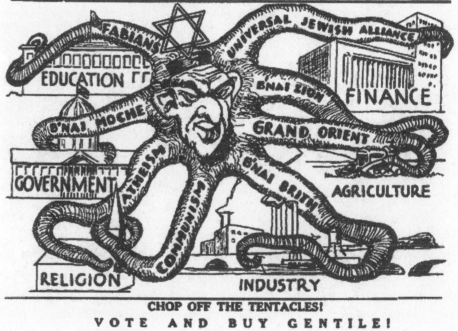

a personal note to Miami developer Carl Fisher, asking for special permission for his Jewish friend to enjoy Fisher's golf course:

> One of the best friends I have on earth, Mr. Wm. Lewin, is staying at Miami Beach at 849 West Avenue. He is the first person that I ever played golf with in my life, and he is anxious to make some connection so that he can play golf at the Beach.
>
> I realize that on account of his nationality there may be some objections but if you can possibly get him the courtesy of your golf club I shall be everlastingly grateful to you.[7]

The fact that the mayor of a major metropolitan city would feel that a personal letter of this sort would be necessary is indicative of the pervasive mood of exclusionism that permeated the new tourist economy of the state. This mode of exclusion was especially prevalent north of Miami Beach, due in part to the construction of hotels catering specifically to the Jewish market. A survey in the early 1950s revealed that 55 percent of hotels throughout the state excluded Jewish patrons, whereas only 20 percent of hotels in Miami Beach and neighboring Surfside had such a policy.[8]

The 1930s witnessed a spate of anti-Semitic activity, centered on a pro-Nazi organization called The White Front, run by a Major Frank Pease. Prolific and energetic, Pease published a brief-lived newsletter called *Nation and Race* that shamelessly borrowed German anti-Semitic propaganda, and mounted rallies in several locations throughout Florida. Northern materials also circulated in Florida at this time, such as the *Nationalist Youth Gazette* from Chicago (with hazy ties to Pease), trumpeting themes made popular by the *Protocols of the Elders of Zion*, a notorious forgery from turn-of-the-century Russia that claimed to "reveal" a Jewish plot to enslave the world.[9] Images of a diabolical Jewish octopus controlling various aspects of American life were disseminated in the *Nationalist Youth Gazette* in the 1930s, but they had little specific connection to the Floridian experience (see figure 5).

Nation and Race, however, was unusual in that it targeted the Jews on specifically Floridian issues. In 1936, for example, Pease played up nativist sensibilities in Florida by portraying the Jews as flotsam from the ocean, floating in with the surf (see figure 6). Jews were seen as pollutants, crowding and desecrating the otherwise pristine beaches of the Sunshine State. Pease's agenda was clearly Nazi in orientation, with a strong Southern flavor: in a White Front leaflet, stated goals included "segregating the Jews" and "disciplining the blacks" (see figure 7). One of the more fascinating images, however, seems to indicate that Mr. Pease had some difficulty convincing other Floridians of his white supremacist agenda. A 1936 cartoon shows a frightened child on the beach with a starfish that has taken on the shape of the dreaded swastika, watching in dismay as a crowd of angry Jews launch themselves on the offending creature (see figure 8). The text of the image is that Jews react violently to the development of Nazi sympathies in America, something that Pease obviously regarded as benign and innocuous.

The Holocaust discredited the activity of anti-Semites like the people behind *Nation and Race,* and Floridian Jews, along with their coreligionists throughout

America, enjoyed a brief honeymoon period in which anti-Semitism was once again an ugly concept. Beginning in 1951, however, a series of synagogue bombings and vandalisms rocked the community, apparently in reaction to the more vocal Jewish support for the civil rights movement, particularly in the northern-southern parts of the state.[10] New anti-Semitic movements sprung up in Florida, some of which would have global impact. One of the more prominent organizations was the Church of the Creator (later known as the World Church of the Creator), founded by Florida legislator Ben Klassen, who referred to himself as Pontifex Maximus. His most important contribution to hatred was the publication of *The White Man's Bible* (Lighthouse Point, Florida, 1981), one of a series of works that later became the core belief structure of Creativity, a church affiliated with the so-called Identity movement (see figure 9). Basic to Klassen's ideas were the notion that Jews and blacks were so-called mud people, descended from animals who may have had some human ancestors. Klassen committed suicide in 1993, but the movement was reorganized and revitalized by a new leader, and is one of the more prominent and active hate groups in twenty-first–century America. The Identity movement had an amorphous relationship with fringe Protestant groups, and the creation of ephemeral churches as fronts for anti-Semitic ranting was not uncommon in Florida. Tampa's Church of the Avenger, for example, was extremely active in the 1990s, producing a prodigious number of hate pamphlets and distributing them widely throughout the state. They also decorated the exterior of the "churches" for maximum propaganda benefit (see figure 10).

Anti-Semitic literature distributed in Florida at this time once again linked Jews to the racial struggle. Borrowing pamphlets from other organizations, Floridian anti-Semites distributed materials like "White and Proud!"—a cheaply reproduced comic strip that advanced the basic thesis that Jews protected blacks from white wrath for their own purposes, namely, to dilute the vitality of the white people

FIGURE 7. *Flyer, circa 1935, Live Oak, Florida. Reprinted from* The Art of Hatred: Images of Intolerance in Florida Culture. *Courtesy the Jewish Museum of Florida. Gift of Mr. Burnett Roth.*

FIGURE 8. *Newspaper illustration,* Nation and Race, *September 1936, Clermont, Florida. Reprinted from* The Art of Hatred: Images of Intolerance in Florida Culture. *Courtesy the Jewish Museum of Florida. Gift of Mr. Burnett Roth.*

through "race-mixing" (see figure 11). Organizations like the Aryan Nations and the National Association for the Advancement of White People made considerable headway in Broward County, a solidly suburban region immediately north of Miami-Dade County, with the Aryan Nations setting up a "Strike Force" in Hollywood.[11]

During the last decade of the twentieth century, another major development in the history of anti-Semitism occurred when Don Black emerged from prison. Newly rehabilitated with the computer skills he learned in federal custody, he proceeded to set up the world's first Internet hate site in his West Palm Beach home. A clearinghouse for anti-Semitism, www.stormfront.org currently hosts hundreds of

FIGURE 9. *Cover of Ben Klassen,* The White Man's Bible *(Lighthouse Point, Florida, 1981). Collection of the Florida Regional office, Anti-Defamation League. Reprinted from* The Art of Hatred: Images of Intolerance in Florida Culture. *Courtesy the Jewish Museum of Florida.*

FIGURE 10. *Church of the Avenger, Tampa, circa 1995. Collection of the Florida Regional Office, Anti-Defamation League. Reprinted from* The Art of Hatred: Images of Intolerance in Florida Culture. *Courtesy the Jewish Museum of Florida.*

links to websites around the globe that support hate. This has led to a remarkable homogenizing of anti-Semitic ideology in Florida and even around the globe, with ominous implications. Stormfront.org allows isolated anti-Semites throughout the state to communicate effectively, propagandizing youth in the privacy of their own homes and making it possible for them to join a virtual community of like-minded true believers, and occasionally gathering in person for National Association for the Advancement of White People rallies (see figure 12).

FIGURE 11. *"White and Proud!" Comic distributed in Florida, circa 1995. Collection of the Florida Regional Office, Anti-Defamation League. Reprinted from* The Art of Hatred: Images of Intolerance in Florida Culture. *Courtesy the Jewish Museum of Florida.*

Finally, Florida has seen its own development of skinheads, disaffected youth looking for an ideological home and finding it in a version of the anti-Semitic movement. Inspired by World Church of the Creator slogans like RAHOWA (Racial Holy War) and puerile codes like 88/14 (88 for the eighth letter of the alphabet, thus an acronym for Heil Hitler; 14 for the "fourteen words" of white supremacist David Lane: *We must secure the existence of our people and a future for white children*), skinheads were known for their brutal violence directed against minorities. Miami had a brief-lived skinhead organization in the late nineties, until its ringleader was apprehended by police for vandalism. Operating under the name SMASH (South Miami Area Skinheads) the group concentrated its activities on propagandizing at rock concerts, with minimal success (see figure 13).

As an ideology, Floridian anti-Semitism has some features that are more or less unique, or at least characteristically unique, to the region. The strong influence of the Klan from the last quarter of the nineteenth century to the Second World War combined with the increasingly important tourist industry to create the silent marginalization of Jews from resorts and hotels in the state. Changing sensibilities and the rapid influx of Jews in the postwar era to the Miami area in particular eventu-

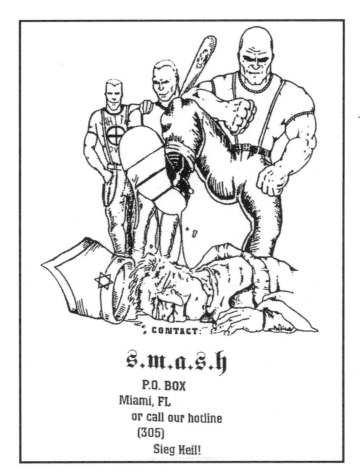

FIGURE 13. *Flyer from SMASH (South Miami Area Skinheads), Miami, Florida, 1996. Collection of the Florida Regional Office, Anti-Defamation League. Reprinted from* The Art of Hatred: Images of Intolerance in Florida Culture. *Courtesy the Jewish Museum of Florida.*

ally overwhelmed this specifically Floridian, and southern, form of anti-Semitism; nonetheless, new influences from other parts of the country caused anti-Semites to turn to ideologies favored by white supremacists in the north and Midwest, from the Aryan Nations to the skinhead movements. While uniquely Floridian elements have largely been lost in this homogenizing process, proponents of hatred in the Sunshine State have been instrumental in using new technologies to deliver their poisonous message throughout the world.

ACKNOWLEDGMENTS

This article is based on research undertaken for "The Art of Hatred: Images of Intolerance in Florida Culture," an exhibit curated for the Jewish Museum of Florida. I am grateful to Ms. Marcia Kerstein Zerivitz, founding director of the Jewish Museum of Florida, for the courage and tenacity she maintained while producing this challenging exhibit. All images are taken from the published catalogue (Miami, 2001), courtesy the Jewish Museum of Florida. Several of the originals come from the incomparable collection of Myrna and Seth Bramson, an assembly of materials that no serious historian of this state can overlook. I am grateful to Mr. Bramson for once again allowing me to make use of his research. I thank the Florida Regional Office of the Anti-Defamation League for sharing some of their valuable materials as well. I am also grateful to my colleague Leslie Siegel, University Archivist at Florida Atlantic University, for technical assistance.

NOTES

1. One of the more remarkable aspects of the history of anti-Semitism is its unusual longevity, due in large part to its unusual ability to adapt to changing cultures with ease, spreading from ancient Greece to modern Japan and mutating in the process. Good discussions of contemporary forms of American anti-Semitism include James Ridgeway, *Blood in the Face: The Ku Klux Klan, Aryan Nations, Nazi Skinheads, and the Rise of a New White Culture*, 2nd ed. (New York: Thunder's Mouth Press, 1995); Michael Barkun, *Religion and the Racist Right: The Origins of the Christian Identity Movement*, rev. ed. (Chapel Hill: University of North Carolina Press, 1997); Carol Swain and Russ Nieli, eds., *Contemporary Voices of White Nationalism in America* (New York: Cambridge University Press, 2003); Carol Swain, *The New White Nationalism in America: Its Challenge to Integration* (New York: Cambridge University Press, 2002).

2. On the "whitening" of Jews in America, see Karen Brodkin, *How Jews Became White Folks and What that Says about Race in America* (New Brunswick, N.J.: Rutgers University Press, 1998). Interesting remarks on this status in the South can be found in Seth Forman, "The Unbearable Whiteness of Being Jewish: Desegregation in the South and the Crisis of Jewish Liberalism," in *Strangers and Neighbors: Relations between Blacks and Jews in the United States*, ed. Maurianne Adams and John Bracey (Amherst: University of Massachusetts Press, 1999), 620–40, and Deborah Dash Moore, "Separate Paths: Blacks and Jews in the Twentieth-Century South," in *Struggles in the Promised Land: Toward a History of Black-Jewish Relations in the United States*, ed. Jack Salzman and Cornel West (New York: Oxford University Press, 1997), 275–294. For more detailed information on the early period, see Bertram Wallace Korn, "Jews and Negro Slavery in the Old South, 1789–1865," in *Strangers and Neighbors*, 147–82; Jayme A. Sokolow, "Revolution and Reform: The Antebellum Jewish Abolitionists," in *Strangers and Neighbors*, 183–197; Bertram Wallace Korn, "The Rabbis and the Slavery Question," in *Strangers and Neighbors*, 198–218.

3. I am grateful to my graduate student, Maury Wiseman, who researched this period in his unpublished seminar paper, "Free Blacks and Jews in Antebellum Florida." See Henry Green, *Jewish Life in Florida: A Documentary Exhibit from 1763 to The Present* (Coral Gables, Fla.: MOSAIC, 1991), Joseph Adler, "Moses E. Levy and Attempts to Colonize Florida," in *Jews of the South: Selected Essays from the Jewish Historical Society*, by Samuel Proctor and Louis Schmier (Macon, Ga.: Mercer University Press, 1984), 17–29; Leon Huhner, "David L. Yulee, Florida's First Senator," in *Jews in the South*, ed. Leonard Dinnerstein and Mary Dale Palsson (Baton Rouge: Louisiana State University Press, 1973), 52–74; Bertram Wallace Korn, "Jews in Eighteenth-Century West Florida," in *Eighteenth Century Florida: Life on the Frontier* ed. Samuel Proctor (Gainesville, Fla.: University Presses of Florida, 1976), 50–59; Cris Monaco, "Moses E. Levy of Florida: A Jewish Abolitionist Abroad," *American Jewish History* 86, no. 4(1998): 377–396.

4. See Martin Shaw, "The Jews of Greater Miami: An Historical Perspective," Master's thesis, Florida Atlantic University, 1992.

5. John Quincy Adams, *Memoirs of John Quincy Adams Comprising his Diary from 1795–1848*, ed. Charles Francis Adams (Philadelphia, 1877), 10:483, cited in Huhner, "David L. Yulee," 61. I am grateful to Mr. Wiseman's research for this reference.

6. The case, described in detail in the Congressional Record of 1869, is treated briefly in my *Art of Hatred: Images of Intolerance in Florida Culture* (Jewish Museum of Florida, 2001), 32. An anecdote with a happier ending, yet still describing more of the nuances of black-Jewish relations in early Florida, is the story of how Isidor Cohen dealt with the

disastrous loss of his entire stock of dry goods due to the clumsiness of the drunken sailors who helped him transport his goods to Miami in February 1896, only to drop it in Biscayne Bay as they were off-loading the boat (taking themselves and Cohen into the bay with them). Rescued by some black bystanders, Cohen offered them each a dollar to retrieve his cargo. The next day when they appeared to receive their due, Cohen offered them instead three dollars' worth of merchandise, and directed them to reimburse him two dollars in cash after they had sold the clothing, turning his loss into profit. The story is discussed in Shaw, "Jews of Greater Miami," 8–9.

7. Personal correspondence dated February 13, 1929, Collection of the Historical Association of Southern Florida, Inc. The original is reproduced in my *Art of Hatred*, 43.

8. See Deborah Dash Moore, *To the Golden Cities: Pursuing the American Dream in Miami and L.A.* (New York: Free Press, 1994), 155.

9. The classic study of the *Protocols of the Elders of Zion* is Norman Cohn, *Warrant for Genocide: The Myth of the Jewish World Conspiracy and the Protocols of the Elders of Zion* (London: Eyre and Spottiswoode, 1967). As a testament to the pernicious nature of this document, there is a steady stream of publications denouncing its validity; see, for example, the recent work by Steven Jacobs and Mark Weitzman, *Dismantling the Big Lie: The Protocols of the Elders of Zion* (New York: KTAV, 2003).

10. Moore, *To the Golden Cities*, 53–92.

11. For examples of their propaganda efforts in the region, see Abramson, *Art of Hatred*, 49, 57.

Stephen Benz

Cuban Jews in Miami

Jews in Cuba: Origin of a Unique Identity

In 1881, when Cuba was still a colony, Spain finally granted Jews permission to enter the island. Jewish religious services, however, were not allowed until 1898, when Spanish hegemony dissolved in the aftermath of the Spanish-Cuban-American War. By 1906, a synagogue was established in Havana. The services were held in English, and most of the members of this "United Hebrew Congregation" were so-called American Jews who had established businesses on the island during the postwar period when Cuba remained a protectorate of the United States. In the decades to come, this community grew in size and stature, but remained insular, interacting only minimally with Cuban society and with the other Jewish groups that soon began to arrive in greater numbers on the island.

The communities that would come to be identified as "Cuban Jews" began to develop at approximately the same time, the first decade of the twentieth century. These communities included immigrants from the Old World: Sephardic Jews from Spain and the former Turkish Empire; and Ashkenazic Jews from eastern Europe. Thus, three distinct Jewish communities were established in Cuba by the start of World War I. Each community spoke a different language (English, Ladino, Yiddish). There was minimal interaction among the groups, a characteristic that would persist for the next fifty years. All told, around one thousand Jews resided in Cuba in 1917. That number doubled by 1919, and doubled yet again by 1923. The size of the permanent Jewish community then remained fairly stable until 1936 when multitudes of refugees from Nazi Germany began to arrive.

At the same time, many thousands of Jews—as many as forty thousand—re-sided temporarily in Cuba. The island became a focal point for Jewish migrants because of its proximity to the United States. Jews hoped to use the island, only one hundred miles off the U.S. coast, as a transition point for easier (often illegal) entry into the United States, which in 1924 had begun to limit immigration strictly. Indeed, Yiddish speakers took to calling the island "Akhsanie Kuba," or Hotel Cuba. For some, however, the hotel became a home. A substantial number of Jews opted to stay in Cuba when they encountered a relatively open, friendly, and welcoming society where they were treated with respect. In the Yiddish phrase, they decided "to make their America in Cuba." George Feldenkreis, president of the Miami United Jewish Appeal (Cuban Division), summarized this history in an interview with the *Jerusalem Post*: "We were European Jews who got stuck in Cuba on the way to Cleveland and New York. We had a very rich tradition. It was very easy living there."

As a consequence of this "easy living," the Jewish communities in Cuba—Sephardic and Ashkenazic—grew steadily as conditions deteriorated in Europe and persecution increased, culminating in the Holocaust and the survivors' subsequent emigration from Europe. By 1959, at its peak, the Cuban Jewish population numbered around thirteen thousand.

In general, Sephardic immigrants initially had an easier time adapting to Cuban culture than did the Ashkenazic. Sephardic Jews came from the Mediterranean and were more familiar with the climate and culture they found in the Caribbean. Moreover, their language, Ladino, was close enough to Spanish to allow for easier learning.

Whether Sephardic or Ashkenazic, most Jews arrived in Cuba destitute. To make a living, they often started as street vendors. They sold neckties, aprons, ribbons,

FIGURE 1. *Cuban Jewish migration (the Brameister family). Many Jews migrated to Cuba from Poland in the 1920s when immigration quotas blocked their passage to the United States, circa 1919. Courtesy Jewish Museum of Florida.*

and even statues of Catholic saints. One popular product was the Eskimo Pie, and Cubans soon took to calling Jewish peddlers "Eskimo Pies." There was, however, no hostility implied in the epithet, and the immigrants were relieved to find themselves in a culture that was far more open and relaxed in terms of race relations than the world they had left behind. Other Jews found work in the factories owned by American Jewish businessmen in Cuba, making shoes and clothing.

While the overall atmosphere was open, there were occasional outbursts of intolerance. As the worldwide economic depression deepened in the 1930s, the Cuban government passed a law requiring businesses to hire a workforce that was at least 50 percent native Cubans. While the law did not specifically target Jews, it had a severe impact on the ability of Cuban Jews to prosper. More serious still, echoes of anti-Semitic fascism, now taking root in Spain, sounded on the Cuban political scene. In 1932, President Machado went so far as to ban Jewish religious activities. Jews were caught in the middle: accused on the one hand of being communist agitators (indeed, some immigrants did have connections with European socialist groups) by the wealthy elite, and deplored on the other hand as strikebreakers and scabs by the common laborers with whom they competed for jobs. The period of intolerance was fairly brief, however. Machado was overthrown in 1933. Religious freedom was reinstated, and by the end of the decade Jews were allowed to become citizens. Many did just that; indeed, Jews were thriving to the extent that 60 percent of the Cuban clothing industry was Jewish-run.

Meanwhile, as the decade of the 1930s drew to a close, a steady stream of refugees arrived from Nazi-controlled lands; some five thousand had entered Cuba by April 1939. Open hostility toward refugees remained rare, but the tone of public debate over Cuba's ability to handle the influx increasingly reflected anti-Semitic, even fascist views. The debate culminated in one of the most infamous episodes of the immediate prewar period: the SS *St. Louis* incident. The Cuban public, stirred to assert national sovereignty, viewed the Jewish refugees unsympathetically. Anti-Semitic demonstrations (fomented by Nazi agents) were held in Havana. After languishing for many days in the harbor, the boatload of refugees was forced to seek another port of call, and the refugees were taken back to Europe. It was a strange episode, considering that Cuba had previously taken in many displaced persons and continued to accept them after the *St. Louis* incident. Indeed, some eight thousand Jewish refugees entered Cuba between 1933 and 1942, but the *St. Louis* incident remains the most emblematic event of the period.

Greater numbers still—including concentration camp survivors—came to the island after the war, when Europe lay in ruins. While the bulk of these immigrants still hoped to get to the United States, a significant number began to think of Cuba as a permanent home. The anti-Semitic stirrings of the prewar years dissipated, and Cuba was once more open and tolerant, a tranquil and inviting place for the war-weary immigrants to contemplate establishing roots.

But even as Jews set about establishing those roots and building a future in Cuba, they did not choose to assimilate readily into Cuban society. Rather, they were intent on maintaining a distinctly Jewish culture within the larger Cuban culture. This intention was especially strong among Ashkenazic Jews. They started Yiddish schools and Jewish social organizations. The first generation of immigrants remained a tight-knit community; indeed, within the wider Jewish community, the boundary lines among Ashkenazic, Sephardic, and American Jews remained firmly delineated.

Stability, however, led eventually to the rearing of a second generation of Cuban Jews. Some arrived on the island as small children. Others were born there. This second generation spoke Spanish as readily as Yiddish or Ladino and absorbed Cuban culture. They grew fond of *café cubano*, rice and beans, and salsa music. They danced the mambo and the rumba at Jewish weddings. They played baseball. They saw themselves as Cubans who were Jews, rather than Jews who had come to Cuba.

Stability also led to economic prosperity. Jewish businesses — numbering in the hundreds — thrived, and some Jews acquired great wealth. The lion's share of the clothing industry was in Jewish hands. So was the largest perfume factory, and Chrysler's Cuba operations. Now more than ten thousand strong, the Cuban Jewish community in 1950 had settled into a prominent role on the island. Their synagogues and community centers grew larger and more impressive. The most significant of these structures, the Patronato, was constructed in the mid-1950s. This large community center was the social center of the Jewish community, where on Saturday afternoons Jews gathered to eat, drink, and take part in sports. El Patronato quickly came to symbolize the prosperity of a community that continued to grow throughout the decade, reaching a population of approximately thirteen thousand in 1958.

That prosperity, however, would factor into the community's rapid dissolution in 1959–60, following the success of Castro's revolution. Having ascended into the middle and even upper classes, Cuban Jews were not inclined to sympathize with the Marxist-Leninist ideology that the revolution promulgated (a somewhat ironic circumstance, given that many of the early Jewish immigrants had been socialist and communist activists in the Old World). A good 70 percent of Cuban Jews abandoned the island in the first two years of the communist takeover. By 1963, only 2,500 Jews remained in Cuba (out of 13,000 before the revolution). Over the next three decades, the population dwindled steadily. Well under one thousand Jews — possibly as few as two hundred — were still living in Cuba at the turn of the new century.

Exile Redux

The overwhelming majority of Cuba's Jews headed into a new exile, this time in the United States. The country that had once refused them, essentially forcing them to settle in Cuba, now accepted them in their flight from communism. The irony of the situation was not lost on the exiles. "Look how things turn out," one told a *Miami Herald* reporter in 1986. "We came to Cuba because it was the country closest to the United States. We came to the United States because it was the country closest to Cuba." The greater percentage of these Cuban Jews opted to settle in Miami, where the climate was similar to Cuba and where a sizeable Jewish population already resided.

Some 3,500 Jews arrived in Miami during the two years following Castro's triumph. Initially, they—like other Cubans—thought of their exile as temporary. Their hopes of an early end to the Castro regime began to fade, however, and it was soon apparent that they would have to establish new lives in a new land.

In Miami, Cuban Jews faced two distinct challenges. The first was economic: they would have to rebuild careers and livelihoods. For many people this meant beginning again at the bottom of a profession or working in nonprofessional fields until they could learn a new language and reestablish credentials. The second challenge was cultural and required Cuban Jews to situate themselves vis-à-vis an already established American Jewish community. In some respects, the latter would prove the more difficult challenge. The majority of Cuban Jews settled in Miami Beach, closer to the American Jewish communities of South Florida than to the other Cuban exiles (who were concentrated on the near south side of the city of Miami, along the soon-to-be-famous Calle Ocho). "They wanted to forge bonds with the Jewish community and went over to Miami Beach," according to Jewish anthropologist Caroline Bettinger-López.

Physical proximity, however, did not result in the intermingling of the Jewish communities. The new arrivals felt isolated from—even rejected by—the established American Jewish community. "The Jewish community reacted with coldness and indifference to them," Bettinger-López says.

Speaking with Bettinger-López, Bernardo Benes, a prominent member of the Cuban Jewish community, summarized the arrival experience this way: "When we arrived in Miami, the local Jewish community basically ignored us. The only person who did anything was Rabbi Abramowitz [of Temple Menorah], who opened his doors to the Cuban Jews."

Rabbi Mayer Abramowitz came to the aid of the new refugees, many of whom had lost everything in Cuba, by offering free synagogue membership until they could become settled. Abramowitz recollected the situation in an interview with a reporter from the *Jerusalem Post Magazine*: "The Jewish community did very little to absorb the fleeing Jews of Cuba. . . . First of all, we thought they were wealthy, and could manage. Second, the U.S. government had a program to absorb all Cuban refugees so the Federation [of Greater Miami] didn't get involved."

In addition, according to Abramowitz and others, there was likely some "anti-Latin sentiment" among the American Jews, who were mostly Ashkenazim. Some Cuban Jews recall hostility toward their use of Spanish: "I felt rejected by the American Jewish community, and I still do," one told anthropologist Bettinger-López. "There are individuals that just can't get over the fact that we've continued to speak Spanish." The sense of rejection was particularly strong amongst Cuban Sephardim, who spoke no Yiddish. As a consequence, they had a difficult time gaining acceptance at the Temple Menorah, a largely Ashkenazim congregation that tended to equate Yiddish language and customs with "true" Jewishness. Most significant, however, Bettinger-López says, "there was a large anti-Cuban mentality, especially from the Ashkenazi, the Jews of Eastern European roots."

In response to this rejection, Cuban Jews felt compelled to split with existing Jewish congregations. By 1961, the exiles had established their own institution to

meet their social and religious needs. This was the Círculo Cubano-Hebreo, or
the Cuban-Hebrew Social Circle. This institution was similar to the Patronato that
Cuban Jews had left behind in Havana, and the leadership of the new Círculo was
substantially the same as the leadership of the Patronato. Initially, both Sephardim
and Ashkenazim entered into membership of the Círculo. By 1968, however, the
Sephardim formed their own Cuban Sephardic Hebrew Congregation, essentially
a continuation of the Sephardic congregation in Cuba, the Chevet Ahim.

At this time, some five thousand Cuban Jews had resettled in South Florida.
The establishment of their own social organizations helped to solidify their standing as a discrete community. They now could worship and socialize within the
context of Cuban Jewish traditions, developing anew the religious, cultural, and
social life they had forged so painstakingly in Cuba before Castro's ascendancy.
The beloved Patronato—the physical and spiritual center of Jewish life on the
island—had been reborn on Miami Beach. Indeed, to this day a plaque on the
wall of the Cuban-Hebrew Congregation refers to the congregation as the Miami
branch of El Patronato.

Socially the Cuban Jews felt a tremendous need to affiliate. Their life in Cuba
had been communal. Jews had rarely wandered outside of the community's social
circle. "When Cuban Jews first came to Miami, they came as exiles like all Cuban
refugees. It was a political identity—exile from communism. They turned that
into a religious identity very quickly, based on their community model in Cuba,
and especially in Havana, where there was a strong Jewish community," Bettinger-
López says. While they had interacted with Cuban society, they had a vibrant community of their own in the island. When Cuban Jews realized their stay in the
United States was not temporary, they began to build a similar community.

In 1964, Rabbi Dow Rozencwaig became the first spiritual leader of the Círculo. A survivor of Auschwitz, Rabbi Rozencwaig had gone to Cuba after the war.
Eventually, he rose to the position of general secretary of the Jewish community
on the island. Under Rozencwaig's guidance, the Círculo became more involved
with other local and national Jewish organizations. An emphasis on *Tzedakah*, or
"righteous action," led the congregation to participate in charitable causes, such as
B'nai B'rith and the Women's International Zionist Organization. By this point, the
exiles had fully established themselves as a functioning, outreaching community.
They also attained greater acceptance among South Florida's Jewish population.
The Greater Miami Jewish Federation formed its first Cuban Division in 1966.
Within thirty years, an Ashkenazic Cuban Jew, Isaac Zelcer, would become presi-
dent of the Greater Miami Jewish Federation.

The fullest measure of the congregation's maturity occurred in 1976, with the
dedication of a new synagogue in Miami Beach. Officially named "Cuban-Hebrew
Congregation of Miami," it is also known as Temple Beth Shmuel. The architect,
Oscar Sklar, was a member of the congregation. With the synagogue's construc-
tion, Cuban Jews finally had a spiritual home to take the place of their beloved
Patronato in Havana. The new synagogue's dedication thus could be seen as the
beginning of the official transfer of Cuban Jewish culture and identity to Miami
Beach. The symbolic affirmation of the transfer occurred in 1980, when leaders of

FIGURE 2. *Cuban-Hebrew Congregation of Miami Beach, circa 1990. Courtesy Jewish Museum of Florida.*

FIGURE 3. *Temple Beth Shmuel, Cuban-Hebrew Congregation, Miami Beach, 2003. Photograph courtesy of Stephen Benz.*

Miami's Cuban Jews revisited the island and El Patronato in order to bring three important religious items—a Torah, a yarmulke, and a talis—to the new congregation in Florida. With the transfer complete, the Miami-based community could see itself as forward-looking, focused on the future more than on the past.

The past was not to be forgotten, however. One of the principal areas of concern for the contemporary Cuban Jewish community was (and remains) the transmission of their history and culture to the new generations now being born in the United States (who have taken to calling themselves "Jewbans" or "Jubans").

The Círculo Cubano-Hebreo de Miami and the related Cuban-Hebrew Congregation have been predominately Ashkenazic from the beginning. Cuban Sephardics, meanwhile, established their own congregation, the Cuban Sephardic Hebrew Congregation, in 1968 and grew quickly. With historically different roots (both in the Old World and in Cuba) and with a different linguistic background, the Cuban Sephardim decided that they needed a space in Miami for their own distinct traditions. Under the leadership of Rabbi Nissim Maya, the son of the chief rabbi of Chevet Ahim in Havana, the Sephardic established a separate Cuban Jewish congregation at the opposite end of Miami Beach from the Ashkenazic Círculo. Economic factors also played a part in the creation of the new congregation. The Sephardim came from a working-class background in Cuba (most had been peddlers and street vendors). Now in Miami, they felt they could not afford the American temples' expensive fees for holy day services, memberships, social activities, and Hebrew school. As a consequence, a new synagogue—Temple Moses—was built at the north end of Miami Beach and dedicated in December 1980.

The two congregations are also divided in terms of ideology. Throughout its history (except during Rabbi Rozencwaig's tenure), the Cuban-Hebrew Congregation has identified itself as a Conservative congregation and has not observed gender separation within the sanctuary. The Sephardic Temple Moses, however, considers itself a Traditional congregation. The sanctuary is divided by a curtain in order to keep men and women separate.

Characteristics of the "Jewbans"

One salient characteristic of the Cuban Jewish community in Miami is its success in meeting the challenge of a double exile. "Consider what it meant that a second time they had to start all over, again with a language problem," Rabbi Barry Konovitch told a reporter in 1986. "But again they built themselves up. They're survivors. They've refused to let anything stand in the way of their progress. They've been up against the biggest odds and they've survived."

Many individual Cuban Jews have not only survived but also thrived in Miami. Numerous examples of success could be cited, but four will suffice. Rafael Kravec arrived penniless in Miami in 1960. "For the first eight months, I sold flowers for an importer, worked at Burdines and even joined a trade mission to the Caribbean as a translator," he told the *Miami Herald*. Eventually, he founded French Fragrances, a publicly traded company of which he is CEO. Marcos Kerbel was twelve years old when he came to Miami. The transition was difficult because he had to live in foster homes until his parents could join him in Miami several years later. But Kerbel, too, was to prove highly successful. He became head of the Miami office of the Israel Discount Bank. Banking was one field open to the new immigrants. Bernardo Benes was one of the first Cuban Jews to become a banker in Miami when he joined Washington Federal Savings and Loan in Miami Beach in the early 1960s. "Among the refugees was a strong professional class, many of them bankers, and the American banks took advantage of this new pool," Benes recalled in a newspaper interview. "They in turn started bringing in clients that they knew from home and the banking character of Miami changed drastically." Later, Benes and Carlos Dascal, another Cuban Jew, started Continental Bank, the first Cuban-owned bank in the United States. Isaac Zelcer, the man who became the first Cuban Jew to be president of the Greater Miami Jewish Federation, is yet another example of individual achievement in the community. In 1960, Zelcer left Cuba and went to New York, where he worked in a tie factory until he became president. In 1980, he moved to Miami and started Isaco Ties, now one of the largest accessories companies in the United States.

Within the Cuban Jewish community there is great diversity. This diversity is the result of the unique historical circumstances that have shaped the community. It is most readily apparent in the linguistic variety found among its constituents. The three distinct generations of the community were born in different countries and speak different languages. The oldest generation was born in either eastern Europe (Ashkenazim) or the Mediterranean (Sephardim) and speak either Yiddish or Ladino as their native language. The middle generation was born in Cuba and is Spanish-speaking. The members of the youngest generation have mostly been born in the United States and primarily prefer to speak English. "It's one of the most unique congregations in this country," Rabbi Barry Konovitch has said. "It's tricultural, trilingual. In any given service, you'll hear four different languages — Spanish, English, Yiddish, and Hebrew — being spoken.

This unique tricultural identity is one of the most notable of "Jewban" characteristics. According to Jaime Suchlicki, a Cuban Jew who is a professor of Cuban history at the University of Miami, "Cuban Jews are a generation in transition with a diluted identity. We identify with three countries: Cuba, the U.S. and Israel." Rafael Kravec says that even though he loves this country and has prospered here he still does not feel one hundred percent American. "I'm still a Cuban and have very strong ties with Israel. I live in Cuba and Israel every day." Businessman Marco Kerbel believes that he enjoys the best of three worlds, being Cuban, American, and Jewish. Kerbel says that at midnight every New Year's Eve at the annual party at the Cuban Hebrew Congregation, everyone sings three national anthems: those of Cuba, Israel and the United States.

For Jewban writer Betsy Heisler-Samuels, the permanence of exile in the United States hasn't kept the Jewish-Latino identity from evolving further. "I have four generations in my family and each one was born in a different country," Heisler-Samuels says. "My parents were born in Europe. I was born in Cuba. My daughter and son were born in the United States, and my grandchildren were born in Colombia. Talk about the wandering Jew."

Of all the disparate elements of Jewban identity, however, Cuban culture remains at the core. Rabbi Eliot Pearlson, explains the nostalgia and persistence of Cuban identity this way: "I understand why, contrary to other immigrants, the Cuban Jewish community has maintained the language, the music and the cuisine of their country of birth. My father arrived from Poland at the age of 17 and the first thing he did was change his name and forget the Polish language. The Poles were anti-Semitic, their interaction with the Jewish community was negative and all he wanted to do was to forget that part of his life. In Cuba, however, from what I understand there was very little anti-Semitism and therefore Jews wanted to preserve the positive aspects of that culture. The tolerant environment of Cuba, in fact, enabled Jews to maintain a positive Jewish identity. It is no surprise that the Cuban Jewish community has now reached the highest levels of leadership in Miami."

While Jewbans insist on keeping their Cuban traditions, they do not necessarily identify with other Cuban exile groups. This tendency is most noticeable where politics is concerned. Most Cuban Jews are apolitical and have not gotten involved in Cuban exile politics. The one notable exception is Bernardo Benes, who during the 1970s was among a group of Cuban exiles that took part in a dialogue with Fidel Castro. The talks led to the release of many Cuban political prisoners. Benes suffered dire consequences, however, for his participation. Many Cuban exiles disparaged him for negotiating with Castro. His life was threatened and his office was bombed. As a result, he largely withdrew from exile politics. Other than Benes's involvement, the Cuban Jewish community as a whole has demonstrated little interest in the passionate political concerns of other Cuban exiles.

Just as the Jewbans maintain an identity distinct from other Cubans, they maintain an identity distinct from other Jews. Certainly this separation is based on historical experience. Their initial relations with the American Jews, or lack thereof, continues to influence how those relations play out. Observing the 1996 installation ceremony of the first Cuban president of the Jewish Federation of Greater Miami, Bettinger-López saw a good example of these worlds at odds. On the night of the ceremony, Cuban Jews filled the auditorium. They applauded and cheered as Isaac Zelcer became the first Cuban Jewish president of the federation, a position traditionally held by a member of the city's established American-Jewish community. To many, the event represented the true integration of Cuban and American Jews at last.

But, as Bettinger-López recounts, no sooner had Zelcer ended his speech, and the applause died down, than the Cuban Jews left the auditorium, walking out on the rest of the program. According to Bettinger-López, "the night was both a powerful symbol of how Cuban Jews have become part of the larger U.S. Jewish community and of the still insular nature of their community, which is often criticized as only caring about their own. It did look on the face of it to be very rude, but I did understand what they were doing. It illustrated the point that Cuban Jews are inward-focused, and in many respects this is largely based on history. They were forced to become inwardly focused when they tried to integrate with the Miami Jewish community and they were slapped in the face."

The Future of an Identity

The Jewbans of South Florida are clearly experiencing a period of cultural transition. While becoming more and more integrated in the broader Jewish community, they cling to the traditions of their unique heritage. The fate of Jewban culture and identity now rests with those generations born in the United States, young Cuban Jews who have never been to Cuba. While they cherish aspects of their heritage and are intent on maintaining traditions, they are also increasingly "Americanized." Synagogue services are now held more often in English than in Spanish. As Rafael Kravec, campaign director for United Jewish Appeal's Cuban Division, told an Israeli reporter in 1991, the younger generation of Jewbans led "an enjoyable schizophrenic life." Inevitably, however, American culture will play a bigger part—as it has for so many immigrant groups. Whether American culture comes to dominate remains to be seen. "When people ask me what I think will happen in twenty or thirty years," says Aron Kelton, former administrator of the Cuban-Hebrew Congregation, "I say I don't know. We have maintained the torch up to now. Now it will be the turn of our young people."

Annette B. Fromm

Sephardic Jews in South Florida

Who are the Sephardic Jews of South Florida? Sephardic refers to a historic separation that led to cultural distinctions between Jewish populations living in different parts of the Balkans, Asia Minor, and North Africa. The Sephardic Jews trace their origins to the Iberian Peninsula, from thirteenth- to fifteenth-century Spain. Their ancestors were a part of the intellectual milieu of Jewish, Muslim, and Catholic thinkers, doctors, jurists, and religious leaders characterized as the Golden Age of Spain. This unique multicultural setting was abruptly disrupted by the Catholicization and incorporation of Spanish states, which led to the eviction of the Muslim rulers and tens of thousands of long-term Jewish residents. This movement took place over the period of one hundred or more years, starting approximately in 1391 with riots against Jews and ending in 1492 with the wholesale expulsion of Jews from a uniting entity of Spain as part of the Inquisition.

The Jewish exiles were driven in several directions. Thousands found temporary refuge in neighboring Portugal. Others went to culturally familiar Southern France. Many others journeyed in a northern direction to the sanctuary offered by the Low Countries. They established a long-lived and well-respected community in Amsterdam, which to this day remains distinct as the Portuguese and Spanish Congregation. Other Sephardic Jews sought refuge in North Africa, across the straits at Gibraltar. Many were rejected and mistreated by the indigenous Jews of Morocco and Algeria. Eventually, however, Sephardic communities were established and prospered there for centuries. The largest number of Sephardic Jews was welcomed with open arms by the rapidly expanding Ottoman Empire in the Eastern Mediterranean. Communities were established in depopulated areas such as the capital, Istanbul, as well as Thessaloniki, Smyrna, and Aleppo. Other Sephardic Jews sought to reestablish themselves in their homeland in such communities as Jerusalem, Tiberias, and Safed. It is in the Ottoman Empire and North Africa, in particular, where they prospered and, moreover, maintained their Spanish-Jewish culture.

The Sephardic culture of the Jews of the Ottoman Empire and North Africa developed in different directions. Nonetheless, they held onto a fierce pride in their Spanish origins. Jewish sacred and secular traditions were clung to and flourished in both locations. One trade carried to Istanbul was printing; the first printing press was established in that city by Sephardic refugees, in order to print prayer books, as they had in Spain. The *yeshivot*, houses of Jewish learning, of the Ottoman Empire were famous. Students were sent to them in the sixteenth through eighteenth centuries from Hungary and Poland. Traditional culture was also maintained as congregations were established by people from the different communities in Spain in their new homeland. Especially well known among the Sephardic folklore of these communities were the rich storehouse of proverbs and ballads, all related in Judeo-Spanish.

Some four hundred years later, the Ottoman Empire reached the end of a socio-political-economic downward spiral. With the rise of European nationalism and other factors, this once strong multicultural superpower lost its role and potency. Rarely harassed under Muslim rulers, Jews and Christians sought new homes where they could carry on their businesses. Many of the Sephardic Jews found homes in Eretz Israel, in the three ancient cities: Jerusalem, Tiberias, and Safed. Others made their ways to European cities such as Paris and Rome. Thousands, however, journeyed to America during the so-called Great Wave of Migration between 1884 and 1924. They established Sephardic communities in Cincinnati, Indianapolis, Seattle, Los Angeles, and Atlanta, as well as the largest in New York City.

Sephardic Jews Come to the United States

In New York, these Sephardic immigrants, who were culturally and historically distinct from the much more numerous East European Jewish immigrants, once again established communal organizations and congregations that met their religious and social needs. They also found the already well established Sephardic congregation, Shearith Israel in Manhattan. After all, the first wave of Jews to enter colonial America had come as a result of the expulsions from Spain

The first individuals were a hapless fifty-six Jews leaving the Portuguese Inquisition, which reached its long arm to colonial Brazil. They were followed by other Sephardic Jews, coming via Holland and England, who sought economic improvement. Early colonial Sephardic congregations had been established in New York, Philadelphia, Savannah, and Charleston. Their order of worship was followed until approximately the mid-nineteenth century when the German Jewish immigrants, considered the second wave of Jewish immigration, took the religious and cultural lead.

The third wave of American Jewish immigration was overwhelmingly composed of eastern European Jews fleeing religious and economic oppression in Russia. A very small component of this mass of people, as already mentioned, were the Sephardic Jews leaving the failing Ottoman Empire. Slowly, the twentieth-century Sephardic immigrants reestablished themselves in their new communities scattered around the country. Those who came as children were educated in the American system. The adults took advantage of the neighborhood settlement houses for lessons in English and Americanization skills, after days of work. Nevertheless, they clung to their traditional heritage. They were staunch traditional Jews. Because the differentiations among the Reform, Conservative, and Orthodox movements did not reach the Sephardic world, their religious expression was often mistaken. Imagine recent arrivals faced with the query if they are "Orthodox" by a well-meaning Jewish communal worker. In their cultural memory, "Orthodox" was synonymous with their Greek Orthodox Christian neighbors in the Ottoman Balkans. This cross-cultural misunderstanding led to misperceptions between Sephardic and Ashkenzic Jews at that time period.

Another misunderstanding between Jews from different geographical origins lay in expressive culture. The Sephardic Jews spoke Judeo-Spanish (also known as

Ladino), their precious "Spaniolit." Other Jews from the Ottoman Empire who emigrated in the same period spoke Greek or Arabic. Many an immigrant was faced
with the question of "How can a Spanish boy read the Sefer Torah?" in the synagogue. Their lack of working knowledge of Yiddish continually raised questions of
Jewish affiliation in the marketplace for Sephardic men, women, and children.

The disparity reached other realms of traditional culture, the culture determined
by *minhag* and shaped by the environment from which the community came. In
the case of Ottoman and North African Sephardim, they had spent many centuries
negotiating within multicultural milieus. Some of the customs of their neighbors
were adopted by the Sephardim, with strictest attention paid to the laws of Judaism. Children were given the names of their living grandparents, the highest form
of compliment to the forebears. Daily and holiday festive foods made use of local
ingredients: thus tastes and flavors were very foreign to their new east European
neighbors. Speech was peppered with proverbs and sayings that spoke of their
distant Spanish origins.

Who are the Sephardic Jews of Florida?

Florida's Jewish "community" has a lengthy association with Sephardic Jews. In
fact, the sequential movement of Jews to Florida mirrors the parallel settlement
nationwide: first Sephardic, then German, then eastern European. The first Jews
who settled in the colonies in the seventeenth century were Sephardic Jews who
came via the West Indies and the Netherlands. Florida's first documented Jews
were three itinerant Sephardic merchants from New Orleans. They purchased
property and opened businesses in Pensacola around 1763. Their tenure was brief
as they moved on to the Carolinas and Georgia, where larger Jewish populations
supported more active Jewish communities.

The nineteenth century was the German period of Jewish immigration and the
actual time when the roots of several Jewish communities were planted in the
north of the territory to become Florida. At least one Sephardic Jew made an impact
on the state. Moses Levy (1781–1854) was a descendant of a significant Moroccan
Jewish family. He and his son David (1810–1886) made a significant impact on the
state (see Zerivitz essay, "Alligators and Matzo Balls," in this collection).

A number of Sephardic Jewish immigrants made their homes in Florida in the
late nineteenth and early twentieth centuries. Like the previous pioneers, they
settled in north and central Florida, as the majority southernmost part of the state
was not populated by non-Indian people until the mid-twentieth century. Alfred
Wahnish (1870–1929) traced his ancestors to medieval Spain, where their name
was probably Juanez. True to migration patterns following the expulsion, the family migrated to England, most likely through the Netherlands. They were probably
conversos or New Christians, Jews who had converted to Catholicism to escape persecution yet forced to go into exile because of their ancestry. There they took the
anglicized name Wahnish. One of the descendents of this family went to North
Africa sometime later, where Alfred was born. He emigrated to the United States,
entering at Boston as a young man in 1885, long before Ellis Island became the

port of entry for millions of immigrants. After some years there, Wahnish moved southward to Pensacola and finally the Tallahassee area in the 1890s. There he purchased some three thousand acres and established a pioneering tobacco plantation and successful business. Wahnish's wife, however, was Ashkenazi. While the family knows its origins and has traced the routes of its ancestors, the descendants were not raised with knowledge of North African Sephardic religious or cultural traditions.

A little further south and west and a few years later, the Dayan family established itself in Tampa where Jews had been living since the late 1880s. The Dayans originally settled in New York after emigrating from Aleppo, Syria, in 1910. The sons married and scattered in the eastern United States. One son went to Washington, D.C. Another struck out for Georgia, then moved south to Tampa. There he established the Dayan Linen Store and, eventually, a car dealership. Haim Dayan and his son Nissim served as the community mohels, ritual circumcisers. Several other Syrian Jewish families followed these early community members. Other relatives of the Dayan family, the Sultans, established a home-decorating business in Southeastern Florida. Other networks led as far as Mexico City, where other family members settled in the early twentieth century.

Another early Sephardi who settled in Florida struck out for the furthest outpost to the south, Key West. This former port of entry was the first community in South Florida where Jews settled. In the mid-1880s, a group of Jews from Romania established their businesses and homes in this town, a common pattern of settlement for immigrants. Mordechai Elias and his son Jack came to Key West in the 1940s from New York City. It is said that Mr. Elias was born in India and lived in Israel. His daughter, Kitty, was born in the Middle East. Elias was a stockbroker and part owner of a bar in Key West. Little of the family's Sephardic heritage was transmitted and preserved by the descendants.

Miami grew from a small settlement along the Miami River to a flourishing city/county with one of the largest Jewish populations in the United States. In the early twentieth century, no records mention any Sephardic Jews among the settlers. Across Biscayne Bay, scarcely a decade later, the community of Miami Beach was established. A handful of Sephardic Jews, immigrants of the early twentieth century and their children, sought to establish themselves economically in this growing new community around the 1940s. Among those who were drawn from New York and other eastern seaboard cities was the Pardo family.

Izzie and Mary Pardo were born in the great Balkan Jewish entrepôt Thessaloniki. When they immigrated to the United States, like many other Sephardic Jews, in the early twentieth century, they initially followed family members to the Midwest, to Saint Louis. By 1916, however, they had moved to New York where Izzie established himself in the garment business. With his uncle, he became active in the United Manufacturing Association. The two men were also involved in Sephardic communal life; they were instrumental in the founding of the Sephardic Brotherhood in America, a Sephardic *landsmanshaft* in New York. In the early 1940s, the Pardos moved to Miami Beach. They had problems finding an apartment because they had children and because of unwritten policies about renting to Jews. So, they invested in real estate. They purchased an apartment house on 15th Street between Alton Road and West Avenue. They also bought the Surf Hotel on the now very popular Ocean Drive. Like other Miami Beach hoteliers, between 1943 and 1946, the Pardos had to relinquish this property to the United States Army Air Corps for troops training to serve in the European arena.

Their hotel customers were primarily tourists; some were repeat customers who would rent by the month in the winter. The property was closed in the summer, as were neighboring hotels, because without air-conditioning, Miami Beach was not a summer attraction. By 1960, they sold the hotel. Their granddaughter, a third-generation Miami Beach resident with school-age children, fondly remembers sitting with her grandmother in the hotel kitchen enjoying traditional Sephardic baked goods, especially during the summer.

More Sephardic businessmen and families settled in Miami and Miami Beach in the third, fourth, and fifth decades of the twentieth centuries. The Esformes family, Nathan and Flora, like the Pardos, were immigrants from Thessaloniki. They came to South Florida after a first stop in New York to establish a commercial tomato growing business. Other Sephardic names known in the business community were Sam Gorman; Mr. Penso, who was the maitre d' at Clover Club on Biscayne Blvd; Albert Behar, who had been known as the knish king for his business on Coney Island; and Mr. Jon, whose women's clothing store Mr. Jon thrived in Biscayne Center in the 1970s. Not all of the early Sephardim in Miami Beach were from Thessaloniki. At least three families were from Kastoria, a fur-trading center in the mountains of northern Greece. These included the Elias family, the Roussos, and the Matalons.

These Sephardic Jews in Miami Beach organized communally to hold services separately from their Ashkenazic coreligionists. At that time, their pronunciation of Hebrew was distinct from that of other Jews. Furthermore, since the start of the twentieth century Sephardic immigration to the United States, their very adherence to Judaism was questioned because their order of service and tunes used to chant the Torah were different. On Miami Beach, services in the 1940s were held in a number of places before a permanent synagogue building was acquired. They were held in a loft area in an unnamed building at Seventh and Washington. According to Steve Cohen, services had been held in the Victor Hotel. The downstairs area of another unidentified location was also mentioned as a site for religious services. In 1951 a building on the east side of Collins Avenue between Sixth and Seventh Streets was bought to serve as the Sephardic Jewish Center of Greater Miami. The Esformes family, Joe Pardo, who was then a young lawyer, and Eli Quain, who owned a fruit and vegetable–shipping shop on Lincoln Road, guaranteed the mortgage for the building.

A Holocaust survivor from Thessaloniki who had come to the United States with his small family took over spiritual leadership of the congregation. Cantor or Rabbi Sa'adi Nahmias had owned a grocery store on Seventh Street. He had been trained as a cantor in his homeland before the onset of World War II. Through tutoring provided by the United Synagogue of Greater Miami, Rabbi Nahmias attained his *smiha*, or certificate to serve as a rabbi. He was able to provide the unique

Sephardic pronunciation and rhythms to their worship. The old-timers still spoke Ladino and the prayer books were written in Ladino. Nahmias was instrumental in obtaining burial sites for his congregants in the northwestern section of Mount Nebo North cemetery.

During the 1950s, '60s, and '70s, the heyday of Jewish life in Miami Beach, the Sephardic Jewish Center flourished. Another wave of Sephardim modestly established themselves in the community. These were the retirees who had immigrated to the eastern seaboard centers from Turkey, Greece, and North Africa in the first decades of the twentieth century. They had raised their families, finished their business lives, and, like the overwhelming number of Yiddish-speaking retirees who made a life in the sun, they too, made the secondary migration south. Scattered among the small apartments characteristic of the South Beach area were numerous older Sephardic couples. While Flamingo Park and the nascent Miami Beach Senior Center or Jewish Community Center were awash with the sounds of Yiddish, the Sephardim congregated at the small synagogue on Collins Avenue. At one point there were six hundred members.

The Sephardic Jewish Center also served as a cultural center. As well as for services, people gathered there to play cards and for other social activities. Joe Pardo remembered that parties were held for every holiday. There used to be constant parties with belly dancers and Greek or Turkish music. No matter what age the partygoers were, everyone got up and danced to the music. The purpose of these festivities was to collect money for the synagogue. In the great Jewish tradition, the women, including Mrs. Nahmias, made borekas and baklava, Sephardic delicacies that exemplified the culinary skills of the bakers. Because the members were predominantly retirees, however, with some business owners, few young people were found in the center. It did not provide activities or programs for the youth.

By the early 1990s, membership in the Sephardic Jewish Center had dwindled to around two hundred members, the last of the elderly immigrants. The anti-preservation developer, fellow Jewish immigrant Abe Resnick, bought the property (for more about Resnick, see Wisser 1995:35–36). He retained the building's facade but gutted the interior to be used for retail. The Torahs were given to other Sephardic congregations in the area. Rabbi Nahmias was provided with a pension.

From the late 1950s onward another wave of Sephardic Jews made a great and more lasting impact on South Florida. They were the Cuban Jews of Sephardic descent. At the same time that Sephardic immigrants resettled from the Ottoman Empire in New York and other North American cities, a number of Sephardim settled in Cuba and several South American locations. Sephardic Jews have a long history intertwined with European settlement in the Caribbean. The first Jews to establish communities in Jamaica, Saint Thomas, Curaçao, Barbados, and Surinam were Sephardic. Their Spanish liturgical traditions have remained in place in these communities. Cuba, however, does not have a lengthy documented Jewish history because of its historical ties with Spain, where the Inquisition remained intact on paper well into the nineteenth century. However, as the east Europeans fled out of Russia and Poland they settled in Cuba alongside the Sephardic immigrants.

The Cuban Sephardim came from two distinct places in the Ottomans. One group came from Syria. There were approximately thirty to forty Syrian Jewish families and they "maintained their own Syrian identity and customs" (Levine 1993:21). The other group emigrated from Turkey proper, particularly the towns of Silivria (Silivri) near Istanbul, and Kirklisse (Kilklareli) near Edirne. Levine (1993:20) wrote that the Jews from Turkey and [Syria] were the "first major Jewish immigrant wave" to Cuba. One of the major push factors that led them to leave their homelands was the institution of universal military service in post-Ottoman Turkey in 1909. The pull factors that led these Sephardim to chose Cuba as a destination was that, like Turkey and Syria, Cuba was a young republic. The promise of economic growth glistened.

As merchants, artisans, and peddlers, the Sephardim tended not to congregate in the capital, Havana, but traveled across the country. They established communal organizations in the provincial towns of Manzanillo, Ciego de Ávila, Camajuani (Santa Clara Province), Colón, Camagüey, Giantanama, Artemisa, Matanzas, and Santiago de Cuba in Oriente. The community in Camagüey was predominantly established by Jews from Silivri. The communal organizations they organized imitated and rebuilt/reconstructed what they knew in Turkey and Syria. The Sephardic Jews who remained in Havana to set up business built the Congregación Unión Israelita Chevet Ahim with several auxiliary groups in 1914. They also founded the Centro Hebreo *Sefardí de Cuba*, a religious and communal center in Havana that resulted from a merger between the Unión Hebreo Sefardí and Congregation Chevet Ahim.

Prior to World War I Sephardic Jews were more populous than Ashkenazic Jews—in Cuba. They assimilated quickly to their new context because of their facility with languages, especially because of their vernacular Judeo-Spanish or Ladino. It appears, however, that because of the proximity of modern Spanish, the ages-old Ladino was dropped as a language of the home except by the elders.

This is a contrast to the Sephardic enclaves in the United States, where Ladino continued to be used in the home. After World War I, parallel to the pattern in the United States, the much more numerous Ashkenazic Jews dominated Jewish life in Cuba. With the change of immigration laws by the United States government in 1924, which greatly restricted the numbers of immigrants entering the country, Jews from both eastern Europe and the lands of the Ottoman Empire were forced to look for other ports of haven. Cuba was viewed as a potential temporary resting place, from which an American visa could be more successfully obtained. Thus, Jews continued to seek a haven there until the onset of the Second World War.

Well before the accession of Fidel Castro's Communist regime in Cuba, some of the Jews of Cuba had business contacts in the United States. With the rise of the repressive Castro regime, Jews were among the many refugees who fled the island. After forty to fifty years in Cuba, the majority of the Cuban Jewish community, Sephardi and Ashkenazi alike, faced a second migration. Many were resettled by the Jewish agencies across the Midwest, yet others remained in Miami-Dade County, eager to reestablish their economic and social lives. Indeed, the whole community was transplanted and their intent was to create a substitute of Havana in Miami, "to reestablish the congregations and Jewish community centers they had maintained in pre-revolutionary Cuba" (Bettinger-López 2000:66). They found that neither cultural part of the community was wholeheartedly welcomed in South Florida. Only one congregation, Temple Menorah, opened its doors to the penniless refugees. The Cuban Jews in South Florida are said never to have forgotten their reception by the established communities.

The Cuban Sephardic immigrants received a mixed treatment at the Sephardic Jewish Center on South Beach. According to Liebman (1977:302), the Cubans were antagonized because the "Sephardi Jewish Center in Miami Beach requested nominal payment." Perhaps it was cultural differences within this minority community that led to the establishment of a new Sephardic congregation by the Cuban immigrants. Few of the older residents were from either the Turkish provincial communities or Syria. As early as the expulsions from Spain, Sephardim have congregated together according to their communities of origin. Some say that the Cuban Sephardim wanted their own way. They set about establishing a separate congregation as soon as possible. The first Cuban Sephardim rented a store on the seven hundred block of Washington Avenue, which they dubbed "La Cueva" to serve as a community center and synagogue. Rabbi Nissim Maya was the son of Gershon Maya, chief rabbi of Havana's Sephardic synagogue, Chevet Ahim. He had been "a professor of Hebrew, a cantor and a *mohel* in the Camaguey province of Cuba." He became the leader of the young Miami Beach community (Bettinger-López 2000:70). Alberto Behar was the first president of the congregation, which attracted 150 families (ibid.). As in Havana, they supported a Sunday school, a Maccabi (sports activities), and a Hevra Kadisha (burial society) with lots in Mount Sinai Cemetery. The Sisterhood, Damas de Buena Voluntad, was founded by Victoria Adouth and Mrs. Ventura in 1969. By 1980, the Cuban Sephardic Hebrew Congregation, better known as Torat Moshe or Temple Moses, moved to its permanent home on 71st Street on Normandy Isle.

The Cuban Sephardim also established businesses in South Florida. The Syrian Habifs manufactured and sold perfume in Havana's Nacional Hotel. They established a jewelry store on 41st Street in Miami Beach. The Turkish Egozi and Garazi families continued to manufacture and sell shoes. These families took an active role in Jewish life as well, becoming supporters of Torat Moshe and selling Israel Bonds.

Another Sephardic synagogue, Congregation Magen David, was established in 1974 in North Miami Beach. Like the Sephardic Jewish Center on Miami Beach, this congregation was founded by "a growing population of Mediterranean Jewish immigrants retiring here from the Northeast" (Taft 1990). Rachel Algaze who had come to the United States from Turkey when she was fourteen, and retired to Miami in 1970 was one of the founders of this congregation.

As the Sephardic population of South Florida grew in the latter decades of the twentieth century, so did the number of Sephardic congregations. Congregation Shaare Ezra, on 41st Street on Miami Beach, has a very active membership with many religious, educational, and social activities. One such program is a monthly series of cooking lessons organized by the women in which varied examples of Sephardic cuisine are introduced. Other congregations include B'nai Sephardim Shaare Shalom of Hollywood, Ner Yitzchak of Highland Lakes, and Beit Edmond Jacob Safra Synagogue of North Dade County and Harambam Congregation.

Prior to the formal establishment of many of these synagogues, a group of retirees attempted to found a Sephardic synagogue in Delray Beach. First, they rented a social hall in one of Boca Raton's hotels to hold High Holiday and Sabbath services. Joe Elias, whose father had been the rabbi at the Monastirli synagogue in New York, ran the services. As their numbers grew, they rented an annex in Temple Emeth for three years. Lack of attendance and support, however, put an end to those services.

Many elderly retired Jews left predominantly Jewish Miami Beach in the late 1970s and '80s as the cultural mix of the community at large changed, and they felt that the community had become dangerous. The retirees looked to north Miami-Dade, Broward, and Palm Beach Counties to resettle. In 1978 a number of Sephardim began settling in Fort Lauderdale and Century Village at Deerfield Beach. More recently, the children of the Sephardic immigrants, many of them living in mixed marriages (that is, Sephardic married to Ashkenazi) have settled in communities such as Century Village in Pembroke Pines. A Sephardic [Social] Club has been organized there. It has drawn sixty to seventy members including non-Sephardim and also Cuban Jews who have now reached the age of retirement. Other more recent influxes of Sephardim are settling in communities in Boynton Beach.

One of the earliest groups of retired Sephardim in Broward County looked to move south from the Bronx in the late 1960s. These immigrants from Greece, Istanbul, Izmir, and a few from Macedonia had settled in the Bronx, the neighborhood of Grand Concourse and 170th Street and established the Sephardic Center in the Bronx. They were looking for an inexpensive retirement place, condominiums catering to lower middle-class life-styles. Dora Strougo, who originally came to the United States from Turkey, did some research and found or stumbled upon the newly established retirement community Hawaiian Gardens Phase I in Lauderdale Lakes. Using funds from an investment club founded in the 1950s, one or two, then ten families were among the first to purchase at Hawaiian Gardens in the late 1960s. This was a word-of-mouth settlement; Sarah Hattem brought a friend and so it continued. Eventually approximately twenty-five other families sequentially followed the first group that moved south over the next decade. In terms of Sephardic traditions, this transplanted community still cooks traditional foods and speak Ladino together. The family language also helps them to communicate with their household help who speak Spanish. Three times a week they still hold their card game.

A similar group of friends, about "forty or fifty men and women who lived in New Lots" in Brooklyn since the 1930s have met for lunch at the Coral Springs Mall in Fort Lauderdale since 1993. These were children of immigrants, according to Halio, whose families had moved to the New York borough from the Lower East Side. Their next destination was South Florida. Annually, this group of lifelong friends holds a dinner dance in Fort Lauderdale (Halio n.d.)

Sephardic culture in South Florida is promoted and maintained not only in the synagogues, but also by a number of social clubs and organizations. One social organization was transferred to Florida from New York, where it was established by immigrants. The Source of Life Benevolent Society is a mutual benefit organization, known as a *landsmanshaft* group among the Ashkenazim, common among many immigrant groups. The Florida branch holds one annual meeting. Their members make all the necessary burial arrangements for members in Menorah Gardens in Davie and Mount Sinai Cemetery in Opa-Locka and make a contribution to the family. This organization also provides scholarships to young people based upon scholastic achievement.

The American Sephardi Federation (ASF), a national organization, has a south Dade Florida Chapter. This group was organized sometime in the 1960s; it was revitalized in 1992, marking the quincentenary of the expulsion of the Jews from Spain. Membership in this group is predominantly Cuban with some participation from North African Sephardim. Most of their efforts have been aimed at education. The ASF has tried to produce and introduce materials relating to Sephardic history, culture, and religious practices into the Jewish day schools in South Florida (see Angel 2000).

Since 1986, the American Sephardi Federation has organized and sponsored an annual Semana Sephardi (Sephardic Week) in association with the Federación Sephardi Latinoamericana (FeSeLa). This organization originally was founded at the Cuban Sephardic congregation, Temple Moses. Programs such as educational lectures, youth kabbalat Shabbats, exhibits, movies, and social events including dinners and picnics are featured in the period between January 1 and Passover.

The Sephardic Federation Palm Beach County was founded in 1992, the year of the quincentenary that sparked interest in Sephardic Jews, their history and culture across the United States. Their membership ranges from 160 to 200 people, primarily from Palm Beach and Broward Counties. The goals of this group include the preservation of Sephardic language and culture, and they sponsor intellectual

and social activities. To reach these goals, the federation publishes a bilingual
newsletter, *Ke Haber*, in English and Ladino. One of their leading members, David
Siman, has run monthly Ladino lessons and socials, Echar Lashon, since the early
1990s. Siman (1992) compiled a *Directory of Sources of Information on Sephardic
Jewry for South Florida* under the auspices of the Commission for Jewish Education
of the Palm Beaches. This directory provides a bibliography, and information on
Sephardic resources both locally and nationally.

Two Sephardic social groups founded in the 1970s and '80s are the Sephardic
Social Club and the Sephardic American Club. The former is older, founded in October 1978. In February 2002, its members celebrated its twenty-fifth anniversary.
One of the primary goals of the Sephardic Social Club was to perpetuate the culture, food, language, and dancing learned when growing up. The members wanted
to get together with other Sephardic people to keep their language and customs.
As one member said, "We're Sephardic Jews, we don't want Yiddish music." By the
end of their first year, the club had attracted approximately one thousand members. Hundreds of people from Miami to West Palm Beach attend their monthly
meetings, which offer music and food and a time to visit with friends. They had
tried to court Cuban Jews in the 1980s, but found that they were more nationalistic
and, in the ages-old pattern of Sephardic socialization, did not join in with others.

The Sephardic American Club was founded in 1986. It grew out a rift in the
leadership of the older group. Like the Social Club, members meet monthly to
socialize, dance, and eat in Broward and Palm Beach County. Both clubs have organized a three-day Spring Getaway every March at Miami Beach's Saxony Hotel.
This event gives members the opportunity to luxuriate in a kosher hotel with a
few Sephardic touches. At the banquet, music is provided by "Sasha," a well-loved
Israeli performer, or Vic Ash(er), a nonagenarian child of Turkish Sephardic immigrants who continues to earn a living as a musician in South Florida.

By the start of the twenty-first century, however, both clubs found that they were
losing members to attrition. Neither was successfully attracting the third generation, the grandchildren of the original Sephardic immigrants to America. In fact,
the overall opinion of many of the Sephardim is that not many young people are
involved in these social activities that were aimed at keeping Sephardic culture in
Florida alive.

Conclusion

So who are the Sephardic Jews in South Florida? They are retired children
of immigrant parents who had originally settled in the eastern cities. They are
businessmen and women seeking economic prosperity who made their homes
in Miami-Dade, Broward, and Palm Beach Counties. According to University of
Miami demographer Ira Sheskin, the Sephardim in South Florida are a small but
growing component of the Jewish community. He measured ten thousand Sephardic Jews in South Florida in 1992 (Sheskin 2002).

By the last decade of the twentieth century a new wave of Sephardic Jews was
making an impact on South Florida's Jewish population. These Sephardim came

to the United States from Israel, North Africa, and the countries of Latin America where an earlier generation of Sephardic immigrants had settled when they were unable to enter the United States. Many of the older Sephardim whose parents settled in the United States in the early twentieth century do not consider these late-comers to be really Sephardic because the heritage of many is not Judeo-Spanish. The newcomers are viewed merely as non-Ashkenazi Jews. A recent article quoted an administrator at one of the South Florida Jewish schools who stated that there is a "nearly 300 percent [Sephardic increase] in the past three years" (Samuels 2002). He is probably referring to these immigrants and their children.

The Sephardic Jews in South Florida have been a minority within a minority as in other locations in the United States. They however, continue to strive to worship and socialize together, determined to maintain their unique heritage and culture.

ACKNOWLEDGMENTS

The author would like to thank the Florida Humanities Council from which she received a 2002 Scholars Grant to conduct research on the history and diversity of the Sephardim of South Florida. Much of this data comes from research and interviews conducted under this grant. Warm thanks are also extended to the individuals who generously shared their family stories with the author.

REFERENCES

Angel, Rabbi Marc D. 2000. *Exploring Sephardic Customs and Traditions.* New York: Ktav Publishing House.

Bettinger-López, Caroline. 2000. *Cuban-Jewish Journeys: Searching for Identity, Home, and History in Miami.* Knoxville: University of Tennessee Press.

Halio, Hank. N.d. "New Lots." *Sephardic Home News.*

Levine, Robert M. 1993. *Tropical Diaspora, The Jewish Experience in Cuba.* Gainesville: University of Florida Press.

Liebman, Seymour B. 1977. "The Cuban Jewish Community of South Florida." In *A Coat of Many Colors, Jewish Subcommunities in the United States,* ed. Abraham D. Lavender. Westport, Conn.: Greenwood, 296–304.

Monaco, Chris. 2002. "A Sugar Utopia on the Florida Frontier: Moses Elias Levy's Pilgrimage Plantation." *Southern Jewish History* 5.

Samuels, Mordechai. 2002. "Yeshiva Elementary School Creates Sephardic Study Room." *Jewish Journal* (December 31).

Sheskin, Ira. 2002. Personal communication.

Siman, David. N.d. Porke Somos Djudios: *Because We're Jewish, A Directory of Sources of Information on Sephardic Jewry for South Florida.* Palm Beach, Fla.: Commission for Jewish Education of the Palm Beaches.

Taft, Adon. 1990. "Sephardim are Entering Mainstream." *Miami Herald.* July 13: p. 1E.

Wisser, Bill. 1995. *South Beach, America's Riviera, Miami Beach, Florida.* New York: Arcade.

Marcia Kerstein Zerivitz

From Swamp to "Shayna Platz": Jewish Life in Broward County

HISTORICAL PHOTOS FROM THE JEWISH MUSEUM OF FLORIDA

In less than a century, a land "unfit for human habitation" has been turned into the permanent home of one and three-quarters million people and the winter residence of tens of thousands more. In the 1920s there was barely a minyan in Broward County. Today about one in six of the people in Broward is Jewish.

FIGURE 1. The Three Friends.
Broward County was formed from portions of Miami-Dade and Palm Beach Counties in 1915 and named for former governor Napoleon Bonaparte Broward. Broward began draining the swamps in 1909; his project promoted settlement of the southern part of Florida. The event that boosted his election as governor in 1904 was his boat that was used to carry supplies to Cuba during the Cuban Revolutionary War. Some of the supplies transported on the filibustering boat The Three Friends were donated by Jews Louis Fine and Louis Wolfson, among others. The Jews remembered the expulsion from Spain in 1492 and donated money, supplies, and arms to the cause.

FIGURE 2. Dave Sokolow built
this house in 1912; it is still
standing.

*Around 1910 a newlywed Russian
couple Gussie Rubinstein and Dave
Sokolow settled in Dania, the first
city to be incorporated. A relative,
Louis Brown, was already there.
Together they opened three stores in
the area and started a tomato farm.*

FIGURE 3. Sarah "Sukki" Lehrman, 1919.
First known Jewish child born in Broward County.

FIGURE 4. Lehrman Family, Fort Lauderdale, 1920s.
Rose Seitlin and Max Lehrman married in 1913 in the first Jewish wedding in Miami and had a daughter, Nell, in 1914. After they had a second daughter, Anne, they moved to Fort Lauderdale in 1916, where they had three more children, the first Jewish children to be born there, in 1918 and 1919. Max Lehrman opened a dry goods store.

Florida's climate attracted new residents and tourists, which created jobs and sparked the interest in real estate.

FIGURE 5. Bill Horvitz holding a photograph of his father, Sam Horvitz, circa 1985.

Samuel Horvitz acquired most of Hollywood in the mid-1920s and by 1937, Hollywood Inc. was building and selling family homes there. The company amassed vast property holdings through the Depression, war, hurricanes, and land booms. Bill Horvitz, Sam's son, continued to expand the company with large residential communities and industrial parks. The business remained in the family until 1988.

FIGURE 6. Ladies from pioneer families of Fort Lauderdale enjoying the Beach, 1920s. *Molly Robbins, Mollie Newman, Rose Reiss and Sadye Katz with daughter Anita Katz [Paris].*

FIGURE 7. Sadye Katz on excursion boat, 1920s.

FIGURE 8. Sadye Katz's store on Brickell Avenue, Fort Lauderdale, 1924.

FIGURE 9. Birthday party with
children of pioneer families,
1930s.
Leonard Robbins, Lester Newman,
Gloria Katz, Lester Epstein, Stuart
Newman, Shirley Blume, and
person unknown.

FIGURE 10. Moe and Mack Katz, founders of Temple Emanu-el in Fort Lauderdale, circa 1938. *There were seven Jewish families when brothers Moe Katz and Mack Katz settled in 1923 to sell real estate, open retail shops, and help found Temple Emanu-el. The first religious service was held September 17, 1926, the night of the big hurricane. Overcoming anti-Semitism in the form of building permit denials and deed restrictions, the congregation built their first synagogue in 1937.*

FIGURE 11. First confirmation class of Temple Emanu-el, 1939.

FIGURE 12. Nancy Newman, Broward's only Jewish majorette in 1942.
Daughter of Mollie and Abe Newman who came in 1927 from Miami to run a shoe store in Fort Lauderdale. Mollie lived to be 101; she died in 1999 in Fort Lauderdale.

Florida offered opportunities for farming.

FIGURE 13. Chicken Farm of Ruth Frank Gross and Ralph Gross, circa 1943.

Ruth Frank was a Florida native from Ocala who moved to Fort Lauderdale in 1939 after her marriage to Ralph Gross. They owned and operated Gross Farms on Broward Boulevard until 1956. Ralph invented this portable chicken coop.

FIGURE 14. Dairy cows of Theodore and Ann Berman, Davie, 1940s.

They moved their farm from Davie to Okeechobee in 1967 and still operate there. Six generations of the Berman family have been farmers.

FIGURE 15. Bill Berman on steer on the Davie farm, 1954. *The farm was located adjacent to the Seminole Indian reservation (note totem pole).*

The white power structure was strong in Broward County in an effort to sustain the "gentiles only" profile in both hotels and apartments as well as property deeds.

FIGURE 16. Sands Apartments with "selected gentile clientele" policy, 1945.

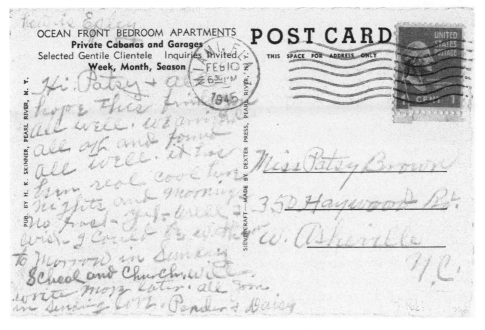

Many Broward Jewish men and women participated in World War II.

FIGURE 17. Captain Leonard Robbins was awarded the Distinguished Flying Cross (DFC) Society Medal for extraordinary achievement during World War II: 1st DFC, May 26, 1944; 2nd DFC, June 4, 1944.

Robbins, standing, second from left, is shown here with his bomber crew. Leonard moved to Fort Lauderdale with his parents Archie and Mollie Robbins in 1926 when Archie opened his men's wear business on South Andrews Avenue and was successful in spite of the pervasive anti-Semitism.

During World War II the airfields were converted to training facilities. After the war thousands of servicemen recalled the nice life in Broward and returned with their families; thousands more joined them and the greatest boom was on. Many Jews who continued to settle were involved in the development of hotels and residential communities, businesses, and farming.

Air-conditioning and airplanes brought increased tourism to Florida and the need for modern hotels.

FIGURE 18. The Hollywood Beach Hotel.
The hotel, built in 1925, was bought from the U.S. Navy in 1945 by Ben Tobin and operated by him until it was closed in 1971. Active in the Jewish Community, in 1956 Tobin donated the Hillcrest Country Club to become Temple Beth El in Hollywood, a breakaway from Temple Emanu-el.

FIGURE 19. The Diplomat Hotel.
The hotel was designed by Norman M. Giller for Sam Friedland in 1958 at a cost of $26 million. Friedland owned Food Fair Stores and in 1958, Giller, a Florida native, had the tenth-largest architectural firm in the nation. The Diplomat was closed in 1993, demolished in 1998, then rebuilt and opened in 2001 on the same site.

Postwar Broward also offered opportunities to expand business.

FIGURE 20. Marvin Wolff
developed Plantation, 1955.
*Aerial photo reflects one example of
the scope of communities developed
by Jews in Broward.*

FIGURE 21. New River Groves, 1957.
Al Roth purchased ten acres of citrus groves in Davie and founded the Groves and Roth Realty, becoming the country's westernmost real estate broker. Roth had been interested in citrus since the age of 10. He operated the grove until 1980 when his son Bob took over.

As the Jewish community grew to about two thousand Jews by 1950, more Jewish institutions were created, Zionism strengthened and traditions were preserved. By the 1970s, the rate of growth of Broward Jews surpassed that of its neighbor, Dade County. The population continued to expand and Jews became even more involved and influential in the general community.

FIGURE 22. Alan Levy at his Bar Mitzvah at Temple Emanu-el, 1953.
Alan is a son of Marie and Richard Levy who settled in Fort Lauderdale in 1942 when there were about twenty Jewish families. The family bought and sold produce in Florida and shipped it all over the United States. Later they got into farming. The fourth generation in agriculture, Alan continues the family business today.

FIGURE 23. Pompano Jewish Circle Sedar, 1955.

FIGURE 24. B'nai B'rith in Hollywod, 1951.
Left to right: *Sam Slater, Herbie Heiden, George Robinson, Lou Charnow, Ira Lieberman, Leonard Robbins.*

FIGURE 25. B'nai B'rith Youth Float, Hollywood, 1950s.

FIGURE 26. Eleanor Roosevelt at Israel Bonds Dinner, 1959. *Leadership of the Jewish Community demonstrate their support for Israel. Back row: Stuart Simon, person unknown, Ben Tobin, Abe Mailman, Commissioner Maynard Abrams; Front row: Mrs. Ben (Jeanette) Tobin, Eleanor Roosevelt, Gertrude Abrams.*

FIGURE 27. Jacob and Ludwig Brodzki sending black children to summer camp, 1961. *As Holocaust survivors, the Brodzkis settled in Fort Lauderdale after World War II, opened a furniture store and became very involved in Jewish Federation and other community efforts. Recalling the discrimination they faced as Jews when they were denied hotel rooms, they became community activists to break barriers.*

FIGURE 28. Mayor Maynard
Abrams as honorary Seminole
Indian chief, 1968.
*Maynard Abrams was mayor of
Hollywood, 1966–69.*

FIGURE 29. U.S. Senator
Richard Stone presenting to
Herman Adelstein his Silver
Star, earned for bravery in WW I
and denied due to anti-Semitism
until 1977.
*Richard Stone was Florida's second
Jewish U.S. Senator elected in
1974.*

FIGURE 30. Coral
Springs Temple Beth Orr
groundbreaking, 1977.
*There were about 40,000 Jews in
Broward in the 1970s. Reflective
of the tremendous growth of
the Jewish community to the
western part of the county that
correlated with the developments
and condominium culture,
new institutions grew rapidly.
Today there are more than fifty
congregations in Broward.*

FIGURE 31. Maria Giulianti was elected mayor of
Hollywood in 1986; she has served seven terms and is still
serving (2004).
*The vast increase in the Jewish population has been especially
evident in the community's heightened political involvement,
which began at the commission level. At least twenty Jewish
men and women have served as mayors in Broward County,
eleven as judges, and twelve as state or federal legislators.*

Florida has been viewed as a paradise for those in their golden years for more than a hundred years. They come for the sun, but refuse merely to bask in it. They see a new kind of opportunity in Broward County and have a fulfilling Jewish Life.

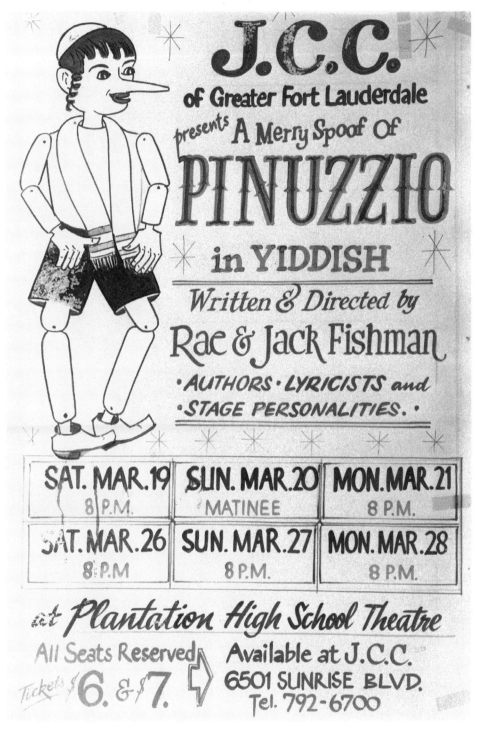

FIGURE 32. Playbill from "Pinnuzio," a Yiddish play produced by the Soref Jewish Community Center, Fort Lauderdale, circa 1980. *Yiddish culture is alive and well in Broward where there are dozens of Yiddish clubs.*

FIGURE 33. Sam and Lillian Mandel becoming B'nai Mitzvot in their eighties at Temple Solel of Hollywood with Rabbi Robert Frazen, 1983.

FIGURE 34. Elderly women dancing.
Many say "people seem to live longer in Florida!" These women certainly know how to enjoy their years of retirement.

FIGURE 35. Richard Simmons leads the way to fitness for retirees in the clubhouse in Century Village at Pembroke Pines, 1990.

FIGURE 36. Children in front
of the Soref Jewish Community
Center, c. 1990.

Jews of Boca Raton

On the sitcom *Seinfeld*, comedian Jerry Seinfeld's fictional parents lived in Boca Raton, where they were at the mercy of condo commandos, loud flowered shirts, and blistering heat. In his book, *Sein Language*, Seinfeld jokes that his real-life folks didn't want to move to Florida, "but they are in their 70s and that's the law."

Dr. Paula Marantz Cohen, an English professor at Drexel University in Philadelphia, affectionately pokes fun at Jewish snowbirds and retirees in her book, *Jane Austen in Boca*. Retirement to Boca might as well be a law, Cohen says, considering how often older folks from North Jersey, Philadelphia, and New York retire to Boca. *Jane Austen in Boca*, Cohen's version of *Pride and Prejudice*, is set among single Jewish retirees in Boca Raton. "I think it's just something older Jewish people do. Of course, there are others who resist it. But mostly, when I think about Jews in Florida, I think about elderly people who want to escape the cold," Cohen said.

Actually though, according to U.S. Census data for the year 2000, the median age for all residents of Boca Raton—Jewish or not—is 42.9 years old. Despite the stereotype among northerners, Boca Raton's Jewish community also has a thriving population of young families and singles. When Aaron Jay Lieberman's parents would come to visit him, he would joke that they were the only people coming to visit younger relatives in Boca. A single, thirty-two-year-old computer programmer, Lieberman moved from Maryland in 1996 at the coaxing of a friend who was enjoying the warm weather. "It was snowing in Maryland, so I moved," Lieberman said. He stayed because "there are job opportunities here, my neighborhood is nice, crime is low, and there is always lots to do. I never need to go more than a mile from my house."

Lieberman, who is involved with many Jewish and secular singles organizations, has found that local women are very much into what a man does for a living, how much money he makes, and what kind of car he drives. But Lieberman said he isn't sure if that trend is necessarily exclusive to Boca and South Florida. Because Boca is centrally located, Lieberman can travel north to singles events in Palm Beach, or south to programs in Dade and Broward. But most of the time, he says, there's no need to leave Boca: "There are plenty of singles events and things to do here." He continues, "I know some people who don't leave Boca. I dated one girl who lived about seven miles west of me and she told me she wasn't interested in a long-distance relationship."

In 1999, the Jewish Federation of South Palm Beach County commissioned Ira Sheskin, a demographer and professor of geography and Judaic Studies at the University of Miami, to conduct a Jewish population study of Boca Raton, as well as the nearby communities of Delray Beach, Highland Beach, and unincorporated south Palm Beach County. Sheskin found that the Jewish population—which has

FIGURE I. *An advertisement selling the virtues of Boca Raton. Courtesy Collection of Myrna and Seth Bramson.*

seen tremendous growth over the last thirty years—makes up 45 percent of Boca's demographics. But if you are talking about city limits, Boca Raton is actually only 20 percent Jewish, says Steve Abrams, the city's first Jewish mayor.

Abrams moved from Philadelphia in 1985 to get a job with a Boca law firm. "I had read a travel story in the *New York Post* that was complimentary about the Boca area. The article called it a very progressive city." What are misconceptions Abrams would like to dispel about his favorite city? He would like people to know that Boca, once labeled a WASP-y town, now has cultural and religious diversity that reaches beyond Christianity and Judaism. Relatively new as a Jewish community, Boca has gone through many changes. In the mid-1970s, Lynn Nobil remembers going to the opening of the Mel Brooks comedy *Blazing Saddles* and being the only one in the packed theater laughing at the Jewish shtick. "We felt like *olim* (Hebrew for immigrants), like pioneers," she said.

In its infancy, Temple Beth El—then called the Boca Raton Hebrew Congregation—borrowed space for seven years from a Moravian church, beginning in 1969. When congregant Stephen Kleinman became a bar mitzvah in December 1971, he shared the pulpit with a Christmas tree (which was temporarily unplugged). Beth El, Boca's oldest congregation began meeting in 1967. In 2003, members celebrated its "double chai" anniversary: thirty-six years. Today, the area is one of the fastest-growing Jewish communities in North America, with nearly 130,000 Jewish households in Boca Raton, Delray Beach, and Highland Beach, according to the Jewish Federation study. Compare that to 1,200 households in 1970. At the time, only one synagogue, Temple Beth El, existed in the community. It wasn't until 1976 when the West Palm Beach–based Jewish Federation of Palm Beach County opened a small, part-time satellite office in downtown Boca Raton.

This is My Shtetl Now

Attorney Rick Gordon works at the Palm Beach office of Arnstein and Lehr, with a magnificent view of the ocean. Still, he is willing to say good-bye to that in order to head the firm's newest location in Boca. In 1985, Rick Gordon was a high school sophomore in Philadelphia, when his parents decided to make the move south. Today, Gordon and his wife—a transplant from New York—are raising a three-year-old and expecting a second baby. "I knew I'd settle in Boca," said Gordon, who began visiting Boca when his grandparents moved to the area in 1976. "This is my shtetl now, my neighborhood. I've seen it grow into what it is today."

What's so great about Jewish life in Boca Raton (which actually means the "mouth of a rat" or "mouth of a mouse" in French)? "It's clean and not overly congested. The schools are good and the area is safe. Plus, there are business opportunities in and around Palm Beach. There's no place else I would live," said Gordon, who is involved at his synagogue and with the Jewish Community Center.

The rest of the United States may think Floridians spent a little too much time baking in the sun after the 2000 election fiasco and the voting problems in 2002, Gordon said. "Some people are also staying away since the news reported that there were terrorists living here and the anthrax scare—all in Boca. They say, 'What is it with South Florida?'"

Lynn Nobil came to Boca from South Miami in 1975. A mother of two and the wife of a physician, she and her first husband (she later married Jim Nobil, a past president of the Jewish Federation of South Palm Beach County) decided Boca Raton's central location made it ideal for his medical practice. At the time, Boca had few choices for worship, no Jewish Federation (the closest was in West Palm Beach), no yiddishkeit and no Jewish schools.

Today, there are 5,800 kids in Jewish schools in Boca, said Dr. Leon Weissberg, executive director of the Jewish Education Commission. The community boasts six congregational schools, five Jewish day schools and six early childhood programs. "The growth of the community and the influx of younger families has been phenomenal in the last decade," he said. Weissberg gives part of the credit to the Jewish Campus in west Boca, a central location that houses the Adolph and Rose Levis Jewish Community Center, the Jewish Federation of South Palm Beach County, Donna Klein Jewish Academy, Hillel Day School of Boca, Jewish Community Relations Council, Ruth Rales Jewish Family Service, and the Jewish Education Commission. The commission was created six years ago by the Jewish Federation to galvanize and coordinate all the Jewish education programs in the south end of Palm Beach County.

"Families invite other families to come to Boca," Weissberg said. "There are a lot from Dade County. Once the Jewish services became available, the Jewish families followed. Thirty-five years ago there were 7,000 Jews in Boca and Delray. Today there are 135,000."

In a short span, things changed dramatically, Nobil said. "All of a sudden every professional young man and his family came here, mostly from up north. The town grew and mushroomed and pushed westward. To go from zero to what we know now is a remarkable climb. The kids have benefited the most. Our children have the good fortune to be in a place where anti-Semitism doesn't have much of a chance. We have created a walled-in city of Jews. We've created our own Jewish ghetto," she said.

For Helen Sendyk, there is comfort in being around other Holocaust survivors. Brockman, Jews of Boca Raton

Today, she is part of one of the largest survivor populations in the country. The author of two books on the Holocaust—*The End of Days* and *New Dawn: A Triumph of Life* (2002)—Sendyk moved to Delray Beach, five miles north of Boca, in 1995. She travels throughout the county and the country educating children about the Holocaust. "Survivors like to be in the company of other survivors and communicate with survivors because there is an understanding between them. Even though we are part of the general community, we have different feelings from the general population. It's important to have different services for survivors," said Sendyk, who was eleven when World War II broke out.

Boca has several survivor organizations and was a research site for Steven Spielberg's Shoah Foundation. Florida Atlantic University in Boca has a Holocaust and Judaic Studies program, as well as two endowed chairs in Judaic Studies: the Raddock Eminent Scholar Chair of Holocaust Studies and the Gimelstob Chair of Judaica. The program started in 1998 and today has nearly four hundred students—with twenty-three majoring in Judaic studies. FAU also has the Molly S. Fraiberg Judaica Collections, one of the largest collections of Judaica in the southeastern United States.

Anti-Semitism: Overt and Covert

Ida and Herman Herst were semiretired when they came to Boca from Westchester County, New York, in 1972. Ida became involved with Temple Beth El, sitting on every committee and was even president in the early 1980s. The eighty-eight-year-old has watched the congregation grow from a handful of members to eighteen hundred families today, and witnessed three building expansions. While there was some discrimination against Jews in those years, Herst said she didn't experience it. "When I moved to Boca, people told me it was restricted, but I didn't pay any attention. People who experienced it didn't talk about it. The hotel at the Royal Palm Country Club was restricted in the mid-1940s, but it was a quiet restriction. Real estate agents weren't allowed to show you a home if you were Jewish. It didn't last long."

Herst and other older residents remember when there was a sign in nearby Delray Beach that said, "No Jews or Dogs." The Boca Raton Resort and Club, originally called the Cloister Inn, was an exclusive, restricted resort built in 1926, said Marcia Zerivitz, executive director and founder of the Jewish Museum of Florida, located on Miami Beach. Excluding Jews ended in the 1940s, when it was bought by J. Myer Schine, a Latvian immigrant turned hotel magnate.

Travel down Yamato Road in Boca and you will see a majestic row of churches and one synagogue, Congregation B'nai Israel. What began with four families meeting in a Boca living room, became more promising in 1984, when the land on Yamato was purchased. Today the Reform congregation, led by its founding rabbi, Richard D. Agler, has 1,150 member families. The first Jew in Boca was Max Hutkin (1895–1987), who came down from Saint Louis with his wife, Nettie, and made many contributions to the area, Zerivitz said. The son of Polish immigrants, Hutkin was the owner of Hutkin's Food Market and one of the founders of Temple Beth El.

Rabbi Kenneth Brander, spiritual leader of Boca Raton Synagogue, came from Lincoln Square Synagogue on New York's West Side eleven years ago. He started with fifty families ten years ago; today the Orthodox shul boasts more than five hundred families and hundreds of children. The Union of Orthodox Congregations named Boca one of the fastest-growing Orthodox communities, Brander said.

Today Boca has an eruv (the creation of boundaries for the Sabbath), which merges distinct domains into one domain allowing people within in that demarcation to carry from one home to another without breaking the laws of Shabbat, Brander said. Why are Orthodox Jews interested in making a life in Boca Raton? Brander said it is due to the established infrastructure that allows an Orthodox Jew to feel comfortable: prayer services, youth programs, Torah programs, kosher restaurants, bakeries and meat markets, and an eruv. "Twelve years ago, there were no kosher butchers or bakeries up to Orthodox standards. Now there are a plethora of restaurants and the number keeps growing. Twelve years ago, we had a small day school that didn't go through all the elementary grades. Now there are 375 kids in the lower school, 150 teens in the high school, and a new elementary school being started. The growth has been unbelievable."

Yiddishkeit on South Beach

The Historical Setting

> *Sixty years ago was a wild island. And the Jewish people came down from the cold country to warm their old bones. —Jack Dintzer*

"I WANT TO BE

WITH YOU TO

SING MY SONGS"

At the end of the nineteenth century, South Beach was truly a "wild island," a mass of untamed mangrove swamps that one enterprising New Jerseyan tried—without success—to fashion into a coconut palm plantation. By the early 1920s, however, Miami Beach was slowly becoming a resort center, seeking "nouveau riche" industrialists in an effort to compete with the old-monied, blue-blood exclusivity of Palm Beach.

While Jews were excluded from most oceanfront hotels above Lincoln Road until the late 1930s (Mehling 121), South Beach experienced a gradual rise in Jewish tourism. Ann Armbruster's social history of Miami Beach (1995) offers some of the richest details of this period. She notes that in 1935, only two South Beach hotels advertised in the *Jewish Daily Forward*, the leading U.S.-based newspaper of Yiddish-speaking immigrants. Just four years later in 1939, a dozen Jewish-owned hotels took out ads. In that same year, the *Forward* also contained an ad (in Yiddish, no less) for a previously restricted hotel that had come to realize the economic benefits of opening its doors to Jewish tourists (Armbruster 79). It was during this period that South Beach gained its now signature small-scale, "Deco"-styled structures, influenced by the decorative arts and "Industrial Moderne" architectural movement of the 1920s and 1930s. In a flurry of construction, three- to five-story hotel and apartment buildings were erected with distinctive ornamentation. Sleek horizontal racing stripes and parapets evoked the fast movement of a train or racing car; round windows simulated huge ocean freighters; and strong, vertical columns replicated the visual prominence of a skyscraper.

As the number of Jewish vacationers gradually increased, anti-Semitism was still pervasive. With Nazism on the rise in Germany, prominent political constituencies in the United States harbored similar anti-Jewish sentiments. Active racist paramilitary groups such as the Ku Klux Klan and the Black Legions flourished in some parts of the country, including South Florida. In the 1920s and 1930s, the Klan regularly marched through downtown Miami and physically ravaged businesses it opposed (Armbruster 76). The nationally broadcast, Jew-hating sermons of Father Coughlin and the Jewish conspiracy theories propagated by Henry Ford's sponsorship of the "Elders of Zion" fueled deep-seated prejudices against not only Jews, but also African-Americans and Catholics. Such racist enmity was visible locally in bumper stickers declaring "It's always 'Jew'n in Miami," and exclusionary hotel signs and advertisements noting "restricted clientele," "gentile-owned and operated," and "No Jews and dogs allowed." Despite such hostility (nothing new to diasporic Jews), the special flavor of South Beach as a seasonal Jewish community with its own cultural and economic infrastructure was beginning.

Deborah Dash Moore's study (1994) of Jewish migration to Los Angeles and Miami attributes the phenomenenal rise of Jewish elders on Miami Beach during the 1960s to their desire to live independently among ethnic generational (41). Most Jews migrating to South Beach came from urban settings where they lived close to shopping, entertainment, and other Jews. Dash Moore suggests that these elders found a sense of safety in living close to their "own kind." Many of the elders I interviewed expressed this sentiment; they sought a community of cohorts with whom they felt "something in common."

The make-up of Jewish South Beach from the 1950s through the 1980s comprised a lower-income community of transient "snowbirds": Jews mainly from the northeastern United States who resided on the Beach for during the winter months. While some settled on the Beach permanently, and could even afford to purchase a condo unit, most South Beach elders spent the "season" in one-room hotel efficiencies with very few possessions. Most had come to the United States as children in the first decades of the twentieth century or after the Holocaust. Most had modest incomes, having worked in factories, retail, or the civil service. On South Beach, they lived on fixed incomes (Social Security or union pensions). Almost everyone spoke Yiddish. Retired, freed from labor, separated from family back home—what rises to the surface?

Outsider Views of South Beach Jews

As a filmmaker and oral historian, I interviewed dozens of Jewish elders from 1985 to 1995, when the population was already waning. Over this ten-year period, it became clear that I was unearthing the collective "story" of South Beach as told by working-class, immigrant Jews who maintained a rich Jewish culture by weaving *Yiddishkeit* into their daily lives.

Most of the Jews I spoke to were of modest means, living in small apartment units as tenants during the winter months. Many were widows or widowers who sought out the pleasures of simple conversation—very often in Yiddish, a language that carried memories of eastern European or early immigrant life. I discovered that despite the very real hardships of aging, there was a utopian quality to Jewish life on South Beach in the 1960s and 1970s. The utopia comprised a rich Yiddish communal life underscored by a glorious tropical climate. These elders used glowing terms to describe the deep sense of place they felt on South Beach. South Beach in its Jewish heyday was not the worst place to live out one's retirement.

Yet, the published materials on the experience of retired Jews on South Beach reveals sharp differences between how these Jews viewed themselves and how others viewed them. Many outsider accounts of Jewish life on South Beach conflate long-term caricatures of the "ghetto" Jew with a disparaging view of aging. Journalistic, business, and government reports generally call attention to the "problems" of South Beach as a "blighted," "seedy" neighborhood of elderly impoverishment and decay:

Born in ghettos, they have moved from one ghetto to another all their lives — from Russia to Rivington Street to Brooklyn, Hoboken, the Bronx, and have come finally to the last ghetto of all, the one from which death is the only escape. Pensioned off by their families, their unions, the state, they come to Miami Beach to spend their last years in the sun, useless, unneeded, unwanted. Who wants to live with an eighty-year-old *bubbe* who barely speaks English? Who needs a retired garment worker? (Redford 1970: 263)

To this essayist, Yiddish-speaking Jewish South Beach is a site of irrelevance, poverty, and death. This constellation of attributes (old, working-class, Yiddish) is evoked in other documents from the period in order to evoke and praise the "good Jew" (young, assimilated, and middle-class).

Even Jewish organizations wanted to transform the behavior of South Beach elders. Dash Moore uncovered a 1940s film commissioned by the Anti-Defamation League (ADL), instructing Jewish vacationers on Miami Beach in appropriate social conduct. As early as the 1940s, "The ADL (was) concerned that Jewish behavior in public places might provoke anti-Semitism. . . . Among the items criticized were schmoozing on street corners (the movie recommended that conversations be held on the hotel porch), playing cards on hotel porches (the movie preferred the game room), elbowing one's way to the front in popular cafeterias (waiting in line was suggested), and engaging in loud arguments in hotel corridors (couples were urged to fight in the privacy of their rooms behind closed doors)" (35).

The ADL's concerns were echoed in other literature about South Beach Jews. In numerous accounts, aged immigrant Jews are depicted as colorful and coarse, loud and uneduated. Mel Zeigler's *Miami Herald* Sunday magazine feature story (1968) describes them thus:

Old Jewish ladies chatter in Yiddish on the street corners. Most have never learned English beyond the rudiments. "When you are living in a ghetto all your life, you use your hands to talk, and three hundred words is sufficient to get you by in a lifetime," explains one social worker. In the shops, the women carefully count pennies from their change purses to buy a Miami Beach T-shirt for their grandson up north. As in any other ghetto, panhandlers shift through the streets, but even they have a peculiarly ethnic style. "Sonny," muttered an old, unshaven Jew with sunken eyes, "could you spare me ninety-five cents so I could get myself a corned beef sandwich? I am waiting on my social security and I am mit out money." (17–18).

Such portrayals evoke stereotypical characterizations of "ghetto Jews" as dirty, coarse, cheap, and loud, paying scant attention to either the history or rich culture of the people under scrutiny.

Calvin Trillin offers a more complicated (and humorous) view of the expressive Yiddish culture of South Beach Jews in this *New Yorker* report (1976):

Washington Avenue, the main shopping street of South Beach, is sometimes called Yenta Alley. In Yiddish, a yenta is a shrew or battle-axe. As shoppers, yentas make the new brand of suspicious and aggressive consumers — those truth-in-packaging advocates and co-op-food-purchasing organizers and unit-measurement freaks—seem like a gaggle of impulse buyers. . . . Some of the shouting that goes on during shopping hours on Washington Avenue must be caused by the impatience and irritability associated with old age; some of it is undoubtedly caused by the anxiety associated with living on a fixed income during a period of terrifying inflation. But I think clerks on Washington Avenue sometimes absorb punishing remarks for the same reason that heavyweights sometimes absorb punishing uppercuts—because somebody good at the game has seen an opening (56).

Trillin observes the lack of self-consciousness displayed by these old Jews as they openly bicker over the cost of goods. Although his account veers to comic carica-ture, he also seems to admire these people. Recalling his own father's preference for shopping on South Beach, he writes:

> Whenever my father was in the Miami area, he used to drive to South Beach to hear women argue with the butcher, the way other people drove down to watch the dogs race. . . . My father preferred the stores on Washington Avenue, particularly the butcher shops.
>
> He had a non-scholarly interest in the development of the Yiddish curse that comes out of the Eastern European ghettos—"May you have itch in a place impossible to scratch" and "May streetcars grow on the back of your throat"—and he thought kosher butcher counters in South Beach were good places for hearing imaginative curses, perhaps because the shoppers were inspired by the added irritant of kosher meat being even more expensive than non-kosher meat. He loitered around butcher counters on Washington Avenue the way American folklorists used to hang around remote Tennessee mountain towns. (57)

Trillin's father, like most outsiders, is fascinated by the highly expressive speech patterns of South Beach Jews. Something of an amateur folklorist, Trillin's father sensed there was more to Yiddish "slang" than met the eye.

And he was right. During my decade-long research, I came to understand that the expressive use of Yiddish by South Beach Jews was related not just to social class and culture, but to how one uses one's body, and, ultimately, to the politics of physical space. The verbosity and physicality of these old Jews eliminated tradi-tional boundaries between private and public behavior. Bickering with merchants about the costs of things, these elders also kvetched openly (and loudly) about physical aches and pains from *kepela* to *tuchus*.

Within the Jewish community, of course, there is much endearing folklore that proudly proclaims the vitality of Jewish speech. The riddle, "What do you get when you put two Jews together?" has innumerable derivations: "Put two Jews together, you have an argument; three Jews, it's a revolution." "With three Jews stranded on a deserted island, why did they build three synagogues—Orthodox, Conservative, Reform? Because they couldn't agree on which one to attend." The folklore I col-lected on the streets of South Beach corroborated the unrestrained, argumentative nature of Jewish conversation suggested in the riddles.

FIGURE I. *Lummus Park, December 1987. Photo by Joel Saxe.*

For example, bustling cafeterias were Jewish daily centers of social life. Yet every story I recorded attributed the demise of cafeterias to Jewish cut-rate conversation: "So why did these places go under? Well, you see, these old people brought their bag lunches. They lived on Social Security and were trying to save a buck. So they ordered a *glezyl* tea and schmoozed all afternoon. No wonder they couldn't stay in business."

A *haimish* relationship between public space and Jewish sociability was a prominent feature of eastern European Jewish experience. According to Mark Zborowski and Elizabeth Herzog, this fabric of connectedness derived from the outsider status of eastern European Jews. Living for long periods of time among hostile Christians, Jews became an "island culture, a minority embedded in and subordinate to a majority group" (Zborowski and Herzog 1962:214). Following centuries of European hostility, the intensification of anti-Semitic attacks under the czarist regime reinforced long-term practices of Jewish cultural and religious autonomy that fostered communication practices oriented toward collective self-preservation. In this culture, talk was a primary resource. Everybody's door was open and there were no secrets among neighbors. Highly expressive speech, both in private and public, was considered normal.

Jack's Song

Miami Beach, I miss you. I want to see you again. . . . I miss that taste of Jewish, the Jewish conversation, Jewish speech that you hear here. Because you can't hear it any place. In Los Angeles, or New York, you can't hear it any longer. You see, but in here, you come out with Jewish . . . —Jack Dintzer, December 26, 1987

Like his generational peers—elderly, eastern European–born, predominantly working-class, Jewish immigrants—Jack lived a transient existence on South Beach. He and his wife, Bettina, stayed in a hotel efficiency within walking distance

FIGURE 2. *Jack Dintzer, Lummus Park, December 1987. Photo by Joel Saxe.*

to the ocean. In addition to enjoying the surf, Jack and Bettina participated in a variety of public and semi-public Yiddish "performances." They and their fellow snowbirds gathered, usually outdoors in parks, to sing, tell stories, read poetry and literature, and make all kinds of speeches.

Having grown up in South Florida in the 1960s, I was very drawn to this scene. Lummus Park, where Jack gathered with his cohorts, left a particularly wondrous imprint. On many weekends in the early 1960s, I took a bus down Collins Avenue to spend the day with my Russian-born grandfather. My mother's father, William Wiener, lived just a block from the ocean at the Edwards Hotel in a "pullmanette," an efficiency with a hot plate and waist-high fridge. After lunch at a cafeteria on Washington Avenue, we often made our way back to Lummus Park. To a six-year old, the scene was captivating.

Every afternoon, hundreds of elderly Jewish men and women walked from their hotel and apartments to meet friends at regular gathering spots in this narrow seaside park. Here they sat in circlelike clusters between the palm trees and sea grape bushes. They brought folding chairs, reading materials, and musical instruments: mandolins, balalaikas, even violins. Fanned by a balmy ocean breeze, these old Jews read, romanced, debated, kvetched, and snoozed. This shmoozefest was a cornerstone of their social life: an outdoor block party, a mellow, daily carnival in which the sounds of Yiddish, English, and Russian swirled in a heady, *haimisha* mix.

Until the early 1980s, there was even a formal outdoor stage in Lummus Park at Ninth Street, located at the coral wall separating the beach from the park. A formally structured performance event, the Ninth Street stage offered local residents the opportunity to attend a free talent show that ran day and night. Anyone who wanted to perform was welcome, and there were often hundreds in the audience. In 1989, Jack Markowitz, the last emcee of the Ninth Street stage, recalled the stage at its zenith two decades earlier:

MARKOWITZ: Well we had, years ago we had all kinds of amusements. All kinds of songs. We had Hebrew songs. We have musicians with violins. We have musicians with clarinets. We have musicians with guitars. There was English songs. There was Jewish songs. There was the best songs of the world. And people didn't have to pay anything! Some people cannot afford to go to Jackie Gleason [Theater of the Performing Arts] for thirty-five dollars orchestra at night. They cannot afford it. They living on Social Security. Social Security. And they have to pay a lot of things. . . . If you know how to sing, you come over there, and we'll put you on the stage, and you'll have a good time for

FIGURE 3. *Lummus Park, January 1992. Photo by Joel Saxe.*

FIGURE 4. *Nina, Lummus Park, January 1992. Photo by Joel Saxe.*

nothing. . . . And from one mouth, from one mouth to another to the other mouth, will spread out and people will come around. That's right.

JOEL: Tell me what this strip of Ocean Drive used to be like, twenty years ago.

MARKOWITZ: Very lively. Verrry, verrry lively. Very, every, in every corner. Young and old in every corner. They used to come from all over the globe. That's it. You never saw any empty places over here. . . . Singing, singing on Eighth Street. Singing on Ninth Street. Down below, Fourth Street. Down below, First Street. Down below, dog track. Down below, dancing. (January 14, 1989)

By the early 1990s, a variety of factors—the 1980 influx of new Cuban "Mariel" refugees, gentrification, and the inevitable passing of this generation of old people—closed the curtain on such scenes. Or as invoked in the refrain to one of the standard Yiddish favorites sung on South Beach: "*Voz iz gevan iz gevan.*" What used to be is what used to be.

In the mid-1960s, 80 percent of South Beach was Jewish. Forty years later, there are virtually no signs of Jewish culture left. Yet, even in its final phase, Jewish elders supported a web of Yiddish cultural spaces. As late as the mid-1980s, one could attend some form of Yiddish cultural event nearly every day of the week. On weekdays, a range of Yiddish cultural clubs and political action groups met in community centers and public meeting rooms. On the weekends, these elders created "Oneg Shabbat" Yiddish talent shows, musical concerts, and an expanded oceanside folksong circle. The Flamingo Park Meeting, a gathering of old radicals that met under a sprawling banyan tree, evoked what I imagined to be the spirit of 1930s soapbox oratory. Indeed, the old Jewish left (or *linke*, as it was called in Yiddish) had a strong presence on South Beach through a range of political, cultural, and fraternal associations that met at the Jewish Cultural Center, a building they erected on Fifth Street in the 1950s.

As the old Jews died and Yiddish declined on South Beach, so did the cultural sensibility of eastern European Jewry the language represented. As the linguistic channel for a generation of immigrants, Yiddish, in simple conversation or as a complex chorus, gave its speakers a sense of safety and a sense of place. So too for Jack, it was not the exact physical space—("I don't miss this edge by the beach")—but rather the opportunity to experience the *ta'am*, the taste of Yiddish.

The stories these elders told of their oceanside gatherings suggest such gatherings functioned as secular rituals that affirmed a shared collective identity among the participants. Whether through everyday conversation or group folksong performance, the use of Yiddish evoked feelings that participants describe in terms that suggest a sense of "the sacred."

JOEL: When you talked about how you enjoyed getting together [at the oceanside gathering] and people playing the mandolins, how does it make you feel when you hear that old Yiddish music?

CHAIM: Oh, we are happy, because this is our, this is our language. See [laugh], Jewish, Jewish, when you hear Jewish playing, Jewish songs, you enjoy it. Because it's from, it's from the childhood. It's from the childhood. We are used to it. And we enjoy it.

For Chaim, Yiddish was the most intimate vernacular; it infused the simplest linguistic exchange with deeply resonant meanings.

During times of shared musical performance, these elders experienced their greatest sense of collective identity as a "Jewish People." The songs they shared represented generational dramas encapsulated in lyrical-narrative vignettes drawn from the palette of modern Jewish life. Singing them connected these elders to one another and to a larger sense of shared historical identity. The songs linked Europe and America, past and present, holy and profane. At these altars by the sea, each song revealed another chapter in the historical experience of the Jews.

Out here on the oceanside, nestled among a half-dozen friendly cohorts, Jack finished the performance of "Miami Beach, I miss you, I want to be with you to sing my songs." In the poem's finale, everyday practices of Jewish sociability contributed to a scene of elderly rejuvenation:

Although the hair is gray and we are graying. But the eyes shine like the dew, the night dew. And the city lives and exists. And I come there, and I forget to count my years. I feel the young years come back to me, because I see them, these people that I seen when I was young. And it come back, the young years come back to me. And I forget to count years when I come over there.

For Jack, it was not the actual physical space that was meaningful, but the revitalizing properties of Yiddish culture, in all its forms. "I don't miss this edge by the beach. . . . I miss the taste of Jewish, Jewish speech, Jewish conversation." Lummus Park, the Ninth Street Stage, the shops and delis become, for Jack and his fellow Jews, metaphorical fountains of youth.

Today on South Beach, there is virtually no sign that these Jewish elders once filled the streets with animated chatter and made music that flowed along the oceanside. As seasonal residents, they became stewards of communal scenes of lively performance, poetry, dance, and politics that stretched from Lummus to Flamingo Park, the pier on First Street to the Miami Beach Library off Twenty-first Street.

The sacredness of such scenes connected the immediate, visceral pleasures of communal performance with reminiscent activity. Yiddish provided a symbolic channel that bridged childhood with old age, melding the past with the present, the individual with the group. Performances in Yiddish served especially vital functions for a marginalized population quite conscious that their language and culture would largely pass with them.

With the loss of this feisty, heroic immigrant generation and their repertoire of Yiddish expressive practices, what will be the materials upon which we draw for a sense of cultural rootedness? Or feeling a sense of place in history?

REFERENCES

Armbruster, Ann. *The Life and Times of Miami Beach.* New York: Knopf, 1995.
Economic Research Associates. "Market Analysis: South Beach Redevelopment Project, Miami Beach." Unpublished report for the Miami Beach Redevelopment Agency, 1977.

Gilman, Sander. *The Jew's Body*. New York: Routledge, 1991.

Gutman, Chaim. "The Real Customers." In *Miami Beach Jewish Omnibus*, edited by Melech Grafstein, 158–159. Ontario: *Jewish Observer*, 1957.

Horowitz, Elinor. "Jewish Poverty Hurts in South Beach." In *A Coat of Many Colors: Jewish Subcommunities in the United States*, edited by Abraham Lavender, 160–166. Westport, Conn.: Greenwood, 1977.

Liebling, Jerome. *The People, Yes: Photographs and Notes by Jerome Liebling*. New York: Aperture, 1995.

Mark, Mary Ellen. *The Photo Essay: Photographs by Mark Ellen Mark*. Washington, D.C.: Smithsonian Institution Press, 1990.

Mehling, Harold. "Is Miami Beach Jewish?" In *A Coat of Many Colors: Jewish Subcommunities in the United States*, edited by Abraham Lavender, 118–127. Westport, Conn.: Greenwood, 1977.

Millas, Aristides, and Claudia Rogers. "The Development of Mobility Criteria for the Elderly Within the Context of a Neighborhood." University of Miami Institute for the Study of Aging. Unpublished research report, 1979.

Monroe, Gary. *Life in South Beach*. Miami, Fla.: Forest & Trees. 1988.

Monroe, Gary, and Andrew Sweet. *Miami Beach*. Miami, Fla.: Forest & Trees, 1990.

Moore, Deborah Dash. *To The Golden Cities: Pursuing the American Jewish Dream in Miami and L.A.* New York: Free Press, 1994.

Nagler, Richard. *My Love Affair with Miami Beach*. New York: Simon and Schuster, 1991.

Redford, Polly. *Billion Dollar Sandbar: A Biography of Miami Beach*. New York: Dutton, 1970.

Rubin, Ruth. *Voices of a People: The Story of Yiddish Folksongs*. New York: Washington Square Press, 1979.

Sennett, Richard. *The Fall of Public Man*. New York: Knopf, 1977.

Singer, Isaac Bashevis, and Richard Nagler. *My Love Affair with Miami Beach*. New York: Simon and Schuster, 1991.

Trillin, Calvin. "U.S. Journal: Miami Beach, Reflections of a More or Less Junior Citizen Shopping on Washington Avenue." *New Yorker* (February 16, 1976): 56–58.

Zborowski, Mark, and Elizabeth Herzog. *Life is with People*. New York: Schocken, 1962.

Zeigler, Mel. "Journey's End in a Promised Land." *Tropic Magazine, Miami Herald* (November 24, 1968): 10–21.

Gary Monroe

Life in South Beach

The hundreds of small hotels and apartments that make up South Beach aged with its yearly and seasonal residents. These people defined a rare ethos. With roots extending back to the shtetls of eastern Europe, survivors of the czarist pogroms and the Nazi holocaust emigrated to America mostly through Ellis Island. After a hundred years of toil, they had established South Beach as the last resort. These elderly Jewish men and women lived communally throughout the isolated small-scale neighborhood in Miami Beach, taking advantage of the tropical climate and therapeutic ocean. Facing the adversity of old age, they lived joyfully and in accord with their religious faith until the advent of the art deco craze. By 1987 the community's tight fabric was loose, becoming unwoven and unrecognizable.

The elderly Jews of South Beach lived in accord with their Old World values. But the ethnic community was out of touch and out of time. The place repelled tourists. South Beach was an embarrassment to the rest of Miami Beach. In a rush to redevelop the southern shore, the powers that be lost sight of an even more powerful entity: You don't tell Holocaust survivors that they will be "relocated."

No one placed value on the refuge whose roots extended back to the shtetls of eastern Europe. No one realized that this legacy was precious. No one stopped to think that the elderly Jews of South Beach had established a culture whose demise was the end of a distinct cultural lineage. Their lives steadfastly maintained their religiosity in a way that would later be forever altered by their children's Americanized Jewry.

Through the 1970s and to the mid-1980s, a shared vision of life went on: card rooms were transformed into makeshift shuls. The ocean was therapeutic. The streets were active. Everything was within walking distance. Social agencies cared for the residents and neighbors cared for each other. On Friday evenings women lit shabbat candles (many hotels set up communal spaces for this ritual, because lighting the candles in residential rooms would be in violation of fire code regulations).

Crime in Miami soared with the 1980 Mariel boat lift and South Beach took much of the wrath. Sunrise swims came to an abrupt end. The final blow was the airing of *Miami Vice*, which imag(in)ed Greater Miami as steamy and sexy. In a classic case of life imitating art, a television show was catalyst for the rebirth of Miami Beach.

Attrition would have taken its toll, but the economy refused to wait. The fever to capitalize on the Art Deco District and to get Miami Beach back into the limelight accelerated fiscal investment. New Yorkers and Europeans couldn't believe the summer-in-winter climate, and an unending stretch of beautiful, undeveloped (by code) beachfront in the middle of it all. As neon lights added a cool glow to balmy nights, South Beach redefined "trendy," and the average age of people there dropped by about fifty years within a decade.

Front porches, where the elderly used to sit and talk about their grandchildren and Israel, became outdoor cafés, while lobbies doubled as restaurants. Old ladies

FIGURE 1. *Before the Mariel boat lift, a large group of elderly Jews would congregate before sunrise at the beach for an early morning swim, circa 1970s. Courtesy of Gary Monroe, from the series* Life in South Beach, *1977–86.*

who had protected their lower lips from the blistering sun with strange sea grape leaves, gave way to supermodels who posed in front of the trees for international advertisements. Rollerbladers replaced mandolin bands along Lummus Park. "Kosher" signs yielded to Versace labels. And croissants replaced rugelach.

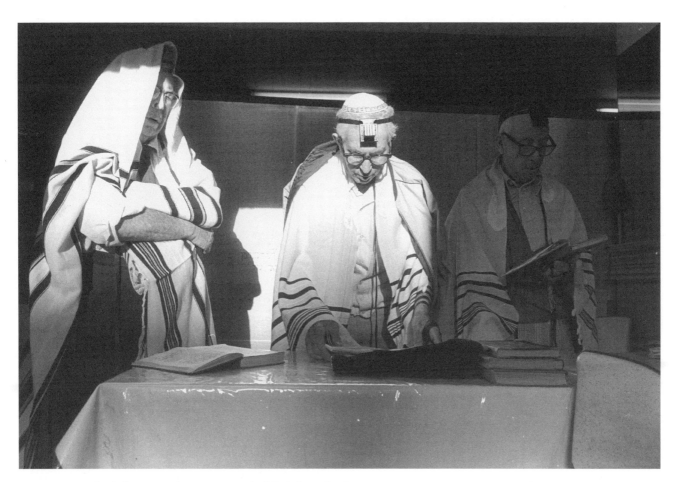

FIGURE 2. *A Lubavitch congregation creates a makeshift shul at a hotel. Courtesy of Gary Monroe, from the series* Life in South Beach, *1977–86.*

FIGURE 3. *This was the largest of a handful of groups that congregated most mornings along Lummus Park—the grassy area between the beach and Ocean Drive—to exercise. Courtesy of Gary Monroe, from the series* Life in South Beach, *1977–86.*

FIGURE 4. *Sixth Street off Washington, circa 1970s.*
Courtesy of Gary Monroe, from the series Life in South Beach, *1977–86.*

FIGURE 5. *Women lighting Shabbat candles.*
Courtesy of Gary Monroe, from the series Life in South Beach, *1977–86.*

FIGURE 6. *A round dance at the pier. It is evident that women outnumbered men. The pier was demolished as part of the redevelopment of South Beach. Courtesy of Gary Monroe, from the series* Life in South Beach, 1977–86.

Newcomers could not appreciate the vivacious life-affirming way that the elderly Jews began the New Year. New Year's Eve parties were thrown for their guests at just about all of the two hundred hotels along Ocean Drive and Collins Avenue. With enthusiasm, the "seniors" cavorted and danced their way into a tentative future.

FIGURE 7. *Hotelfront porches provided a sanctuary for its seasonal residents. At times, it offered them social opportunities or solitude. Courtesy of Gary Monroe, from the series* Life in South Beach, *1977–86.*

With each year, however, there were fewer and fewer celebrations. Morale, more than increased age, slowed them down as they saw their community withering away. The party atmosphere, as if a barometer, measured the community's demise to the point where in 1986 only three hotels held parties, and those were lackluster.

FIGURE 8. *An elderly South Beach resident stands in front of a photo of herself from younger days. Courtesy of Gary Monroe, from the series* Life in South Beach, *1977–86.*

South Beach has become a metaphor for everything that it wasn't. The few square miles that had given refuge to the elderly Jews is now "the American Riviera," attracting the rich and famous. Yiddish is now the exception, with seemingly every other language being spoken there. Costs have escalated so much that Hollywood filmmaking has pushed aside high-end photo shoots for glossy print ads.

FIGURE 9. *An impromptu gathering of musicians who maintain their interest in Old World music, as seen by their use of the mandolin and accordion. Courtesy of Gary Monroe, from the series* Life in South Beach, *1977–86.*

The hotels have again been transformed. Even the backdrop is different: the small buildings that had formed a pedestrian community are dwarfed by high-rise condominiums. Today all the hotels and most of the apartment buildings have either been beautifully renovated or razed. And no trace remains of the precious legacy that the elderly Jews created—a forgotten epoch.

FIGURE 10. *Women with grape leaves in their mouths.*
Courtesy of Gary Monroe, from the series Life in South Beach, 1977–86.

FIGURE 11. *Elected officials and those who sought public office would heavily lobby the elderly South Beach residents. This community was quite politically active. Courtesy of Gary Monroe, from the series* Life in South Beach, *1977–86.*

FIGURE 12. *Women exercising on the beach.*
Courtesy of Gary Monroe, from the series Life in South Beach, 1977–86.

PART II Individuals & Institutions

Jewish Gangsters Starring Meyer Lansky

The phrase "Jewish gangsters" seems to many Americans an oxymoron, a clash of words truly or seemingly contradicting each other. The early, mythopoeic gangster films—the three most popular (or notorious) were *Little Caesar* (1930), *The Public Enemy* (1931), and *Scarface* (1932)—did not depict them. Neal Gabler has demonstrated that the burgeoning film industry's mainly Jewish "Hollywood moguls," were careful about the images of Jews and Jewish life their companies projected (or, more ordinarily, did *not* project) on the screen. Though the stars of *Scarface* and *Little Caesar*, Paul Muni and Edward G. Robinson, were Jews, they portrayed Italians. James Cagney's magnetically sociopathic Tom Powers in *The Public Enemy* was according to Harry Hossent "likely . . . based on 'Little Hymie' Weiss, a Polish Jew" (22; ellipsis mine unless otherwise noted), but portrayed as a generic, deracinated American.

New York's pre–World War I Jewish gangster bosses and small fry have been the best tracked: some that Albert Fried lists are Monk Eastman (born Edward Osterman in the Williamsburg section of Brooklyn around 1873), Max Zweibach (the original "Kid Twist"), Big Jack Zelig, Benjamin "Dopey Benny" Fein, Joseph "Joe the Greaser" Rosenzweig, Hyman "Little Hymie" Bernstein, Benjamin "Nigger Benny" Snyder, and Jacob "Tough Jake" Heiseman.

An authoritative, anti-Semitic study published in 1897 claimed the East Side Jews were "the worst element in the entire make-up of New York life" (Joselit 6) and an article by Theodore Bingham in the prestigious *North American Review* for September 1908 declared that these Jews just did not like to work hard. Jacob Riis suggested a saner, environmental view in his landmark *How the Other Half Lives* (1890), that much crime stems from the foul, hard, crushingly overcrowded, impoverished, violent conditions many newcomers including Italians and Jews, were forced to endure (or succumb to) in urban America.

Arnold Rothstein, Dutch Schultz (b. Arthur Flegenheimer), Benjamin "Bugsy" Siegel, Louis "Lepke" Buchalter followed, along with Meyer Lansky, who would become the only legendary, big-time gangster associated with the South Florida area, bringing along with him his far lesser known brother Jacob ("Jake") Lansky.

Sparsely settled postwar South Florida communities lacked most of the environmental and historical qualities crowded, tenemented New York and Chicago possessed as fertile breeding grounds for the growth of gangsters. The trauma of disruption many Jewish immigrants and their children experienced had been lived through and its impact dissipated with time and changed conditions. The South Florida Jews were generally more prosperous and more Americanized, somewhat older. Young criminal gangs were not a major part of the South Florida scene as they were in New York—where even Eddie Cantor as a kid had once "belonged to 'Pork-Faced Sam's' outfit" (Fried 39).

As befitted the Miami area's blossoming image during the 1920s as a pleasure dome, gambling and the illegal alcohol industry were the region's two chief criminal businesses, complementing each other to produce in Miami what the *Macon Telegraph* called "a Frontier town harboring criminals and rascals" (Muir 139). An urban business not controlled by WASPs that Jews could enter needing little capital (like the early motion picture industry), gambling is particularly germane to the Jewish gangster story. "Big Tim Sullivan, a Tammany boss of the nineties" is reported telling Arnold Rothstein "and his friend Herman Rosenthal: 'You're smart Jew boys . . . and you'll make out as gamblers. That business takes brains'" (Howe 99). Rothstein and Meyer Lansky could be considered gambling moguls almost as Sam Goldwyn and Harry Warner and Carl Laemmle were film moguls. Except of course, the gambling industry would often—though not always—be illegal.

The fact that at one time "Miami was the only place [along the eastern seaboard] for midwinter racing in America accounted for the influx of gangsters and gamblers into the area." Fortunes could be made—though usually not by the bettors. "A man known as Ace-Deuce Solomon, for instance, who rose to the top of Miami's gambling hierarchy in the fifties, came to town during the boom to run a jitney line out to the track," which was legal, and then launched a bookmaking enterprise, which was not. Illegal gambling could be glamorous in nightclubs, and a bet placed in the Olympus Theater "under a dome studded with a tropical moon and stars" possessed its own Miami cachet. Lansky's associate "Detroit gambler Mort Wertheimer establish[ed] a casino nightclub [whose] opening-night show featured" among others the highly successful Jewish entertainer Sophie Tucker (Armbruster 47, 48), a gambling showman's favorite because she often left more at the tables than she gained in salary for performing. But crime could also pay in blood: "a small-time gambler named Leo Bronstein [was] mowed down by bullets as he answered a telephone call in a Miami Beach apartment lobby one night" during the 1934–35 season (Muir 188).

Throughout the Depression, payoffs and constant customer desire kept, in the idiom of the day, the gambling gravy train on track, with only temporary reformist derailments. Pressure from some of the public forced the closure of Wertheimer's gambling rooms, while presumably other public pressure moved them to the hotel's top floor, up a flight of stairs, and behind a closet door (Armbruster 48). The glamorous Deauville, built in 1924, might boast of the Beach's "biggest dining room, the biggest gambling room [and] the biggest pool." In 1936 the *Chicago Tribune* claimed, "the area offered more gambling than any other place in the nation" (Armbruster 40, 58).

Al Capone, referred to by the *Miami News* as "the notorious beer and brothel baron" (Muir 164), discovered Miami in the late 1920s and moved to an ornate Spanish-style home on Biscayne Bay in 1929. He is reputed to have thrown a large party February 13, the evening before the Saint Valentine's Day Massacre. Capone was Italian but his associate Jake "Greasy Thumb" Guzik (whom he introduced to Mayor Sewell) was Jewish, as were Lansky, Buchalter, Dutch Schultz, and Abner

"Longy" Zwillman, who sometimes "wintered" in Miami the years Capone threw other parties at his island retreat, and supposedly maintained an interest in the Villa Venice, a "bathing-turned-gambling-casino at Fourteenth Street," Miami Beach (Armbruster 69; Messick, *Silent Syndicate* 348).

Even though they might not establish permanent homes there, the Jewish gangsters who stayed in the area provided their own ambience to the region's high-rolling, louche image, adding spice along with their poison. Benny Siegel, whose bootlegging operation with Lansky stretched along South Florida's coast, once went "in his twenties . . . to Miami Beach for a vacation, and there, to his embarrassment, he was grabbed in a gambling raid." Calling himself Harry Rosen, he pled guilty and was fined one hundred dollars. This was the "first and last conviction" he would receive "on a long and bloody record" (Jennings 27). After his release from Sing Sing in 1936, "Kid Twist" Abe Reles, one of the most murderous of the Jewish gangsters, traveled "to [South] Florida to relax" on the sixteen hundred dollars he had "put away." According to Burton Turkus, he would be arrested in Florida that year, and again in 1938 (55). November 12, 1941, Reles's body dropped "five stories, forty-two feet" from his room in New York City's Half Moon Hotel where he was guarded constantly by police when he was testifying daily against his former gangland associates (Cohen 225). His death was never solved: in grim jokes its cause was Newton's Law of Gravity.

Allie Tannenbaum "sang" along with Reles about the same time, after being picked up in Miami. Allie had good connections. He attended the bris of Charlie Workman's son on the East Side in 1935 with Buchalter, Jake "Gurrah" Shapiro, Zwillman, and Reles. He had become good friends with Workman during the time the two "spent together at the Park Beach Hotel in Miami," at the tracks, and at local gambling casinos (Cohen 106–9). He had also earlier "wintered in [South] Florida" and Burton Turkus states, worked there "as a strong-arm in gambling joints" such as the "Deauville in North Miami Beach." Workman said "Lepke sent me down" (154).

Charlie "The Bug" Workman "customarily celebrated New Year's Eve with" Tannenbaum and Al Capone" (Joselit 154). A particularly vicious killer, Workman supposedly gunned down Dutch Schultz in 1935 in a legendary killing allegedly agreed upon by mob bosses, including Meyer Lansky, because Schultz had become dangerously obsessed with eliminating prosecutor Thomas E. Dewey—an act the gang leaders felt would cause increased pressure upon them and do their interests far more harm than good. After the murder, Workman distanced himself in Miami from police probes. According to Hank Messick, in 1939, Workman also murdered Tootsie Feinstein, a gunman who had once worked for Lepke Buchalter but now wanted to go straight. Workman tracked him down through help supplied by Allie Tannenbaum who found and talked to Feinstein's wife in Miami (Turkus 197). Workman would be successfully prosecuted in 1941 partly on evidence supplied by Abe Reles.

By the time the Kefauver Committee (investigating organized crime in the United States) held hearings about the region in 1950, it could be claimed that "the most vicious criminals in the U.S.A. were now making Miami Beach their winter capital" (Muir 224). The Wofford, on the Beach, owned by Frank Erickson's lawyer Abe Allenberg, was known as (suspected to be) a meeting place for big-time gangsters (Muir 224). A best-selling crime chronicle labeled Miami as one of the cities where Murder, Inc. could "wax fat and flourish" (Turkus 493). A group headed by Erickson that included both Lansky brothers supposedly operated the Greenacre and Club Boheme, and Mert Werthehimer still operated around town (Turkus 496). A bagel shop linked to Jake Lansky on 163rd Street in North Miami had apparently transmogrified into "a syndicate message center" (Messick, *Silent Syndicate* 289). "Jewish leaders" along with Senator Kefauver "demand[ed] action" (Armbruster 228).

Meyer Lansky has become the Jewish criminal most associated with Miami and South Florida history and myth. Ethnically and culturally he was thoroughly Jewish, though religiously secularized. His community, whether of friends or gangland associates (some were both), was mainly of Jews. He seems never to have forgotten he was a Jew, and others whether Jewish or not seem always to have seen him as a Jew. In many ways, Stephen Birmingham notes in *The Rest of Us: The Rise of America's Eastern European Jews*, with the major exception of the criminal route that he took, Lansky can be seen as a typically successful American Jewish immigrant of his day—though he was ultimately not without dissatisfactions.

He was born around 1902 as Meyer Suchowljansky in Grodno, an undistinguished Russian city of about forty thousand inhabitants, "[n]early 70 percent" of whom were Jewish (Lacey 16). His grandfather Benjamin was a traditionally, deeply religious man, respected and successful at business. He took Meyer to *chedar* and served as an example to him of how to be a man. Meyer always idolized him. During the decade when Nicholas II's huge, frangible empire was disintegrating, the Grodno region offered Jews no fortress of safety and peace. Cossacks hacked off Meyer's uncle's arm. To escape oppression, the family emigrated in 1909: Meyer's father Max leading his family to what he thought might be the haven of America; Meyer's grandfather—more cynical and hard-headed, distrustful of any *goyische* nation—and grandmother emigrating to an enclave in Palestine already established by Grodno Jews. They died there not long after arriving.

Lansky associated his grandfather with determination and strength, like the young man he remembered, perhaps a soldier, who had said at a meeting in his grandfather's house, "Jews should stand up and fight" (Joselit 170) and not just behave "like stupid sheep" (Cohen 42).

By 1911 Meyer's father was able to save enough money as a garment presser to bring over his wife Yetta, Meyer, and Meyer's younger brother Jacob who arrived at Ellis Island on April 8, 1911. Meyer, soon a "Lansky," did well at school, especially mathematics. Learning the culture of his adopted country, he could recite the Gettysburg Address and, he later claimed, *The Merchant of Venice*.

In 1914, the family resettled to Manhattan's Lower East Side—not an economically upward move. As the Hollywood studio bosses chronicled in Neal Gabler's *An Empire of Their Own*, Lansky revered his mother, and as a child dreamed of growing up rich, protecting and providing the best for her. For his mother and the memory of his grandfather he went to *cheder* and was bar mitzvahed. Later, however, when

FIGURE I. *Meyer Lansky and his two sons, circa 1940. Courtesy Jewish Museum of Florida.*

his father urged him to send his own sons along the same path, Meyer demurred: taking extra academic tutelage would serve them better. He rarely spoke of his father, and after his death in 1939 never lighted a candle annually to commemorate his death as Jewish custom suggested. In his mother's old age he hired a private nurse for her after an eye operation, and eventually saw her comfortably placed in a retirement apartment in Hollywood, Florida, not far from his own home.

Lansky's formal schooling at East Side schools ended after he graduated from the eighth grade. He also frequented libraries at the Seward Park branch of the New York Public Library, and at the Educational Alliance. When not in school he used his developing powers of observation and fact retention and his skill at numbers to study and master basic street-gambling games like craps. He would learn that the big winners were not bettors but those who controlled the games. He would also meet two tough hoodlums with whom he would become entangled in life and gangland legend: flashy, mercurial, violent Benny Siegel; and the crafty, more thoughtfully murderous Charles "Lucky" Luciano.

Lansky apprenticed as a tool-and-die mechanic after his schooldays ended. He also acted as a strong-arm man at East Side gambling joints, and as a goon in local labor disputes where his weapon of choice was a lead pipe. Garnering in October 1918 a felony charge (later dismissed), found guilty a month later of a misdemeanor disorderly conduct for which he was fined two dollars, in 1921 he quit his mechanic job and was on his way to becoming a wiseguy, "never again employed in a conventional 'job'" (Lacey 43).

Lansky's career and particularly colorful episodes in it, true or not, have often been haphazardly and sensationally reported on. In that fashion his myth has grown. A detailed, accurate, temperate, full-length biography did not appear before Robert Lacey's *Little Man* in 1991, long after the mythic version had congealed. In some ways, Lansky became a captive to his myth not simply as a tough Jew, but as a criminal mastermind, diabolical as Christopher Marlowe's infamous and anti-Semitic caricature of Barabas in *The Jew of Malta* (c. 1589).

The toughness, ambition, and intelligence he displayed as a freelance thug and small-time gambling entrepreneur brought him to the attention of Arnold Rothstein, the best-known and most successful Jewish gangster of his day, a smooth, debonair gambler and bankroller for promising criminals. Lansky met him at a friend's bar mitzvah. Around the same time, during the early days of Prohibition, Lansky ran a car and truck rental business as a front for his bootlegging operation with Benny Siegel. His friend Lucky Luciano—as boys they had both fought against the same Irish cops—ran a similar operation, and occasionally the two worked with each other on liquor importation or distribution deals.

Lansky came to have the reputation among gamblers and other bootleggers of relative honesty, neither cheating associates by skimming profits nor greedily plotting bloody takeovers. Years later, he told a journalist (probably a bit disingenuously), "Shooting and killing was an inefficient way of doing business. Ford salesmen didn't shoot Chevrolet salesmen. They tried to outbid them" (Eisenberg 122). Yet it is quite possible that in 1931 Lansky gave advice to his friend Luciano on how to deal with Luciano's rival Salvatore Maranzano, a competition that ended with Maranzano's assassination by what the underworld grapevine considered Jewish hit men. The film *Lansky* shows young Lansky himself plugging away at Maranzano's wounded body, but this interpretation seems dramatic license and is unsupported by evidence. Nor are allegations in several of Hank Messick's often unreliable books about Lansky and organized crime (though frequently copied by other sources) that a Lansky-Siegel gang existed as a murder squad for organized crime, and that Lansky was one of the evil geniuses of so-called Murder, Inc. Lan-

Greetings from the Colonial Inn

FIGURE 2. *Colonial Inn. This brochure shows one of the Jewish-owned properties on what was once Motel Row, north of Haulover Beach. The hotel was frequented by Lansky. Courtesy Collection of Myrna and Seth Bramson.*

sky seems not to have been particularly repelled by violence committed by others; after a time, however, he found it distasteful or just inexpedient to participate in it directly.

Prohibition's demise on December 5, 1933, forced a turn back down an old avenue in Lansky's illicit businesses: gambling. He would not be a gambler himself, but he would facilitate the (usually illegal) gambling of others. Here again, he became respected for not rigging games, for running good-looking operations (pleasant surroundings, good food, often quality entertainment). He seems not to have tolerated dishonesty except, of course, that his entire enterprise might be outside the law and corruptive of public officials.

At first he operated, ordinarily with partners such as Frank Costello and Joe Adonis, around Saratoga, New York. He entered the South Florida scene in 1936 following the steps of Julian "Potatoes" Kaufman, a Chicago bookmaker who needed more capital and brains for developing "carpet joints" such as the Plantation in Hallandale, just south of Fort Lauderdale in Broward Country. Lansky and his (and Lucky Luciano's) boyhood friend Vincent Alo ("Jimmy Blue Eyes"), provided the capital. Lansky used a tricky legal loophole by which land might be legally purchased for a nightclub and payment made to nearly all the service clubs in town, and assorted city officials would permit transformation into carefully regulated (but still illegal) gambling rooms. Soon the Plantation (or the Farm as it was now called) was joined in the region by classier gambling houses (no "B girls" allowed) such as the Colonial Inn, the Beach Club, and the Hollywood Yacht Club offering good food and often good shows with stars like Paul Whiteman and Joe E. Lewis. As Miami Beach prospered during the Depression's waning, so did Meyer Lansky's South Florida gambling empire. Not yet forty, a young man many of whose early colleagues were in jail or dead, he gave the people—the ones who wanted to gamble—what they wanted, and gave it to them in clean, well-lighted places.

In 1938 he helped clean up legal gambling in Fulgencia Batista's Cuba by replacing shady, local pit crews at Oriental Park with his own apparently honest Floridians, who in the evening after the park's races ended, Lansky moved to the Gran Casino Nacional. His friend Frank Erickson saw that the local bookmaking was honest too. The situation seemed strange, perhaps paradoxical: crooks needed to run things straight. Lansky recognized other ironies: the Israeli journalist Uri Dan quoted him saying, "If Socrates and Plato had trouble defining what morality was, how can people come along, just like that, and lay down that gambling was immoral?" (Lacey 109). It wasn't—*if* the state profited.

He aided Zionist activist Nathan Perlman in disrupting pro-Nazi rallies in the mid-1930s, and on a tip from Walter Winchell broke up a pro-Hitler meeting in the heart of New York's heavily German Yorkville section. (After the war he would co-opt Winchell from writing damaging reports about gambling in Miami, by securing him a $5,000 gift to his Damon Runyon Cancer Fund and supplying him with a good meal and compliant Texas showgirl at the Colonial Inn). He saw to it that some arms destined for Arab use against Israel were lost in transit after their assembling on New York docks, and even had them diverted to the embattled Promised Land. He acted as a go-between in the Navy's covert plan to gain prisoner Lucky Luciano's help in enlisting New York dockworkers to maintain free flow of shipped war goods and perhaps provide information about plots to impede wartime transportation of supplies and men. Luciano was later paroled—to Italy—for his cooperation in this plan and for further contacts he made with Sicilian gangsters that facilitated America's invasion of that island stepping-stone to mainland Italy.

But this kind of information never appeared in the newspapers. Instead, the greatest publicity Lansky received in the war or postwar years, came in June 1949, when the *New York Sun* ran a story about him complete with photograph and a résumé of his brief record of arrests and much longer chronicle of charges and allegations about his life in crime, his associations with Bugsy Siegel and Luciano and Johnny "Cockeye" Dunn, who was about to die in the electric chair—while Lansky, with his second wife, Teddy, was blissfully sailing to Europe. The *Sun* was apparently alerted by narcotics agents who promised Lansky secrecy when he agreed to an interview with them in his New York hotel apartment. The story was ill-informed and devastatingly negative, including the remark originally made in 1938 by former New York police chief Lewis Valentine but never substantiated, that Lansky was "the brightest boy in the [syndicate] combination" (Lacey 176). That Lansky was bright and that he engaged in criminal activities was true. That he was officially a member of some kind of nationally organized, coherent, ruling body of crime, would often be repeated. The statement's validity would remain fuzzy as a cloud, but it stuck like glue.

The February 13, 1948, *Miami News* estimated the number of gambling establishments in the Miami region from the mid-1940s until 1950 at around thirty-two (Lacey 140). Clubs that Lansky participated in dominated. After the war he had also helped Frank Costello run the Beverly Club outside New Orleans, and in 1945 invested sixty thousand dollars in his old friend Benny Siegel's El Cortez in Las Vegas, which later was reinvested in the ill-fated—for Siegel anyway—Flamingo.

South Florida, however, remained Lansky's center of interest and operation with the exception of the years from 1953 until 1960, when he was increasingly involved with gambling in Cuba again, following Fulgencio Batista's return to power. He apparently advised Batista on how to reform gambling operations that had fallen into shoddy and corrupt practices, and ran casinos at the Nacional and the Montmartre. His dream for this legal gambling paradise was to be embodied in the Riviera, whose construction and control he was responsible for: a top-flight, world-class casino. The hotel-casino opened December, 1957, with Ginger Rogers starring in its floorshow. The Riviera was an immediate success but its fate was as insecure as Batista's control of Cuba. When Fidel Castro's revolution succeeded, Batista left the country immediately. Lansky, physically sick and emotionally dispirited, stayed and tried to negotiate the survival of the splendid Riviera, a behemoth moneymaker but also a nightmarish symbol of decadent, filthy capitalism. He lost a great deal of money and considerable heart when the Riviera was confiscated and nationalized in October 1960. He would recoup some of both, but perhaps never be a cock of the walk again.

The trajectory of a film gangster's life starts low, hits a garish peak, and then, as his power is switched off, concludes abruptly: the gangster is extinguished. Meyer Lansky's life was nothing like that. Called in 1951 "one of the three leaders of the 'eastern crime syndicate,'" (Lacey, quoting Estes Kefauver, 299), and in the March 17, 1967, *Miami Herald* "the most publicized organized crime figure in the world today," his financial gains after the Cuba debacle were increasingly undercut by losses. He was often sick, his control over his businesses (many legitimate such as area motels) and personal life diminished. His life was full, but not always with triumph. He would always be comfortable financially, but the often repeated claim that his wealth hovered around three hundred million dollars—first declared by Hank Messick in the December 12, 1967, *Miami Herald* and endlessly repeated—was more and more obscenely ludicrous.

Government officials and the police harried him. J. Edgar Hoover, who had formerly declared organized crime a chimera, labeled Lansky as one of its heads, and so the FBI incessantly monitored his activities. Senator Estes Kefauver had him subpoenaed in October 1950, as a witness in his fascinating, highly popular, often televised, but arguably insubstantial attack on crime. As a witness Lansky revealed little, though in a private off-camera exchange with Kefauver he claimed he discovered the senator's ethnic insensitivity when Kefauver admitted that though he himself gambled, he did not want "you people"—arguably the mob but to Lansky, Jews—to control the institution. A combination of Kefauver fever, crusading newspapers, and public-spirited citizens generated a cleansing if not purging of Miami's image as a den of gambling vice by scrubbing away its glittering casinos. Miami was for families, not high rollers.

In 1953 Lansky experienced his first extended stay in jail, on a gambling charge. His lawyer thought the accusation could be proven false but Lansky did not want to go into court and testify about others, so he spent two months in a Saratoga County prison (time off for good behavior). Released, he still had the Immigration and Naturalization Service to worry about. They would deport Joe Adonis in 1954, but never could quite untangle the potential case against Meyer Suchowljansky (who had hidden the fact of his criminal record in his citizenship application), though they tried hard, and let Lansky know they were trying hard. He made money for a time, but not millions, starting in 1964 in a legitimate oil and gas business in Michigan, but this gain did not come close to recouping his Cuban losses. His interest in the Las Vegas Sands hotel is typical. In 1967 he sold out perhaps for a million, before the boom that would have increased his share's worth many times. His fate would have been far worse had not the FBI bungled wiretapped conversations — disallowed as evidence because they were illegally obtained.

His personal empire was shrinking. In 1965 he entrusted an unknown but large part of his cash savings to the International Credit Bank, whose director he greatly admired: Tibor Rosenbaum, a Jew who seemed to be in higher finance to aid the fledgling Israeli state. In 1974 Lansky lost everything in his account when the bank failed.

Lansky was in the last decades of his life a marked man, a high-priority target for clucking journalists, J. Edgar Hoover, and local police authorities. His complicity in the 1947 murder of Benny Siegel is still assumed though never faintly substantiated. He did not attend the infamous 1957 congress of top syndicate criminals at Joseph Barbara's estate in Apalachin, New York, but this was because, undisclosed wiseguys claimed, he had "tipped off the cops" in order to embarrass Vito Genovese with whom "[h]e had been fighting a low-grade war" (Cohen 137). New York police yanked him off the streets after his recent arrival from Miami one wintry day in February 1958, to grill him about Albert Anastasia's murder. In 1970 he was arrested in Miami on drug charges (pain suppressants prescribed by his doctor) that were dismissed as soon as brought to trial (in the 1990s an FBI agent suddenly claimed Lansky had been a heroin addict in the 1930s, Cohen 142). An article about him in the May 1970 *Reader's Digest* called him "Public Enemy No. 1." Yet in 1975 the Public Enemy could not even get a promised better rate at a Miami motel for two men with whom he had agreed to discuss a projected Lansky biography.

Perhaps the most painful experience Lansky endured during his later years involved his long-standing interest in Israel. Still a secularized Jew, never insisting that his two sons (one severely disabled from birth, the other a West Point graduate!) and his daughter undergo religious training, and certainly not running a kosher household, he supported Jewish synagogues and charities, and from time to time donated money privately to persons or institutions such as a deaf children's home in Israel. In 1948 he held a benefit at the Colonial Inn raising ten thousand dollars for the Haganah. Of course he admired the national strength Israel demonstrated in its wars with Arab nations, particularly after his first visit to the country in 1962, and backed up his admiration and possibly identification with cash.

In 1970, beleaguered by what he considered harassment in the United States, he visited Israel again, discovering his grandparent's grave. He found the people and lifestyle very much to his liking. So he applied for Israeli citizenship, essentially open to all Jews born of a Jewish mother and lacking "a criminal past" and "likely to endanger the public welfare." For a person of Lansky's background, the latter strictures were matters that would have to be decided through the legal system.

Lansky's lawyer decided that while what had been alleged publicly in newspapers, magazines, books, and even films about Lansky showed him a monster of criminal control, the proven record was relatively mild, certainly nothing faintly to suggest public endangerment. U.S. files on Lansky were leaked to Israel, filled with many legally unsubstantiated charges and further allegations that Lansky's lawyers felt would actually prove him no public threat. And then there were the undeniable services he had provided the state before it had even become a state.

The intricate, tangled situation lasted almost two years, during which time it became clear, in Robert Lacey's words, that the U.S. government—which had previously attempted to deport Meyer Lansky—now "was devoting its best efforts toward getting him back" (329). Several subpoenas demanded his appearance before a grand jury in Miami, and ultimately he was charged with failing to appear. Hank Messick publicized Lansky's criminal career further in his simply titled but greatly embellished and highly unreliable *Lansky*, a book replete with extraordinarily re-created, imagined mobster dialogue and hunches parading as facts (not that Lansky had been an angel) that Israeli newspapers picked up and debated. The issue traveled up to Prime Minister Golda Meir, then negotiating as Lacey points out, for ongoing aid from the pro-Israel but anti-Semitic Nixon administration. Despite numerous encomia from church leaders and members of the South Florida Jewish community, Lansky's request was turned down. Legally, he could enter no country save the United States, unless some other nation voluntarily agreed to accept him. In Lacey's book (362) and in David Mamet's film *Lansky*, he is rightly called "a wandering Jew" whom no country except the prosecutorial United States would accept.

None of the charges against him stuck, nor did further government accusations throughout the 1970s result in convictions against the elderly, often ill, self-confessed retired Jewish man whose alter ego occasionally returned to public consciousness as Public Enemy No. 1. He appealed in 1977 to the Israeli Prime Minister Menachem Begin once more for admission to the state as a citizen, but was again rejected, this time perfunctorily. In 1980 he tried for the last time to enter the country merely on a visit, but was told he must post a $100,000 bond to ensure his good behavior. Still a feisty Jew, he angrily declined.

A member of AARP, he lived modestly (as he had always lived) in Hallandale and then Miami Beach the last years of his life, reading books from the public libraries—usually not novels, Spinoza at least once—walking his dog, schmoozing mainly though not exclusively with Jewish friends such as Yiddy Bloom and Jimmy Blue Eyes, playing gin rummy, eating at Wolfie's in the Art Deco district, perhaps a tongue on rye sandwich, the Syndicate's ace money man as *alte kocker*. He died January 15, 1983, and in accordance with Jewish custom was buried the next day in West Miami's Mount Nebo cemetery. His wife Teddy, brother Jake, sister Esther, and a few fellow Wolfie's *noshers* (he was never a *fresser*) attended graveside services. Perhaps out of respect for the dead, a police car with a detective and police photographer in it, was parked some distance away.

FIGURE 3. *A dapper-looking Meyer Lansky walking his dog in Miami Beach, circa 1970s. Courtesy Historical Association of Florida Miami News Collection. Reprinted with permission from the Jewish Museum of Florida.*

Meyer Lansky was a real person and criminal, but also a creature fabulated in the public imagination through insistent presentation in the media, which reflected and projected his image throughout the 1940s. He was written about in magazine articles, books, and ultimately depicted in feature or documentary films whose sources were questionable. In the process, factoids—nonfacts generally accepted and parading as facts—reinforced one another and became accepted gospel. He clearly engaged in many illegal activities and was enmeshed in civic corruption and surrounded by considerable criminal violence. But as Robert Lacey's definitive 1991 *Little Man* would ultimately, richly document, his life and criminal stature were greatly distorted as his myth as the country's number-one rich, Machiavellian Jew outlaw evolved.

Murder, Inc.: The Story of "The Syndicate" coauthored by Burton Turkus and Sid Feder was a best seller in 1951. Its subject is "the fantastic ring of killers and extortionists that *is* organized crime in the United States," an organization that "controls and operates, as big business, every racket, extortion, and illegitimacy across the nation . . . responsible for the unbelievable total of approximately a thousand murders in the decade up to 1950" (xi). Key words in this fevered introduction are "fantastic" and "unbelievable," as the matter of "Organized Crime" as it exists in dramatic portrayals and thus lodged in the public consciousness, as a neat, orderly structure akin to Coca Cola or IBM, almost godlike, with clear lines of communication and a complex hierarchy "just like Bethlehem Steel" (Turkus 20) is very questionable. In Norval Harris and Gordon Hawkins' words:

A perplexing and elusive problem does indeed confront anyone seeking infor-

mation about organized crime. It concerns the concept "organized crime" itself.
A curious feature characterizes almost all the literature on this subject. . . . That
is that a large proportion of what has been written seems not to be dealing with
an empirical matter at all.

   It is almost as though what is referred to as organized crime belongs to the
realm of metaphysics or theology. (203)

Gourmet mobsters in out-of-the-way Italian restaurants were portrayed debat-
ing like Supreme Court justices potential murders. Mob hits in reality frequently
bungled transmuted to models of efficiency time-study expert Frederick W. Taylor
would have admired: "But when it was a killing for the Syndicate, everything was
meticulously planned. Nothing left to chance. The killers were chosen as carefully
as the starting lineup for a World Series team" (Cohen 91). Such are only a few of
the more absurd images depicting "Syndicate" folkways. Who could doubt New
York City prosecutor "Burt Turkus . . . easily the best-informed man in the United
States on this incredible countrywide network of organized crime," an attorney
"suave, dynamic, in conversation sharp," who looked "like the movie version of
a D.A.," whom gangsters called "Mr. Arsenic" (Turkus xi)? Surely Lansky was, as
Turkus asserted, a syndicate director, one of the board of directors who sat with
Lepke Buchalter at the head of the table during conferences that starting in 1934
"governed the underworld" (Cohen 135) and "dictate[d] all policy" (Turkus xiii).

   Hank Messick further embellished Lansky's role as syndicate leader and trea-
surer in four books combining groundbreaking details of Lansky's activities, with
suppositions, conjectures, and flat-out misinformation. Dialogue Messick never
heard casts Lansky as a devious, deadly master criminal, a kind of American
Dr. Mabuse. Around Miami, Lansky is perceived as a stealthy, lurking spider who
"controlled a web of criminal activity—in jukeboxes, hotels, motels, laundry, services" and the like (Armbruster 167). Linking Lepke Buchalter's execution in 1944
(resulting, according to Messick, from Lansky's betrayal of him), the impossible
"suicide" of Longie Zwillman in 1959, the clearly gangland murder of Anthony
Carfano the same year, the mysterious, permanent disappearance of Tony Bender
in 1961, Vito Genovese's death in prison in 1969, Messick ratified public opinion
and anointed Lansky "Chairman of the Board of the National Crime Syndicate"
(*Lansky* 219). The immigrant, East Side hoodlum now combined in his image old
anti-Semitic cartoon figures of intrusive, octapul, corporate moneymaker, and evil,
arachnoid crook, two stereotypes fused into one, creeping into American business
and society.

   Robert Lacey reports (282–85) that Sunday, May 27, 1962, David Susskind presented on his *Open End* show a panel discussion on organized crime. The FBI
was taping conversations in Lansky's hotel room at the Volney in New York City,
on orders from J. Edgar Hoover. Family conversation was taped, then transcribed,
paraphrased, by a FBI agent. The tapes were not retained. The agency learned
that Lansky liked matzos and sardines, and was reading alternately "a history
book, a grammar book, and a book of French quotations." The agent paraphrasing

Lansky's response to the show (mostly silence) wrote that at some point a panelist said that "organized crime" was "second in size to the government itself." Hearing this, Lansky said something to his wife like—whether snorting derisively or not is unknown, as are his exact words and tone of voice—"organized crime was bigger than U.S. Steel." Leaked to the media—no one knows how—whatever he said was transmuted into the definite and arrogant statement, "We're bigger than U.S. Steel." This infamous factoid still haunts articles, books, and films about Lansky. The *New York Times* quoted it in its obituary of Lansky, and as late as 2002 *Life Magazine* accepted its validity in a special issue devoted to famous mobsters. Apparently it reflects an attitude many wished Lansky to take, summing up the kind of person they wanted him to be.

The line was picked up in Francis Ford Coppola's 1974 masterpiece *The Godfather, Part II*, spoken clearly by Lee Strasberg in the character of Hyman Roth, to Al Pacino's Michael Corleone. Strasberg apparently studied aspects of Lansky's life for his thinly disguised portrait of Lansky as possibly America's most powerful gangster. Lansky's discreet behavior, his (criminal) sagacity, and above all else his Jewishness are all on display. On the surface he is an honorable ruler of the mob, though he covertly plots Michael Corleone's death. He seems to run gambling in Cuba, and he is sickly. He is far more powerful, far more in charge than facts indicate Lansky ever was. Lacey notes that the film repeats legend rather than reality by indicating Lansky/Roth knew accurately in advance when Cuba would collapse and escaped the resultant chaos in a private plane. In the pumped-up milieu of Coppola's regal gangland myth, Roth's chilling assassination upon his return to Miami from a fruitless attempt to secure a homeland in South America, may be dramatically appropriate, even if historically misleading.

Sergio Leone's 1984 epic *Once Upon a Time in America* did not directly concern Lansky or base a character upon him, but it does brilliantly and convincingly present a view of tough Jews, children of immigrants, growing up hard on the East Side the first years of the twentieth century and sometimes in their fight for survival and success rolling drunks, becoming criminals, and joining Italian gangs during Prohibition.

Mafia, The History of the Mob in America (Empire of Crime) released in 1993 is typical of many documentaries offering a version of syndicate or organized crime in America and featuring Lansky as a prime agent of the Mob. It describes Lansky's friendship with Siegel, laughably enough to anyone familiar with their real lives, as "like they were lovers" who "would complete each other's sentences." Correctly enough Lansky is "a Jewish mobster . . . much smarter than most gangsters" though one wonders why his ethnicity needs specific labeling. The film erroneously credits him with establishing in Saratoga the model for Benny Siegel's Las Vegas dreams and notes that along with Frank Costello and Lucky Luciano he "grumbled" at Siegel's increasing losses at his grandiose Flamingo Hotel and claims Siegel's execution was coolly determined at a meeting of gangland investors in distant Cuba at which Lansky pleaded for delay. No known facts support this familiar contention, and much evidence points to a local killer acting on his own: another example of the film adage, that if history and myth disagree, print the myth.

La Cosa Nostra. Mafia, an Expose: Vegas, a 1997 documentary distributed by the Madacy Entertainment group, also declares that Lansky was instrumental in inspiring the creation of Las Vegas as a gambler's legal paradise. "1941. That's when Las Vegas caught the eye of two men, Meyer Lansky and Ben Siegel." Actually, Las Vegas never excited Lansky, who did not share Siegel's grandiose vision of it. Talking heads for what seems a quickie film include a one-time maitre d' at the Copacabana (the once-fabled New York nightclub), and "Joe 'Dogs,'" identified as a Mafia informant, whose face is blacked out as he speaks. Lansky is called Siegel's "closest friend" who "must have known" about a Mafia contract on Siegel as Lansky was the organization's "money man." The film also features cameo performances by comedian Charley Callas, Joan Rivers, the Osmonds, Tony Martin, and Siegfried and Roy, though not as mafiosos.

Lansky (HBO 1999) written by David Mamet, is the fullest and most sympathetic film presenting Lansky or his image. Three actors play Lansky at different stages of his life. The oldest Lansky (Richard Dreyfuss) is first seen at his grandparents' graves, wearing a yarmulke, tenderly feeling their tombstones' lettering, saying he would like to buy a plot nearby. Periodic flashbacks dramatize earlier episodes in Lansky's life (or purport to do so). Following the cemetery scene, almost subliminal cuts show an old Jew being beaten by east European anti-Semites, a Cossack chopping down the door to a Jewish peasant's house, and a Jew about to be split open with an axe. This horror fades to a few years later with the Lanskys in the East Side. Yetta Lansky, speaking Yiddish, tells Meyer to pick up the traditional *cholent* from the baker. He returns home chagrined, having gambled and lost the money she gave him.

Scenes showing young Meyer growing up in the rough new world alternate with depictions of the older Lansky wandering about Israel, awaiting the verdict that increasingly he knows will go against him. As a boy he links up with Benny Siegel to learn crafty ways on the East Side's mean streets, and fights with Irish kids who call him kike and Christ killer. Siegel advises him always to "wade in and never fight fair." Lansky tells Benny they don't need the loaded dice "Irish kids use" in alley play, because the odds favor whoever runs the game anyway. Back in Israel, the old, cynical Lansky converses with a storeowner who was in the Haganah in 1948 when Lansky supplied it with guns, asking, "think your Supreme Court will remember that in their arguments today?"

In periodic trips to the past, the film portrays a maturing Lansky (Max Perlich) bootlegging but also reading an economics text, performing difficult business mathematics in his head while his friend Bugsy grows increasingly murderous. A suave Arnold Rothstein is Meyer's mentor. When the film shifts again to the present, Lansky talks about the vendetta President Nixon, Attorney General Mitchell (soon to be indicted himself), and J. Edgar Hoover (that "old woman") have waged against him, pulling his passport and subverting his chances for Israeli citizenship.

Mamet had displayed in his 1997 novel *The Old Religion* his interest in American violence, Jewish culture, and indirectly his own Jewishness through examining the Leo Frank castration and lynching in 1915 Georgia. Frank is seen as innocent of any criminal act, but passive, predominately a victim. Lansky to the contrary is shown in Mamet's film as a criminal who at least once actively engages in murder, as an accomplice in Salvatore Maranzano's killing—a scene of doubtful reality. He is portrayed as a fighter, standing up to Luciano when he calls young Lansky "Jewboy," and to Senator Estes Kefauver who asks him "Do you consider yourself an American or a Jew" (as though he could only be one or the other) and "What did you do for your country?" ignoring Lansky's wartime services. Lansky wonders what Joseph Kennedy did for the country, "ready" as he was "to sell England to Hitler." Mamet also includes humanizing episodes from Lansky's private life, such as his despair learning that his first son "Buddy" will always be badly crippled. But he does not sentimentalize Lansky here: he also shows him turning away from his bedridden wife Anne who cries, "weh ist mir!" (woe is me) after him.

The narrative technique of the film in effect divides Lansky in three: young Jew living a hardscrabble existence in an almost hostile land; tough, crooked, even murderous Jew smartly plotting and fighting to the top of the crime heap; older Jew engaged in illicit gambling. He is cynical and witty, beleaguered by one government in part because he is a Jew, rejected by another government whose birth he had amply supported (once, he says derisively to his Israeli lawyer, "Every Jew on earth has a homeland"). The oldest Lansky dominates.

Toward the film's end in "Miami Beach, 1978," Lansky is being interviewed by a Jewish journalist (Uri Dan, whose writing on Lansky is a prime source for the film). Lansky says "I'm a gambler, nothing more." What about violence in his life? "The Cossacks are coming. What do you do? You do what you have to do." Standing outside Wolfie's restaurant he claims, "I never stole. . . . I never killed." What would he do if he could do it all over again? "I wouldn't change a thing."

Almost comically, the last shot of Lansky shows him walking his dog on Collins Avenue. The one-time *macher gonoff* now a retiree. The screen states, "He was never convicted of a major crime." Which is true.

REFERENCES

Armbruster, Ann. *The Life and Times of Miami Beach.* New York: Knopf, 1995.

Birmingham, Stephen. *The Rest of Us: The Rise of America's East European Jews.* Boston: Little, Brown, 1984.

Cohen, Rich. *Tough Jews.* New York, Simon & Schuster, 1998.

Eisenberg, Dennis, Uri Dan, and Eli Landau. *Meyer Lansky: Mogul of the Mob.* New York: Paddington Press, 1979.

Fried, Albert. *The Rise and Fall of the Jewish Gangster in America.* Rev. ed. New York: Columbia University Press, 1993.

Gabler, Neal. *An Empire of Their Own: How the Jews Invented Hollywood.* New York: Crown, 1988.

Griffith, Richard, and Arthur Mayer. *The Movies.* New York: Bonanza Books, 1957.

Harris, Norval, and Gordon Hawkins. *The Honest Politician's Guide to Crime Control.* Chicago: University of Chicago Press, 1969.

Hossent, Harry. *The Movie Treasury. Gangster Movies.* London: Octopus Books, 1974.

Howe, Irving. *World of Our Fathers.* New York: Simon & Schuster, 1976.

Jennings, Dean. *We Only Kill Each Other: The Life and Bad Times of Bugsy Siegel.* London: John Long, 1968.

Joselit, Jenna Weissman. *Our Gang: Jewish Crime and the New York Jewish Community, 1900–1940.* Bloomington: Indiana University Press, 1983.

Lacey, Robert. *Little Man: Meyer Lansky and the Gangster Life.* Boston: Little, Brown, 1991. Details of Lansky's life not otherwise attributed are from this absolutely indispensable book.

Messick, Hank. *Lansky.* New York: Putnam's, 1971.

———. *The Silent Syndicate.* New York: Macmillan, 1967.

Muir, Helen. *Miami, U.S.A.* Gainesville: Univesity Press of Florida, 2000.

Turkus, Burton, and Sid Feder. *Murder, Inc.: The Story of "The Syndicate."* New York: Farrar, Strauss and Young, 1951.

Leon Kronish

MIAMI BEACH'S

TWENTIETH-

CENTURY

PROPHET

Rabbi Leon Kronish was a significant presence in the communal life of greater Miami from the 1940s to the mid-1980s. A tireless activist on behalf of Israel from before its founding in 1948 until his near fatal stroke shortly before the first intifada, he was affectionately dubbed "Mr. Israel" in Miami. A prominent exponent of the Liberal variant of Reform Judaism in the post–World War II era, his vision and congregational practices had a profound impact on Diaspora Jewry. Tall, handsome, and an engaging public speaker, he was warmly embraced by his congregation, Temple Beth Sholom of Miami Beach, one of the largest Jewish congregations in the southeast United States.

Leon Kronish was born in New York in 1917 into an Orthodox family, the eldest child of Max and Lena Kronish. Both sides of the family had immigrated to America prior to World War I: Max from Zborow, Ukraine, and Lena from Most, Lithuania. Leon attended a public school and an after-school Talmud Torah where modern Hebrew was an important part of the curriculum. As a teenager, he was a member of Hashomer Hatzair, a socialist Zionist youth movement, and experienced both the aspirations for a Jewish homeland and the threat to all Jews represented by the rise of Hitler and Nazism. Kronish writes, "As a child I lived and grew up on the edge of a non-Jewish neighborhood. To walk to public school or go to Talmud Torah meant walking through "the enemy camp." I was afraid because I had already been beaten up many times by non-Jewish children who ganged up on me."[1] By the time he finished high school, his education was a lively mix of Orthodox, *Yiddishkeit*, socialist, Zionist, and assimilationist tendencies typical for so many families of his generation.

After graduating from Brooklyn College in 1936, Kronish became aware of his calling to be a rabbi. First, he attended the Jewish Theological Seminary (1937–38), where he encountered Mordecai Kaplan, the founder of Reconstructionism. Then, he was ordained at the Jewish Institute of Religion (1938–42), where he became a close disciple of the institute's founder, Stephen Wise.

In 1940 the young rabbinical student married Lillian Austin, and they had three children: Jordan in 1942, Ronald in 1946, and Maxine in 1951. While a rabbinical student at the Jewish Institute of Religion, Kronish was offered and accepted the position as student rabbi at the Huntington Jewish Center on Long Island in 1941. From September 1944 until his severe stroke in January 1984 Rabbi Leon Kronish served first as the rabbi of the Beth Sholom Center, a storefront Conservative synagogue, and then as the spiritual leader of Temple Beth Sholom, the Reform synagogue he founded in Miami Beach. Following his stroke, he became Founding Senior Rabbi until his death on March 23, 1996.

The following essay portrays the institutional contexts—religious, political, social, and congregational—in which Leon Kronish was formed, and which he, in response, did so much to re-form. In the process he served as a catalyst in the transformation of his community, South Florida, and American Jewry.

OVERVIEW: INSTITUTIONAL CONTEXTS

The first and most important of these institutional contexts was *Liberal Judaism*, a movement whose basic template was Reform Judaism's emphasis on "prophetic mission" and social justice, but which differed from standard Reform Judaism in significant ways. From the beginning, Liberal Judaism was pronouncedly pro-Zionist and was considerably less hostile than Reform to traditional elements of the Jewish liturgy and custom.

The second of these contexts was *Zionism*. Stephen Wise was one of the few enthusiastic advocates of both Reform Judaism and Zionism—a combination he bequeathed to his young student Leon Kronish. For Kronish, the Six-Day War in 1967 evoked a marked expansion and intensification in his commitment to Israel, one that was to remain his lodestar from the late 1960s.

The third framework for Leon Kronish was Miami Beach, which he termed "the American Negev." Kronish's special genius was to sense from the beginning how the overall growth of the entire South Florida region could be especially rewarding to the Jewish community, not simply in Miami-Dade County, but also in the United States and the State of Israel. Kronish was a leading Jewish figure in the main social struggles roiling the 1950s and 1960s: civil rights and desegregation; the separation of church and state; as well as the "ban the bomb" movement for peace and disarmament.

The final institutional context was the small congregation he turned into one of the major forces in South Florida Jewish life: Temple Beth Sholom. Kronish imparted to his congregants a strong commitment to the social values of Liberal Judaism, featuring a prominent and public role for women in Jewish community life. In addition, he forged a new relationship between the members and Israel: the "Israelization" of American Jewry, which engendered deep personal links between his congregants and Israelis.

Liberal Judaism

STEPHEN WISE: MIXING REFORM JUDAISM, AMERICANISM, AND ZIONISM

Rabbi Leon Kronish's formative rabbinical training was under the tutelage of Rabbi Stephen Samuel Wise (1874–1949), a tireless advocate of the "prophetic mission" of social justice. An articulate and powerful ally of workers' movements agitating against exploitative conditions in the workplace, Wise was nationally recognized as an incisive and moral voice. Wise founded his own congregation, the Free Synagogue of New York, after the board of trustees at Temple Emanuel in New York City denied him complete freedom of speech from the pulpit. Later, he created the American Jewish Congress (1917) in reaction to what he perceived as the conservative elitism of the American Jewish Committee; he emphasized "the prophecy of tomorrow" rather than the "survival of yesterday." In Wise's view, there was no contradiction between Zionism and an equally fervent embrace of Americanism. Every Jew, Zionist and non-Zionist, could participate in a national revival of Klal Yisrael (people of Israel) in their ancient homeland.

Most important for Leon Kronish, Wise established the Jewish Institute of Religion (JIR) in 1922. While the atmosphere was predominantly Reform, there were many among both the faculty and students who were either Conservative or Orthodox (including the future rabbi of Miami Beach's Temple Emanu-El, Irving Lehrman). Samson Benderly served as a lecturer in education, Salo Baron acted as director of advanced studies and Harry Wolfson (Harvard University) regularly delivered guest lectures. Wise felt that a "liberal" spirit in the Jewish context meant an openness to embrace all forms of Jewish religious practice—the theological basis of his commitment to Klal Yisrael. Samuel Karff has commented that "nearly all of the Institute's graduates harbored a lasting affection for their one-time mentor."[2] This was certainly the case with Leon Kronish. Much of his rabbinical style and substance for decades to come was molded in the image of Rabbi Stephen Wise.

From Wise, Kronish inherited three main concerns: a strong commitment to the Reform mainspring of the "prophetic mission" of social justice; a fervent activist-oriented Zionism; and an ecumenical approach to those members of Klal Yisrael who were Conservative or Orthodox. These legacies were central for Kronish in his own rabbinic career.

MORDECAI KAPLAN: CONCERN FOR JEWISH CULTURE AND LITURGY

The second major influence on Kronish was Mordecai Kaplan, the founder of Reconstructionist Judaism. Kronish encountered Kaplan in 1937 at Teachers' College, Columbia University. There, Kronish was exposed to Kaplan's *Judaism as a Civilization* (1934). In this book, Kaplan conceived of Judaism as an evolving civilization with its own culture and ethos, which needed to fit into American society. Theology is replaced with cultural anthropology, and Judaism is reconstructed by sociological thinking.

Like Wise, Kaplan was a strong Zionist and adopted the position that one could embrace Zionism and Americanism. In contrast to Wise, however, who had little intuitive empathy with ritual matters, Kaplan emphasized the religious civilization of Judaism, a concern that led him to seek to reinvigorate contemporary Jewish religious practices and liturgy in a variety of ways (e.g., the *New Haggadah*, 1941). Kaplan argued that it was crucial for all denominations of Judaism to revitalize their theological, ritual, and liturgical dimensions. Kaplan's insistence on the centrality of a living liturgy profoundly influenced Kronish's thinking. Kronish came to understand that Liberal Judaism was "Torah for the twentieth century":

> Torah should be honored but it should not tyrannize. A return to ritual, to ceremony, strengthens Judaism. To separate the Sabbath from the rest of the week increases attendance at temple services. [But] Liberal Judaism is democratic. No family is excluded because of financial circumstances. There are no assigned seats and no tuition fees for Jewish education.[3]

ZIONISM AND AMERICANISM

The most important concept for understanding Leon Kronish's Zionism was that of Klal Yisrael, the idea emphasized over and over again by Wise. The Jewish people, whatever their differences (whether political, religious, or cultural), were all indissolubly bound together in a community of fate; this collective identity had to be at the forefront of the criteria by which any action was evaluated. There was no contradiction between being strong Zionists and strong Americans.

SOCIAL JUSTICE AND LABOR ZIONISM

Kronish's passion for social justice was internalized long before he became familiar with Reform Judaism and the activities of Stephen Wise. His father was a committed union member. Thus, it is hardly surprising that Kronish was allied with the dominant Labor tendency within the Zionist movement. The national redemption of the Jewish people could only be accomplished by their simultaneous social and economic transformation. Labor Zionists argued that there was little point in eliminating the oppression of Jews as a people, only to reproduce oppression in the workplace and economic relations of that new society they were involved in building.

In this context, it is easy to understand why Kronish brought into being in 1965 the Histadrut Foundation of the United States, an American support group for the Labor Federation in Israel. Drawing from his father, his youth in Hashomer Hatzair, and the need for Jews in the United States to understand and appreciate that in the 1960s nine out of ten Israeli workers belonged to the Histadrut, Kronish took the lead in linking his socialist values to Labor Zionism. He served as chairman of the board of the American Foundation and played a leading role in the thinking and programming of the Labor Zionist Alliance in the United States.

ALEXANDER DUSHKIN AND CULTURAL ZIONISM

While Stephen Wise created the political and ideological framework, it was Alexander Dushkin, another mentor from the Jewish Theological Seminary, who infused a strong cultural content into Leon Kronish's Zionist identity. Similar to Ahad Ha'am, the leading theorist of cultural Zionism, Dushkin believed that the teaching of the Bible as literature, and Hebrew as a living, modern language were major elements in the nurturing and maintenance of a strong Jewish identity. Teaching Jewish culture would impart a profound spiritual aspect to Zionism, one that would make it a viable alternative to assimilation. Dushkin's mission was to create a "state of mind," then fill it with content.

For Kronish, Zionism would have a strong cultural dimension: one that highlighted Jewish education in general, and encouraged a direct encounter with the Hebrew language as a structural feature of the concept of the Zionist mission. Both his theological point of view and his liturgical innovations were developments of cultural Zionism (e.g, *Explanatory Notes to Shofar Services for Rosh Hashanah* [1970] and *Passover Supplementary Haggadah* [1974]).

FIGURE I. *Leon Kronish, national chairman, Israel Bonds, inspiring the troops at the National Bond Conference, Fontainbleau Hotel, Miami Beach, 1980. Archive picture courtesy of Temple Beth Sholom, Miami Beach, Florida.*

A ZIONIST ACTIVIST

Leon Kronish had a multifaceted conception of what it meant to be a Zionist, one simultaneously collective (Klal Yisrael), egalitarian (social justice and Labor Zionism), and rooted in the themes of cultural Jewish education, and Hebrew as a living language.

Kronish visited Israel frequently. His first trip, during the War of Independence (1949) as part of a United Jewish Appeal Federation fact-finding mission, led to the reacquaintance with his teenage Hashomer Hatzair friend, Julius Freeman. Julius had made aliyah, established a kibbutz (Kfar Menachem) and now called himself Yehuda ben Horin. Kronish also met with James McDonald, the ambassador of the United States to Israel. Returning home to Miami Beach, Kronish asked himself: "Was the planting and nurturing of a Jewish temple as valid as establishing a kib-butz and rebuilding the state of Israel? Was migration to Miami to colonize a Jew-ish tropical oasis of equal significance in perpetuating *Klal Yisrael* as making *aliya* to the new Jewish state? What is my role as an American Zionist?"[4] In the coming years, Kronish was able to give positive answers to these questions by building one of the most vibrant synagogues in American Jewish life.

Another concrete way of solidifying the connection between Diaspora Jewry and Israel was through Israel Bonds. From its inception in 1951 Kronish became a South Florida leader in the bond drives of the 1950s and 1960s. By the 1970s he had earned the prestigious position as chair of the Rabbinical Cabinet of Is-rael Bonds in the United States. Under Kronish's direction, some twelve hundred congregations in the United States participated in bond appeals. In the 1980s, in recognition of his efforts, Leon Kronish served as national chairman of Israel

Bonds. For Kronish, bonds quite literally became the way in which he could help achieve his long-sought goal of the redemption of Israel.

THE SIX-DAY WAR: A SHIFT IN DIRECTION

With Israel's stunning military victory in the June 1967 Six-Day War, Kronish's Zionism, like that of many American Jews, underwent a profound transformation, a metamorphosis chronicled in two major documents he wrote: *Yisrael Goralenu* (Israel is our destiny [1968]), and *What Are the "Zionist Mitzvot"?* (1977). In *Yisrael Goralenu*, Kronish argues that the Six-Day War had irreversibly altered the dynamics of Jewish life.

> Never before in the history of our movement has the oneness, the unity, the interlocking destiny of the Jewish people been so sharply and simply stated. . . . As Richard Hirsch has phrased it: "In June, 1967, it became clear that the destiny of *Am Yisrael* [literally, "the people of Israel," in the sense of *Klal Yisrael*] was inseparable from the destiny of *Medinat Yisrael* 'the State of Israel.'"[5]

For Kronish, the war brought an end to what he called the "equivocating" of the American Jewish community in general—and Reform Judaism in particular—with regard to relations with the State of Israel. Henceforth, his mission would be to link (1) his congregation Beth Sholom to Reform Judaism as a whole; and (2) the entire American Jewish community not simply to the State of Israel, but, in a very specific way, to the policies of the Israeli government, whatever its political coloration.

The substantive aim of Kronish's new program was to refocus the "prophetic mission" of Reform Judaism from social justice and Klal Yisrael, to the well-being of the State of Israel, and the aims of the Israeli government. The strategy he chose to realize these new goals was to develop a myriad of close, personal connections (*gesher vakesher* [bridges and bonds]) between the institutions of Reform Judaism in North America in general, and Temple Beth Sholom of Miami Beach in particular, with a wide variety of individuals and institutions—religious, political, social, and cultural—in Israel.

We term this program the "Israelization" of American Jewry, a calling Kronish pursued in the post-1967 period with his characteristic energy as his agenda shifted from the Reform "mission" of seeking social justice in America to forging ever more numerous, tighter, and intimate bonds between Jews in America, and the people and polity of the State of Israel. Many of the programs and institutions that exist on the American Jewish landscape today are indebted in some way to Leon Kronish. These include, among others, the Israel Committee of the Central Conference of American Rabbis (CCAR), the Israel Committee of the Union of American Hebrew Congregations (UAHC), the rabbinical year-in-Israel for Hebrew Union College–Jewish Institute of Religion students, the Association of Reform Zionists of America (ARZA), and the Alexander Muss High School in Israel Program.

Miami Beach

When Leon Kronish arrived in 1944 to become rabbi of the Conservative Beth Sholom Center, he found a small Jewish community on Miami Beach. Although a few Jews had participated in the building of hotels in the Art Deco district and an Orthodox congregation, Beth Jacob, was established in 1927, anti-Semitism kept the total Jewish population small, and their geographic domain limited to the lower reaches of the island.

KRONISH AND THE "JEWISH EXPLOSION" OF THE 1950S AND 1960S

Kronish was well positioned to take advantage of the changing Jewish demographics of Miami Beach. By the early 1950s, Miami Beach was starting to transform from "snowbirds" into permanent residents. During the "season," the handsome and personable Kronish was able to multiply severalfold attendance at his Sabbath services by drawing on those snowbirds who wanted to maintain some sort of active Jewish identity while in residence on the Beach. By the end of the 1950s, membership had climbed more than twentyfold.

One unpredicted outcome of greeting snowbirds was that they told their friends up north about the charismatic, "Liberal" rabbi on Miami Beach. Thus, when many visited the area they sought out Temple Beth Sholom and developed denominational allegiance (e.g., Rabbis Rubin, Richard Hirsch, and Alexander Schindler). In this way, Kronish and Temple Beth Sholom, located on 41st Street ("uptown" when he first arrived), both encouraged and benefited from the dramatic upward mobility of American Jewry. Located just a twenty-minute walk from hotels like the Fontainebleau (1954) and the Eden Roc (1955), Beth Sholom became a visible symbol of the increasing prominence—both socioeconomic and physical—of Jews in the life of Miami Beach.

By the 1960s, Jews were the dominant and majority ethnic group on Miami Beach (four thousand in 1940; sixty thousand in 1960) and instrumental in securing high profile events: the Miss USA and Miss Universe pageants (1960), the Jackie Gleason television show (1963), and the Cassius Clay (Muhammad Ali) heavyweight champion fight (1964). In contrast to synagogues around the country that had few programs for seniors, everywhere Kronish looked was the "world of his fathers and mothers." According to Polly Redford, a Miami historian, Miami Beach was 85 percent Jewish and 80 percent over age sixty-five."[6]

TROUBLE IN PARADISE

The growing Jewish presence in Miami Beach led to increasing tensions with some of the other communities on the Beach. Most notable were those with the Catholic community that was also centered around 41st Street, symbolized by Saint Patrick's Church, between Alton Road and Meridian Avenue. From the mid-1940s through the late 1950s, Saint Patrick's was at the center of efforts to stop the building of three visible Jewish institutions in the 41st Street area.

The first was construction of Temple Beth Sholom itself, on an empty lot across from Saint Patrick's, a project that eventually did come to fruition, but in a different location, a few blocks east and north of 41st Street on Chase Avenue. The second was the building of the mammoth Mount Sinai Medical Center—today considered the most distinguished medical facility on Miami Beach—just west of Alton Road at 41st Street. And the third was the proposed Hebrew Academy, an

Orthodox educational center, which was unable to overcome Catholic opposition, and was finally completed much further south on Dade Boulevard.

In addition to these specifically Jewish projects, Catholic individuals and institutions, among others, also opposed the building of the Julia Tuttle Causeway. Completed in 1959, the causeway linked the mainland to Miami Beach right at 41st Street, just south of the Mount Sinai complex and passed by Beth Sholom on the way to the Fontainebleau on the ocean. Detractors argued that the causeway would only increase the already (in their view) too large numbers of tourists and others who were turning what had been a pleasantly sleepy backwater into a densely populated, urban neighborhood. Implicit in this argument, many felt at the time, was hostility not just to the increasing Jewish presence, but a fear that a causeway would also give increased Beach access to Miami's large black population, centered in the Liberty City and Overtown neighborhoods just north of downtown Miami. The decline of anti-Semitism encouraged both Jews to live on the Beach, and African-Americans to attend public schools on the island.

Those who held such fears felt them confirmed when the civil rights movement in the 1960s advocated busing children from schools in those black neighborhoods to Miami Beach. While Jews endorsed civil rights legislation in principle, they themselves became apprehensive at the thought of having their local schools integrated.

By the time Miami Beach High was integrated in 1970, black/Jewish relations were disintegrating, owing (1) to the lack of black support, in the Jewish view, for Israel in the wake of the Six-Day War and (2) to what black activists and then others in the black community saw as a paternalistic attitude on the part of Jews. To compound this already turbulent situation on Miami Beach, the arrival of Cuban refugees in the 1960s, followed by the Marielitos in the late 1970s, further tended to heighten the often tense dynamics among the ethnic communities living cheek by jowl on an increasingly densely populated sandbar.

Temple Beth Sholom

On June 3, 1942, a storefront was leased at 761 Forty-first Street for the Beth Sholom Center, a Conservative-oriented synagogue. The center served the twenty inaugural members and the needs of the several hundred Jewish servicemen billeted in hotels in the Art Deco Miami Beach district.

Rabbi Leon Kronish's arrival for Rosh Hashanah in 1944 heralded a new era. The following year, he quickly transformed the Conservative center into a Reform temple, Beth Sholom. Shortly, thereafter, the temple moved from the storefront on 41st Street, to a site just north on Chase Avenue, former home of the stables of Carl Fisher's restricted Nautilus Club polo fields.

BUILDING AN INSTITUTION: 1945–1957

Explosive growth in the newly established Reform temple occurred over the next decade. Membership multiplied from forty or so family units to more than seven hundred and fifty. Very quickly, the temple developed the whole panoply of institutional infrastructures characteristic of American Reform congregations during this efflorescence of organized Jewish life. The Sisterhood, the Men's Club, an active adult education program, Zionist youth clubs for both girls and boys, a nursery school, a Sunday religious school, a weekly Hebrew school, a lecture series on Jewish current events, weekly library activities. Among the many youth who passed through Temple Beth Sholom's doors and were bar mitzvahed during these years was Robert Rubin, secretary of the treasury in President Clinton's cabinet.

The ideological matrix generating the flurry of productive activity was Kronish's unique mixture of Reform Judaism, Zionism, and Reconstructionism—what he termed Liberal Judaism. Each week the *Temple Beth Sholom Bulletin* identified itself as "the Liberal congregation on the Beach" to its members and the community. The culmination of this era came with the dedication on November 29, 1957, of a completely new sanctuary on the Chase Avenue site designed by Percival Goodman. With this came the inauguration of a new period of activism.

THE ERA OF "PROPHETIC MISSION": 1957–1967

Temple Beth Shalom continued to grow. By the mid-1960s, its membership exceeded twelve hundred households. Many were former snowbirds, who had decided to relocate permanently to Miami Beach. This new blood was of great help to Kronish and the synagogue as they together encountered three of the many great social challenges confronting American society at this time: the civil rights movement; the "ban the bomb"/peace and disarmament movement; and the separation of church and state, especially relating to the issue of prayer in the public schools. These challenges provided ample opportunity to test the congregants' internalization of Kronish's teachings of Liberal Judaism, and their commitment to his new meaning of prophetic covenant and mission.

Civil Rights. Kronish's attitude and behavior toward incidents of blatant racism was unequivocal, and he inaugurated social action programs in civil rights as a regular feature of Beth Sholom life. Members of the synagogue joined local black activists working to desegregate hotels and restaurants on the Beach, efforts crowned later by passage of municipal and state laws requiring the desegregation of buses (1957), beaches, parks, and hospitals (1958), and public schools (1960).

In 1960, following the decision of the Reform umbrella Union of American Hebrew Congregations (UAHC) to build a Religious Action Center in Washington, D.C., Beth Sholom established an Interfaith Institute to encourage communication between Jews and non-Jews. In 1963, members of the Interfaith Institute actively participated in a unity march for civil rights jointly sponsored by the Rabbinical Association of Greater Miami, the Catholic Archdiocese, and local Protestant clergy.

Kronish became friends with the Reverend Theodore Gibson, head of the Miami chapter of the NAACP, and invited him several times to speak at Temple Beth Sholom. From the pulpit, Kronish criticized political figures, and especially Floridian national legislators, who spoke out against drives to register black voters. For Kronish, the commitment to battle segregation had a religious basis:

The story of segregation is a sordid and sinful one. Who is there among us who, in the tangled realm of race relations, is so righteous that he doeth good always, and sinneth not through his own acts of exclusion and segregation? . . . If this problem has no relevance to Judaism, if we refuse, no matter how many statements we have previously made, to continue to "cry aloud and spare not," if we fail to take such action as may be within our power to end every vestige of discrimination, then Judaism itself really has no meaning or relevance to life itself.[7]

Nuclear Disarmament.   Throughout the 1950s, Kronish took a visible public role in the campaign for nuclear disarmament. In 1950, he wrote a public letter to President Truman protesting the construction of the H-bomb, arguing that "the time has come for the American Eagle and the Russian Bear, and even the British Bull, to find a way of living together," sentiments he continually repeated from the pulpit, encouraging his congregants to write similar letters to members of Congress.[8] By 1962, Kronish was one of a handful of clergyman interviewed by *Life* for the magazine's cover story on "The Drive for Mass Shelters." Kronish's statement, published along with his picture, echoed his sermons. "Shelters delude people into accepting the inevitability of war . . . and the possibility of survival. Belief in safety is a hoax."[9]

In 1964, Kronish was invited to the "Washington Conference on Disarmament and World Peace," and in 1966, to the "National Inter-Religious Conference on Peace." The goal of both conferences (organized by the UAHC Religious Action Center) was to recommend how religion could play a role in governmental decisions affecting war and peace. Out of the 1966 conference came a declaration to promote peace in Vietnam, and to consider an "immediate halt to the bombing," both moves fully supported by Kronish and the social action committee on nuclear disarmament he had established at Beth Sholom.

Separation of Church and State.   Throughout the 1950s, the question of a formal, Christian presence in public schools simmered both nationally and in Florida. In Miami, things came to a head when the American Jewish Congress, representing Jewish students, brought a suit challenging certain programs in Dade County Schools, such as the reenactment of the crucifixion of Jesus as part of the Easter holiday programs and the morning recitation of the "Lord's Prayer." As vice president of the American Jewish Congress's South Florida chapter, Kronish had worked tirelessly behind the scenes to eliminate such practices. But when these efforts failed, he became a leading public critic of the mixing of church and state, a practice he repeatedly condemned from the pulpit.

The case was heard in July, October, and November of 1960, attracting national media attention. Kronish was a key witness for the plaintiffs. The suit was successful in the Dade County Circuit Court and, two years later, was unanimously affirmed by the Florida Supreme Court.[10]

A SOUTH FLORIDA CULTURAL CENTER

At the same time, due to the heroic exertions of one congregant, Judy Drucker, and Rabbi Kronish's emphasis on cultural Zionism, the temple began a cultural affairs program that would soon lead to its recognition as the foremost musical arts center in greater Miami, secular or religious. From the late 1960s well into the 1980s, Temple Beth Sholom became known throughout South Florida for its prestigious winter concert programs featuring world-renowned instrumentalists, singers, and dancers. Among those who appeared under the rubric of the Culture and Fine Arts Series—renamed Miami's Great Artist Series in 1970—were Pinchas Zuckerman on his first U.S. tour, Leonard Bernstein, Itzhak Perlman, Yehudi Menuhin, Zubin Mehta, Vladimir Ashkenazi, Richard Tucker, and the Israeli Philharmonic, in addition to leading chamber music ensembles and others.

The temple established a unique art gallery featuring the work of Jewish artists from all over the world, and especially Israel. A Jewish cultural arts program was also integrated into the educational curricula. In addition, the Leon Kronish Institute for Living Judaism was established for formal and informal education and culture. The institute especially targeted adults with Jewish culture classes, including Bible and Talmud classes, a Great Book Series, and a Distinguished Lecture Series. The Lecture Series sponsored a parade of national and international notables over the years: Isaac Bashevis Singer, Amos Oz, Martin Gilbert, Howard Sachar, Jacob Timmerman, Herman Wouk, Emil Fackenheim, Elie Wiesel (annually), Yosef Yerushalmi, Haim Herzog, Yitzhak Rabin, and Golda Meir were just a handful of the personalities that spoke at the temple.

THE "ISRAELIZATION" OF THE TEMPLE AND AMERICAN JEWRY

While Temple Beth Sholom was becoming known both regionally and, as a result of the continuing snowbird presence, nationally as a center of high culture, Rabbi Kronish was also leading it to a much deeper connection with a myriad of Israeli individuals and institutions. As noted above, the stunning events of the Six-Day War marked a significant shift in the political orientation of Leon Kronish and Temple Beth Sholom. From 1967 Kronish became focused almost exclusively on linking the temple to many aspects of Israeli life, including, but not limited to, support for numerous policies of the Israeli government, even those not headed by the Labor Party. *Yisrael Goralenu* (Israel is our destiny [1968]), and *What Are the "Zionist Mitzvot"?* (1977), outlined the linking initiatives, and Temple Beth Sholom became Kronish's laboratory to exercise the programmatic features of the process we call "Israelization."

In Kronish's view, Reform Judaism needed to translate the concept of covenant into support for Progressive Judaism (Reform Judaism's identity in Israel), enabling American Reform Jews who decide to live in Israel to exercise their religious beliefs in according with their conscience. Some members of the Central Conference of American Rabbis responded that Kronish was advocating nothing less than the "exporting" of non-Orthodox ways of expressing Liberal Judaism. But Kronish appreciated that in the postwar period, Six-Day War, and Yom Kippur War, a new Liberal Judaism had to be framed to inspire a new generation, one that had experienced neither the Holocaust nor the birth of the Jewish state.

The "Israelization" of American Jewry was a powerful revival of Zionism as well as an extension. It modernized the connection between the Diaspora and Israel,

FIGURE 2. *Rabbi Leon Kronish leading a mission to Israel in the mid-1970s. Archive picture courtesy of Temple Beth Sholom, Miami Beach Florida.*

taking account of the current status of youth, American Jewry's infrastructure and Reform Judaism. "Israelization" had five main dimensions. The first was "bringing Israel to America." Kronish began this practice in the immediate aftermath of the Six-Day War by inviting Israelis to come and live with members of his congregation. By exposing Israeli and American Jews to each other in an American Jewish environment, Kronish believed that both the Israeli and the American would come to understand each other better. This "Israelis-in-Residence" program became a model throughout the country.

The second was "bringing American Jews to Israel." In contrast to the traditional goal of Zionist travels or Federation missions, these trips were established to bring American youth and their parents. In Kronish's view, the best way to strengthen their sense of Jewish identity was to have them spend several weeks in Israel, getting to know firsthand the land and people. Thus, he established the confirmation trip to Israel for teenage boys and girls at age fifteen and adult missions that were thematically designed. Many of these adult missions included sites in Europe of Jewish significance, especially Holocaust-related. Current programs like "March of the Living" and "Birthright" are an outgrowth of this "Israelization" dimension.

The third "Israelization" component was to make American synagogues and temples into visible centers for the promotion of Israeli life and culture. All institutions were encouraged to include festivals celebrating Israeli culture. Toward this goal, Kronish assisted in bringing a *schaliach*, an Israeli emissary without portfolio, to Miami. The *schaliach*'s mandate was to expose the community, and in particular youth in synagogues and centers, to Israel. The first *schaliach* arrived in 1969, the year after *Yisrael Goralenu* was published.

The fourth component of Israelization was in catalyzing major Jewish organizations in the United States to develop significant and systematic relationships with

FIGURE 3. *Israel's Twenty-third Independence Anniversary, 1971, Fountainbleau Hotel, Miami Beach.* Left to Right: *Ambassador Yitzhak Rabin, Lillian Kronish, Leon Kronish, and Mike Litvak.* Archive picture courtesy of Temple Beth Sholom, Miami Beach, Florida.

Israel, including growing links with Israeli institutions of similar orientations. The Alexander Muss High School in Israel, the Association of Reform Zionists of America, the launching of Reform kibbutzim and the development of Progressive Judaism in Israel are all examples. In this sense, the "Re-Forming" of Israel was as important for Kronish as the "Israelization" of American Jewry.

The fifth and final aspect of "Israelization" revolves around the establishment of permanent links among political, social, and economic institutions in both Israel and the United States — institutions not linked solely to American Jewry, that is, but to the United States as a country. Toward this goal Kronish played a significant role in helping the State of Israel organize the Miami-Israel Chamber of Commerce and the Consultants for Israeli Industry in the mid-1970s, pave the way for direct flights between Miami and Tel Aviv in the late 1970s, and establish a consulate in Miami (1982).

In these and several other ways, Kronish moved to expand and extend the relations between American Jewry (and especially Reform Judaism) and the State of Israel. "Israelization" challenged national Jewish organizations to adopt polices that represented an Israel-centered focus for Jewish life in America. "Israelization" went far beyond the traditional Zionist goal of bringing Jews to live in the Land of Israel. Its purpose was to develop a wide array of interconnected relations between Israeli and American Jews — a web that would, in Kronish's view, redound not only to their mutual benefit, but also to the benefit of both Israel and the United States as interdependent, cooperating democratic nation-states.

"RE-FORMING" JUDAISM IN THE STATE OF ISRAEL

At the same time Kronish was undertaking these, and indeed other, efforts to "Israelize" Temple Beth Sholom (and, by implication, all of American Jewry), he was also attempting to upgrade the status of Reform Judaism within Israel itself.

FIGURE 4. *Jerusalem mayor, Teddy Kolleck, with Leon Kronish following his presentation at the Fountainbleau Hotel in recognition of the unification of Jerusalem as the capital of Israel (Jerusalem Day), Miami Beach, 1970. Archive picture courtesy of Temple Beth Sholom, Miami Beach, Florida.*

As one of the leading lights in binding Reform Judaism with Zionism, Kronish felt it was his duty to bring Reform rabbis to Israel. As chairman of the Committee on Israel of the Central Conference of American Rabbis in the heady days after the Six-Day War, he asked his colleagues to consider joint pilgrimages to Israel, programs to encourage aliyah for Reform rabbis, and projects leading to the establishment of more institutions for American Jews to experience Reform Judaism in Israel.

Not surprisingly, these efforts to legitimize Reform Judaism in Israel aroused the antagonism of the Orthodox religious establishment there. They were especially bothered by what they considered the lax *halachic* (Jewish law) standards applied by Reform rabbis to those wishing to convert to Judaism, and the Reform insistence on recognizing the right of women to become rabbis. Kronish stood apart, however, from many of his rabbinical colleagues by opposing the CCAR and

UHAC decision in 1983 to adopt the policy of "Patrilineal Descent." In Kronish's view "Patrilineal Descent" would not strengthen the pulse of Liberal Judaism.

Leon Kronish: The Man

Kronish was considered a man of the people. A tireless and effective organizer, he was also viewed as a great conciliator. This ability to find common ground, to reconcile opposing positions was undoubtedly influenced by the work he did to overcome the crises in his own life. Although the story frequently told is one of triumph and transcendence, there was tragedy, too, experiences Kronish used to inspire him further. His grandfather was lost during the Holocaust, his first child was challenged in a variety of ways and died before reaching adulthood, and Kronish suffered a major heart attack in 1978. Yet he persevered until a stroke in 1984 finally left him paralyzed.

Throughout it all, Kronish never lost his own sense of mission, especially with his congregation, whom he sincerely saw as the members of his extended family. Indeed, he was a role model for a whole generation of religious, political, and community leaders. Several members of his congregation became presidents of the Greater Miami Jewish Federation (Jules Arkin, Harry Smith, and Donald Lefton), others became cantors (Rachelle Nelson and Stephen Haas), a handful became rabbis (Marty Lawson, Ronald Kronish, Gregory Marks and Gerald Serotta), and many others rose to leadership positions in national organizations such as the National Council of Jewish Women (Nan Rich, national president). In honor of his achievements, Temple Beth Sholom named its school the Rabbi Leon Kronish School for Living Judaism, the city of Miami Beach named a street the Kronish Plaza, and the Hebrew Union College–Jewish Institute of Religion hosts a Leon Kronish Memorial Lecture in Jerusalem. In March 2002, the lecture was delivered by Rabbi David Ellenson, president of Hebrew Union College–Jewish Institute of Religion, before several hundred Reform rabbis and guests.

Leon Kronish is further distinguished, even within the vaunted circles he frequented, not simply by his magnetism to outsiders, but by the extent to which he was able to pass on his brand of principled commitment to values to his own children. His son Ronald Kronish followed in his father's footsteps, without ever feeling that such a path was preordained for him. He became a rabbi at the Hebrew Union College–Jewish Institute of Religion, after completing his degree in humanistic psychology at Brandeis. In addition, he earned a Ph.D. in education from Harvard University—testaments to his desire to carry on the tradition of teaching that he learned at his father's feet.

Most important, Ronald Kronish lived out his father's deep commitment to the State of Israel, and made *aliyah* in 1979. Since then, he has served in several positions, including as codirector of the Melitz Centers for Jewish Zionist Education in Jerusalem, the director of the Israeli office of the American Jewish Committee, as well as a lecturer at both the Hebrew University of Jerusalem and Tel Aviv University. Currently, he is director of the Inter-Religious Coordinating Council in Israel. All this activity reflects a wholehearted embrace of the principles modeled by his father.

And, finally, as Leon Kronish's daughter Maxine Kronish Snyder—one of

many beneficiaries of Kronish's deep commitment to the equality of women in
the Temple, and the notion that a loving family life is the basis of a vibrant Jewish
identity—so eloquently put it in a volume of essays in honor of her father:

> With all my father's commitments and activities as a rabbi and communal
> leader, I am sure that I—and the rest of the extended Kronish family—revere
> him most as the patriarch of our family. And we know that the feeling is mutual,
> that family for him is always the top priority—it always has been, and it is so
> now, more than ever before. . . . It is my privilege to share in his dreams—for
> our family, for the Jewish people, and for all of God's children—and I fervently
> pray that I will be able to continue to fulfill many of his dreams and hopes for
> the future, along with the rest of his family and his many friends and followers,
> who have become his devoted disciples in the Jewish world.[11]

NOTES

1. Sermon, April 23, 1959.
2. Samuel Karff, ed., *Hebrew Union College–Jewish Institute of Religion at One Hundred Years* (Cincinnati, Ohio, 1976), 151.
3. *Temple Beth Sholom Bulletin*, March 26, 1954.
4. Interview with Kronish, August 1989. Notes to himself February 17, 1949, and April 13, 1978, and letter to Ephraim Shapira, April 17, 1978.
5. "Yisrael Goralenu," *CCAR Journal* 16 (June 1968): 31.
6. Polly Redford, *Billion Dollar Sandbar: A Biography of Miami Beach* (New York, 1970), 263.
7. Sermon, May 10, 1957.
8. Letter to President Truman, March 15, 1950.
9. *LIFE Magazine* (January 12, 1962), 36.
10. *Chamberlain v. Dade County School Board*, 17 Florida Supp. 196, 1961 and 142 So. 2d, 21; *American Jewish Yearbook* 62 (1961): 89–90; 63 (1962): 184–85; 64 (1963): 123–24.
11. Maxine Kronish Snyder, "My Father and My family: Growing up Jewish," in *Towards the Twenty-First Century: Judaism and the Jewish People in Israel and America*, ed. Ronald Kronish (Hoboken, N.J., 1988), 334–35.

REFERENCES

Allman, T. D. *Miami: City of the Future.* New York: Atlantic Monthly Press, 1987.

Bettinger-López, Caroline. *Cuban-Jewish Journeys.* Knoxville: University of Tennessee Press, 2000.

Didion, Joan. *Miami.* New York: Simon & Schuster, 1987.

George, Paul. *The Event of the Decade: Temple Emanu-El Of Greater Miami, 1938–1988.* Miami Beach, Fla., 1988.

Green, Henry A. *Gesher Vakesher, Bridges and Bonds: The Life of Leon Kronish.* Atlanta, Ga.: Scholars Press, 1995.

Green, Henry A., and Marcia Zerivitz. *Mosaic: Jewish Life in Florida.* Miami, Fla.: Hallmark, 1991.

Karff, Samuel, ed. *Hebrew Union College–Jewish Institute of Religion at One Hundred Years.* Cincinnati, Ohio, 1976.

Kleinberg, Howard. *Miami Beach.* Miami, Fla.: Centennial Press, 1996.

Kronish, Ronald, ed. *Towards the Twenty-First Century: Judaism and the Jewish People in Israel and America. Essays in Honor of Rabbi Leon Kronish on the Occasion of his Seventieth Birthday.* Hoboken, N.J.: Ktav, 1988.

Meyer, Michael. *Response to Modernity.* New York: Oxford University Press, 1988.

Moore, Deborah Dash. *To the Golden Cities.* New York: Free Press, 1994.

Munroe, Gary, and Andrew Sweet. *Miami Beach.* Miami, Fla.: Andrew Sweet Memorial Foundation, 1990.

Portes, Alejandro, and Alex Stepick. *City on the Edge.* Berkeley and Los Angeles: University of California Press, 1993.

Redford, Polly. *Billion-Dollar Sandbar.* New York: E. P. Dutton, 1970.

Rieff, David. *Going to Miami.* Boston: Little, Brown, 1987.

Singer, Isaac Bashevis. *My Love Affair with Miami Beach.* New York: Simon & Schuster, 1991.

Tebeau, Charlton. *Temple Israel of Greater Miami.* Coral Gables, Fla.: University of Miami Press, 1972.

Zev Ben Beitchman

Synagogues in the Sand

In its era, up to the late 1970s, there were approximately thirty-five shuls on Miami Beach up to 85th Street. As demographics shifted, with an influx of the Hispanic population, and as the elderly Jewish population began to die out or relocate to Broward and Palm Beach counties, Miami Beach synagogue congregations began to dwindle. Congregations could no longer shoulder the financial burdens of their synagogues, and many buildings were abandoned or sold. The collapse of each synagogue signifies a loss, an erasure of memory of Jewish culture in South Beach.

FIGURE 2a. *Jacob C. Cohen Synagogue, 1535 Washington Avenue.*

FIGURE 2b. *Location became a series of nightclubs.*

FIGURE 3a. *Congregation Etz Chaim, 1537 Washington Avenue.*

FIGURE 3b. *Now a retail store.*

FIGURE 5a. *Temple Beth Raphael dedicated to the Holocaust, 15th Street and Drexel Avenue.*

FIGURE 5b. *Turned into residential lofts.*

As the photographs in this chapter demonstrate, many of these shuls have taken on new identities, becoming nightclubs, retail stores, and restaurants, while some buildings have been demolished.

FIGURE 6a. *Beth T'filah, 935 Euclid Avenue.*

FIGURE 6b. *In the process of becoming lofts.*

The Jewish Museum of Florida, however, which was formerly an orthodox synagogue, is a praiseworthy example of adaptive reuse: the preservation of the original building for the continuance of Jewish culture in Miami Beach.

FIGURE 7a. *Beth Jacob Congregation, 301 Washington Avenue.*

FIGURE 7b. *Now the Jewish Museum of Florida.*

Susan Neimand

Jewish Education in South Florida

The story of Jewish education is one that parallels the growth of the South Florida Jewish community while representing a microcosm of national Jewish trends. Although the Jewish community of South Florida is more than a hundred years old, it is only since the 1940s that permanent Jewish residences have rooted in South Florida. With permanence came the need for the education of the children and adults in the forms of synagogue congregational schools, Jewish high schools, early childhood education, day schools, and adult education. Today, South Florida has the third-largest concentration of Jews outside of Israel. Jewish influence in Florida is part of everyday life, and Jews continue to contribute to the South Florida culture.

Synagogue Congregational Schools

Many unsuccessful attempts were made to develop a plantation economy in Miami beginning in 1840 by the Acostas, in 1870 by the Lums, and in 1894 by John Collins. Carl Fisher completed the bridge that united Miami Beach with the mainland in an effort to create another Atlantic City that would be "for gentiles only." The southern tip of Miami Beach was developed by the Lummus brothers who attracted wealthy Jewish businessmen in the 1920s. The 1920s tourist boom ended and financial collapse occurred, aggravated by the hurricane of 1926. In 1930, the failure of the Bank of Bay Biscayne plunged Miami into the national depression. It was the semiretired Jewish businessmen who saw this as an opportunity to amass property and transform Miami Beach into an extension of their northern communities. They built synagogues, schools, restaurants, and hotels.[1]

In 1938, the Miami Jewish community opened the Greater Miami Jewish Federation (GMJF). Its primary focus was to organize philanthropy in the Miami area and to help plan for the development of the community systematically. Jewish communal life in Miami grew up around the congregations. It was the synagogues and rabbis of the major congregations in Miami who assumed strong leadership roles in the community. Beth David Congregation was the pioneer congregation in Miami, founded in 1912 as B'nai Zion, and changed to Beth David in 1917. Next came Temple Israel, the breakaway Reform group from Beth David, founded in 1922. Beth Jacob Congregation, today's Jewish Museum of Florida, was built in 1936 on 3rd Street in Miami Beach. The Miami Beach Jewish Center, today's Temple Emanu-El, was founded in 1940. Temple Beth Sholom was founded in 1942. These were the first Jewish organizations in existence in South Florida.[2]

Providing religious education for its children, including the children of the poor and fatherless, had always been the responsibility of the Jewish community. In Europe this took the form of private *chedarim* (supplementary Jewish classes). In the New World, however, it was the Sunday school, the Hebrew school, and the day school models that took root. Sunday schools were based on the Protestant model of religious education taking place one day a week and reflected the conviction of Jews of the time to become more "Americanized." The conception of Jewish education was the preparation of the children who would find both the Jewish and secular worlds compatible, but clearly defined.[3]

The rise of the congregational school coincided with the sociopsychological need for belonging to one's group in light of the Holocaust and the founding of the State of Israel. From the inception of Jewish education in Miami, each of the synagogues in Miami ran its own religious, supplementary schools. In 1941, Rabbi Jacob H. Kaplan, president of the Greater Miami Rabbinical Association, called for the centralized operation and supervision of Hebrew schools rather than the support of individual synagogues running their own programs. An association called the Jewish Educators Association (JEA) was formed. The JEA became the Bureau of Jewish Education (BJE) and ultimately evolved into the Central Agency for Jewish Education (CAJE), which marks its inception date as November 1943. Its role became one of coordinator of Jewish educational activities among religious schools and other educational agencies, rendering a variety of services to the schools, and assisting with the development of a Hebrew high school, adult education, and curriculum. Moreover, it was the role of the JEA to provide financial assistance to schools in order to raise their standards.

In 1944, four synagogues—Miami Beach Jewish Center, Beth David, Temple Israel, and Beth Sholom—joined the BJE, while Beth Jacob, Shaarei Zedek, and Miami Jewish Orthodox did not. Miami Jewish Orthodox and the Arbeiter's Ring (Workmen's Circle School) affiliated in 1946; Beth Jacob affiliated in 1948; and the United Jewish School (sponsored by the Coral Gables Jewish Center, West Miami Jewish Center, and the Flagler-Granada Jewish Center), Temple Isaiah Sunday School, and the Miami Hebrew School affiliated in 1949, representing an educationally unified Jewish community.[4]

In the 1944–45 school year there were approximately 3,000 children in the Miami and Miami Beach communities, but only 1,140 received either Hebrew or Sunday school education. However, by the 1948–49 school year the number of children who received a Jewish education leaped to 2,537 of 4,300 children in the Miami area; a 30 percent increase in the total child population in the community netted a 45 percent increase in school population.

To address the attrition rate in enrollment after bar mitzvah age, a central Hebrew high school program for graduates of Hebrew schools was developed. It was begun in 1945, and only through recruitment efforts were there ten male students registered in 1945, and twenty-one in 1949 at the locations of Beth David, Miami Beach Jewish Center, and Beth El.

The 1950s heralded tremendous growth in the permanent population of Miami; public schools were the only accessible means of education for the school-age Jewish population, except for the Hebrew Academy on Miami Beach. The Dade County Public Schools conducted Christian religious practices in the schools just as all public schools of that era did: daily Bible reading, usually from the New Testament, daily recitation of the Lord's Prayer, and elaborate celebrations of Christ's birth at Christmas and the Crucifixion and Resurrection at Easter. Anti-Semitism took the form of the bombing of Tifereth Israel Northside Jewish Center in the spring of 1951, dynamite being found at Temple Israel of Miami in the fall of 1951, the bombing of the Miami Hebrew School and Congregation in December 1951, and dynamite found at the Coral Gables Jewish Center in December 1951.[5]

The postwar years soon became a period of widespread religious revival among Jews. National statistics estimated that in 1959, 80 percent of Jewish children attended a Jewish school, although not all completed their elementary course of study. Jewish education was defined as afternoon Hebrew school meeting three to five afternoons per week and the Sunday school. The 1950s brought an increase in the percentages of girls who attended Jewish schools.

In the post-Sputnik era of the 1960s, American parents became increasingly conscious of the importance of education, the need for higher standards, and greater intensification of learning. The secular school year was lengthened from 162 days in 1920 to 180 days in 1965 and concerted efforts were made to improve classroom methodology, teacher training, and supervision. These developments impacted greatly on Jewish education.[6] The curricula of the Hebrew schools were revised and new texts were presented to the teachers through the work of the BJE. The curricula of the Sunday schools were also revised and time was provided to train the teachers how to use the curricula effectively. A plan for the accreditation of Hebrew schools was also developed in 1962 in an effort to raise standards in the schools in administration, curriculum, teaching staff, supervision, and physical facilities. Efforts were made to set licensing standards for teachers and to lengthen the time of schooling.

In 1962, more stringent requirements were suggested for bar and bat mitzvah by the BJE and endorsed by local rabbis. The new requirements were a minimum of three years of satisfactory attendance at a Hebrew school with four or more hours weekly of instruction, the ability to read Prayers, the understanding of Customs and Ceremonies, an understanding of the early chapters of Genesis, and a knowledge and understanding of the major historical events and personalities in history and current Jewish events. (The 1949 standard had required only two years of Hebrew school attendance.) Beth David, Temple Emanu-El, and Beth Torah, the major synagogues of the time, were in full compliance and support.

In the 1950s there was a shift in attendance from the one-day Sunday school model to the multiple-day Hebrew school model with 70 percent of Jewish children receiving some form of Jewish education. Additionally, more synagogues were being built and more students were able to attend. Attendance exceeded national standards. In 1962, the smallest schools had between seventeen (Tifereth Israel and Miami Hebrew School) and thirty-six students (Beth Israel and Workmen's Circle). The largest Hebrew schools were Temple Menorah with 205 students, Beth David with 603 students, and Beth Torah with 685 students.

Two major national trends began in the 1960s and 1970s, a rise in the intermarriage rate (to 30 percent and beyond) and a decline in the birth rate. These trends led to a spirit of religious revival that began infiltrating the Jewish community in the 1960s, and by the 1970s had taken root in Jewish communities across the United States. Increased attention was given to Jewish education, which witnessed a peak enrollment. There were shifts in the type of Jewish education favored. By the 1970s synagogue schools were being criticized nationally and locally for their lack of substantive Jewish education.[7]

The late 1980s brought forth a myriad of studies that attempted to answer the questions, What characterized American Jews in the 1980s? Studies showed that contemporary Jews were highly educated, relatively affluent, very mobile, geographically dispersed, and had high rates of intermarriage; the Holocaust and Israel were key to the Jewish psyche. American Jewish identity was characterized by a decline in denominationalism and practice of rites and rituals, but stability in synagogue affiliation and participation. Such indicated acceptance of the concept that rabbis of the era were trying to inculcate in their congregants: that the center of Jewish life was the synagogue.

JEWISH HIGH SCHOOLS

The central Hebrew High School, a community-sponsored institution, differed from the previous Hebrew High School, which was conducted by individual congregations. In the 1949–50 school year, the central high school was first sponsored as a centralized school with all of the classes in one building, the Peninsular Institute. The first graduation was held on May 23, 1950 and two students graduated. Growth of the high school was slow. In 1963, the program was moved to four different locations in Miami at Beth David, in Miami Beach at Temple Emanu-El, in Coral Gables at Temple Zion, and at Beth Torah in North Dade. The Hebrew High School was accurately named: it strongly emphasized Hebrew language and the study of classical Jewish texts. It was designed for the most interested and motivated students from the schools. Widespread support of post–bar mitzvah education emerged in the late 1960s and the high school changed from its Hebraica orientation to a Judaic Studies orientation. For a few years, this conception of the high school lingered on as a parallel system to the Judaica system that was developed, but the Hebrew High School gradually faded out.

The goal of the Judaica High School, created in 1971, was "to reach out to the unmotivated and indifferent Jewish teenager, committed to involve him in learning experiences, and to strengthen his sense of Jewish identity." The Judaica High School established its program as a communal structure with the intent of extending across all ideologies and denominations of Judaism. It involved the synagogues and youth organizations and utilized diverse methodologies including formal classes, rap sessions, weekends, and drop-in centers. The content of the program was expanded to include Jewish sources, cultural arts, current events, and Jewish thought. Every major synagogue, Adath Yeshurun, Beth David, Beth Sholom, Beth Torah, Temple Emanu-El, Temple Or Olom, Beth Am, Beth Moses, B'nai Raphael, Temple Sinai, Temple Zion, Temple Israel, Temple Judea, Temple Menorah, and Ner Tamid all participated. In 1975, the number of hours studied was intensified from three to seven hours weekly. The program was changed to three trimesters and college credit courses through Miami-Dade Community College were offered for the first time. A Jewish Identity Survey comparing teenagers in the Judaica High School with those not involved found that Judaica High School students reflected higher Jewish identity, were less likely to interdate, had the lowest rate of negative self-identification, and were more aware of major Jewish issues.

The Greater Miami High School in Israel (later renamed the Alexander Muss High School in Israel program) was one of the major avenues for the development of knowledgeable and committed Jewish adolescents. This educational commitment resulted in the establishment of educational trips to Israel. The first trip was in the summer of 1973. Students traveled to Israel and studied within the sites that they visited. They also received college credit for the courses through Miami-Dade Community College.

As of 2002, the Judaica High School operates junior and senior high school educational programs in cooperation with local synagogues, a college credit program in cooperation with Miami-Dade Community College and Broward Community College, the Akiva Leadership program, and the March of the Living Program.

The Akiva Leadership Program was instituted in 1973 in an effort to cultivate knowledgeable, committed future leaders for the Jewish community. Participation requirements were enrollment in at least four hours weekly of Judaic studies (with a minimum of two hours of Hebrew) and recommendations by principals, youth directors, and teachers as to students' Jewish commitment and motivation. Students met on Sundays for two hours to discuss history and sociology for which they earned three college credits, and to discuss Jewish current events and problems. Students participated in a variety of community service programs to raise money for the Combined Jewish Appeal and educational programs. The number of students in Akiva remained between seventeen and thirty, and the educational programs, community service components, and topics of study varied.

In 1988, the CAJE initiated the "March of the Living" program, a programmed march from the concentration camps of Auschwitz to Birkenau on Yom Ha'shoah, Holocaust Memorial Day, which culminated in a trip to Israel for Yom Ha'Atzmaut, Israel's Independence Day. Avraham Hirshenson, a member of the Likud party in the Knesset, had run a contest in Israel that dealt with student knowledge of the resistance movement and martyrdom during the Holocaust; while many international students participated, students from the United States was poorly represented. In 1987, conducting the contest in Poland in 1988 was contemplated as it was the forty-fifth anniversary of the Warsaw Ghetto uprising. Additionally, more participation on the part of American Jewish students was sought. During the discussions between Israeli contest leaders and New York and Miami Bureau of Education leaders, the topic of the March of Death out of Auschwitz (where sixty thousand people started and six thousand survived) led to the concept of the March of the Living, having the students march into Auschwitz, instead of coming out. Thus, the idea was born. On April 14–23, 1988, the contest was held in the Opera House in Warsaw for 1,500 people who came from all over the world, 700 from Israel, and 150 from the United States. A delegation of fifty-two teenagers from South Florida participated. The power of the march was immediately noticed by the leadership of the CAJE as students were markedly affected and changed in a very short time. Psychologists who were later consulted called this a "spontaneous emotional growth spurt."

Specific goals were set for the program. The first goal was to instill a sense of Jewish pride and identity in each march participant. The second goal was to impart the concept of *achdut* (unity), that all the students were Jews regardless of their ideology or affiliation. The third goal was fostering community involvement, becoming involved in the Jewish community through social service actions. The fourth goal was the awareness of rootedness, where each Jew is a link in the chain of history and that each is the beginning of the next generation.

A documentary based on the March of the Living experience was coproduced by the CAJE with Jewish Federation Television (JFTV) and WPBT 2 (the Miami affiliate of PBS). The program was based on the writings of the participants during the experience and the CAJE book *Reflections on the March of the Living*. It was authored by the director of operations and executive producer of JFTV. Two of the narrators were Colleen Dewhurst and Jonathan Silverman. The Florida Chapter of the National Academy of Television Arts and Sciences (NATAS) nominated the TV documentary *March of the Living* as a finalist in three categories: producer, director, and individual achievement/camera. The documentary also won three Illinois State Film awards: the Wilbur Award, the Louie Award, and a PBS award.

The March of the Living program continued every two years with a wide representation of students from Dade County. In 1994, the CAJE was the Southern Regional Coordinating Office for the March of the Living.

EARLY CHILDHOOD EDUCATION

In 1955, the BJE planned to set up a resource department for preschool education available to all Jewish schools and in 1956, preschool teachers were included in seminars for teachers. This was the first time early childhood education was addressed, acknowledging that "Jewish education needs extension downward to the pre-school age."

In 1961, the Jewish Congregational Pre-School Teachers Association of Greater Miami was formed by Naomi Brandeis, who became the chair of the Pre-School Council. The increases in the enrollment in preschool attested to its growing importance in the community. The Pre-School Council planned seminars for early childhood teachers; licensing of early childhood teachers by the BJE (and eventually the CAJE) went into effect in 1961. Most teachers, however, did not have teaching credentials and many had insufficient backgrounds and were ineligible for licenses. The organization still is in existence today: the Helene and A. B. Weiner Early Childhood Education Department of CAJE provides services to more than one thousand early childhood education professionals annually through the Jewish Council of Early Childhood Educators. These services take the form of pedagogical resources to support ongoing personal and professional development.

DAY SCHOOLS

Day school enrollment in the 1940s was negligible; by the 1970s, however, 25 percent of Jewish children attended Jewish elementary and secondary day schools.

The changes in Jewish patterns of education were seen in Miami in the growth of the day school movement and the commitment of the Greater Miami Jewish Federation to education. By the 1970s, Miami's communal agencies and rabbis saw the possibilities in Jewish continuity and in day schools.

The Greater Miami Beach Hebrew Academy (today's Rabbi Alexander S. Gross Hebrew Academy), the first all-day Hebrew school, opened in February 1947, with six first-grade students at the YMHA building at One Lincoln Road on Miami Beach. Earlier that year a kindergarten and prekindergarten class had opened. By September 1947 eighty students were enrolled in the dual studies program and the school purchased a building at Sixth Street and Jefferson Avenue. This was the latest venture of Torah U'Mesorah, the national Orthodox governing board. The school was officially dedicated in January 1948.

The day schools opened in Dade County. Joining Rabbi Alexander S. Gross Hebrew Academy (1947) was Lehrman Day School of Temple Emanu-El in 1960. Dr. Irving Lehrman, founder of the school, recognized the need for Conservative Jewish education and established the day school. Landow Yeshivah Community School on Miami Beach was founded in 1967. In 1970, Beth Am Day School, the first Reform day school in Dade County, illustrated the population shift away from Miami Beach to South Dade, while the opening of the Samuel Scheck Hillel Community Day School indicated the same in North Dade. Greenfield Elementary (formerly South Dade Hebrew Academy), Goldstein Academy (the community day school of South Dade), and the Mesivta of Greater Miami on Miami Beach were founded in 1971. Community schools were defined as those without affiliation to a stream of Judaism.

Beth David Congregation opened a satellite campus in South Dade to facilitate the needs of the community of young families. It subsequently opened a preschool and then a Solomon Schechter Day School in 1972. Beth David Congregation split into two congregations in 1984: Beth David in downtown Miami and Bet Shira in South Dade. The Solomon Schechter School became part of Bet Shira Congregation; due to attrition in the population after Hurricane Andrew in 1992, however, it closed its doors in 1994.

Toras Emes Academy, an Orthodox day school on Miami Beach, began in 1978. Sinai Academy, the second Reform Jewish day school and the first such school in the North Dade community, opened in 1981. Yeshiva Toras Chaim opened on Miami Beach in 1984 and Yeshiva Elementary in 1987. In 1989, Beth David Congregation once again opened a day school, the Gordon Day School at their site in the downtown section of Miami. In 1995, Temple Bet Breira opened a first-grade class and established their day school, a Reform Jewish day school west of South Dixie Highway. Beth Torah Adath Yeshurun, the merged congregations of Beth Torah and Adath Yeshurun, opened the BTAY Solomon Schechter Day School, the same year as Aventura Turnberry Jewish Center added the Tauber Day School to its congregation, 1996.

Jewish communities began spreading throughout all of South Florida, away from Miami and Miami Beach. By 1948, a number of synagogues opened in Broward County. Subsequently, day schools opened: David Posnack Hebrew Day School, a community day school, opened in 1975. Initially a single campus was opened with an elementary school located in Sunrise. The school grew to include two elementary schools located at two different campuses, one in Sunrise and one in Davie. In 1998, the David Posnack Hebrew Day High School held its first classes. Since then the high school has grown to more than one hundred students. In August 2002 the middle and high schools moved to a new facility.

Additional schools opened: Brauser Maimonides Academy, an Orthodox day school in Fort Lauderdale (1980); the Hebrew Academy Community School in Margate (1986); and Temple Kol Ami Day School, a Reform day school (1997).

Palm Beach County's Jewish population dates back to the 1940s, the opening of synagogues in the 1950s and communal agencies in the early 1960s. Day schools followed. In Palm Beach County, Donna Klein Jewish Academy, a community day school opened in Boca Raton in 1979, a branch of Hillel of North Dade opened in 1990 to facilitate the Palm Beach county families wishing for an Orthodox Jewish education without the travel to North Dade. This branch of Hillel became autonomous in 1993. As the Orthodox community grew in Boca Raton, the Yeshiva High School opened in 1997 and Torah Academy, an Orthodox day school, opened in 1998. The Solomon Schechter School of South Palm Beach County opened in 2001 to fill the void for the Conservative population of Boca Raton.

The center of Florida Jewry was in the Miami–Fort Lauderdale area. Forty percent of southern Jews (320,000) lived there in 1990. This center was the third largest Jewish community in the United States behind New York and Los Angeles.[8] Miami was also 29 percent Jewish. Each of the day schools opened to meet the needs of a unique population. The first day schools were Orthodox in their orientation, which did not represent the needs of all of the community: hence the opening of the first Reform Jewish Day School in Temple Beth Am's day school and Beth David's Conservative Solomon Schechter Day School. With the spread of the population and the diversity of each community more and more schools opened to meet the needs of the community, from Orthodox to Reform to community. In 2002, there were eighteen Jewish day schools in Dade County, five in Broward County, four in South Palm Beach County and ten outside of the tri-county area, totaling thirty-seven Jewish day schools in South Florida.

What was unique about the day schools was their commitment to providing a quality education in both general and secular studies. Day schools were characterized by their mission to ensure that each student's academic, social-emotional, and physical needs were met in a warm, nurturing environment. Day schools attempted to provide a holistic view of life as a Jewish American, a citizen who could function in each world comfortably. Conservative and Reform day schools were dedicated to an integrated approach to curriculum and created many opportunities for interdisciplinary activities in their curricula. Studies ultimately proved that it was day school education that ensured connection to Judaism and that day school graduates continued to be part of the Jewish community through their involvement and participation in synagogue life and religious practice.

In August 1992, Hurricane Andrew, the costliest disaster in American history, tore through Dade County, destroying much of South Dade and its Jewish community. Thousands of families were temporarily displaced and others lost their homes and property. Many moved away, creating a change in the nature of the community. A once thriving Jewish community suffered shifts. Synagogues began to note attrition in their memberships, and the JCC and day schools noted drops in their enrollments. In 1994, Bet Shira Solomon Schechter Day School closed and its students moved to Greenfield Elementary School and Temple Beth Am Day School. Both Greenfield and Temple Beth Am opened middle schools in 1995. Beth Am closed its middle school in 2002.

Conversely, the North Dade community saw a revival of young families moving in. In the year 2000, Jacobson Sinai Academy opened its upper school for students in grades six through eight and saw a steady growth over the years. Shortly thereafter, Aventura-Turnberry's Tauber School also opened a middle school with equal success.

One of the objectives of the Day School Survey of 1977 conducted by the GMJF and CAJE was the exploration and planning for a community day high school. The Hebrew Academy had developed a Girls' High School in the 1950s and established a Boys' High School in the late 1970s on Miami Beach. Attempts were made by the CAJE to create a unified Orthodox high school system by joining the Rabbi Alexander S. Gross Hebrew Academy High School, the Mesivta of Greater Miami, and Toras Emes Academy of Miami. The Mesivta was not interested in this venture and Toras Emes agreed not to open a high school, but rather to send their graduates to the existing schools.

The Community High School was opened in September 1981 at the site of the Michael-Ann Russell JCC in North Miami Beach. Simultaneously, Hillel decided to open a tenth grade at its site. Although it graduated its first class in 1983, and opened a new building in 1985, by the end of the 1986–87 school year, the Jewish High School of South Florida was not considered viable as a separate entity and therefore merged with the Samuel Scheck Hillel Community Day School; operation as a unified school began in the fall of 1987.

As the Jewish community grew in South Dade, the need for a community day junior high school was examined. Plans began being developed in the 1979–80 school year with a tentative opening date of September 1981. It was hoped that with the establishment of a junior high school in South Dade, a high school would soon be established. The site of the Alper JCC was selected for the school and the South Dade Hebrew Academy was asked to give up its junior high school in favor of a community junior high. The school opened in September 1982 with eighty students. In December 1983 its name was changed to Brandeis Academy with plans to open a tenth grade for the 1984–85 school year. By August 1984, however, Brandeis was in an emergency situation owing to low enrollment. By 1985–86 only twenty-seven students were enrolled and debts amounted to almost $200,000. The GMJF, which had already spent more than $800,000, discontinued funding. Brandeis was subsequently closed in August 1985.

With so many day schools in the community, the Greater Miami Jewish Federation called upon the CAJE to supervise the day schools, and in 1977, the Day School Department was established. The department would set guidelines for funding, financial auditing, tuition allocations, and teacher services such as licensing of Judaic Studies teachers, and interschool activities. The CAJE set forth a personnel code and a teacher salary scale that all funded schools needed to adhere to in order to receive their allocations from the GMJF. A principals and administrators council was established to set the agenda for the day schools as a unified body.

ADULT EDUCATION

Adult education was always important within the South Florida Jewish population. The first attempt at adult education was an experimental program conducted by Beth David and Temple Israel in 1948. By 1949, an Institute of Jewish Education was set up and offered courses in Hebrew, Yiddish, Jewish History, the Bible, and Zionism at Temple Beth El, Beth David and the "Y," while the Miami Beach Jewish Center and Temple Sholom conducted their own programs of adult education. Courses such as advanced Hebrew, the Bible, Mishnah, and Hebrew Literature continued to be offered through the various synagogues in conjunction with the BJE through the 1950s and 1960s. This organization eventually was called "The College of Jewish Studies" although it was never accredited nor ever affiliated with an accredited institution of higher learning.

As the nature of Jewish education changed, so, too, did the College of Jewish Studies. It was decided by the GMJF to establish a chair of Jewish Studies at an institute of higher learning. Subsequently, a cooperative program with the University of Miami was established and Barry University also began to offer courses in comparative religion and Jewish Studies. Eventually, all the South Florida universities, including Florida International University, Nova Southeastern University, and Florida Atlantic University created departments of Jewish Studies that offered a variety of courses and workshops in all aspects of religion and religious study.

Adult education, however, continued to be a focus of the synagogues that created programs within their individual congregations. Additionally, the CAJE created both the North Dade and South Dade Midrasha programs. These offered classes in Bible study as well as Modern Hebrew. Reviews determined that these courses remained at the beginning level and never progressed to an intermediate or advanced level.

Family education programs were undertaken in 1981 through the Home Start program sponsored by the AAJE, whose goal it was to bring observance back into the home. The program featured published materials on how to celebrate Jewish holidays in the home with young children. Seminars were run by the CAJE in 1980 and serviced families in Dade. Stepping Stones, a program of outreach to unaffiliated, intermarried parents and their children from ages five to fifteen was undertaken as a pilot program in 1993. The program provided knowledge of the basic elements in Jewish life, traditions, and history in an enjoyable, informal atmosphere.

In 1945, plans were made for the Jewish Library of Greater Miami, a library that would serve the community but would not be in competition with other existing libraries; it would contain Judaica references, pedagogy for teachers, pamphlets, Jewish Studies books, periodicals, and holiday books. The library started with

1,000 volumes; by 1971, the BJE reported 14,000 volumes in Hebrew and Yiddish, with a circulation of 17,000 books to 1,200 borrowers. In the 1950s, the library was located on northwest 3rd Avenue in the Old Beth David Building. Because the community was geographically less spread out, this location was central and became a constant place of gathering. It moved to 940 Lincoln Road in Miami Beach and was used by teachers for materials, but it was not a community library and it was not used as well as it should have been. Some questioned the actual numbers visiting the library at the Miami Beach location and thought that it should be moved to a more central location. In its subsequent (and present) location at 4200 Biscayne Boulevard, it was difficult to reach; while it is centered in the three Jewish areas of Dade County (South Dade, North Miami Beach, and Miami Beach), it is not located in a Jewish area.

The library was transformed from a repository for books to an outreach service of multimedia resources for teachers and students in the community and was named the Educational Resource Center. During the twenty-five years of its existence, the library had amassed a substantial collection of Judaica, "the largest collection of general interest Judaica in the South." In 1973, it began to broaden its holdings and included filmstrips, records, tapes, maps, transparencies, records, sheet music, and teacher materials such as curriculum guides, courses of study, units of instruction, and thematically related materials.

Recognizing that the move to 4200 Biscayne Boulevard left a high concentration of Jewish population, especially the elderly, without adequate library resources, arrangements were being made to transfer the collection of Yiddish books to a location on Miami Beach. The books were to be the property of the South Beach Branch of the Miami Beach Library for as long as it remained opened. Bunny and Sam Adler expressed an interest in endowing the library and naming it after their parents. They offered $150,000 for this honor, to be paid over seven and a half years at the rate of $20,000 a year. On March 9, 1986, a dedication ceremony was held to change the name of the center to the Esther and Morris Adler and Ruth and Samuel Shinensky Library as a result of the bequest made by the Adlers.

The new millennium has brought educational changes and challenges to the South Florida community. Similar to the emigration of Russian citizens and the Resettlement Program for Soviet Refugee Families in 1989–90, Latin American families from Argentina, Venezuela, and Colombia continue to move into South Florida. These families have created their own synagogues and cultural centers. In cases where they have joined synagogues and enrolled in existing day schools, they have established their own unique groups.

As in the secular world of education, Jewish education has entered a period of a critical teacher shortage. With expanded opportunities for women, and with little financial incentives to attract talented people to Jewish education, educators in South Florida are actively discussing methods for attracting and retaining talented teachers in the schools. Once again the concept of a College of Jewish Studies is being discussed with opportunities for Jewish leaders in education to take the lead in creating a corps of knowledgeable teachers. A renaissance of Jewish commitment is required to address the needs of future generations.

This essay is based on my doctoral dissertation "The Central Agency for Jewish Education: Fifty Years of Jewish Education in Dade County."

1. Irving Lehrman and J. Rappaport, *The Jewish Community of Miami Beach*. New York: Jewish Theological Seminary, 1956.

2. G. Rosen, "The Rabbi in Miami," in *Turn to the South: Essays on Southern Jewry*, ed. N. M. Kagonoff and M. I. Urofshy, 33–43. Northvale, N.J.: Jason Aronshon, 1979.

3. L. Gartner, *Jewish Education in the United States: A Documentary History*. New York: Teachers College, 1969.

4. J. Pilch, *A History of Jewish Education in the United States*, 119–76. New York: American Association of Jewish Education, 1969.

5. D. D. Moore, *To the Golden Cities: Pursuing the American Jewish Dream in Miami and L.A.* New York: Free Press, 1994.

6. Alvin I. Schiff, *The Jewish Day School in America*. New York: Jewish Education Committee Press, 1968.

7. Alvin I. Schiff, "Jewish Education in the United States: Three Comments," in *Jewish Education World—Cross-Cultural Perspectives*, ed. Harold S. Himmelfarb and Sergio DellaPergola, 123–29. Landham, Md.: University Press of America, 1989.

8. E. S. Shapiro, *A Time for Healing: American Jews since World War II*. Baltimore, Md.: Johns Hopkins University Press, 1992.

Joanie Glickstein

A History of the National Council of Jewish Women, Greater Miami Section

For more than 120 years, the National Council of Jewish Women, the oldest Jewish women's volunteer organization in the United States, has provided a framework for women committed to the Jewish principle of *Tikkun Olam* (repairing the world) to carry out their mission of improving the quality of life for women, children, and families, and striving to ensure individual rights and freedom for all. Through programs of research, education, advocacy, and community service in sections around the country, NCJW volunteers have touched hundreds of thousands of lives, both through direct services to specific populations in need and to the community at large.

In South Florida, the Greater Miami Section, in addition to Kendall Section and several sections in Broward County, has been the training ground for women who have gone on to positions of national leadership in NCJW, as well as other organizations, and to elected offices locally and statewide. This pattern is not unique to South Florida: one can find women around the country who attribute their professional skills to the training they received as volunteer leaders in the National Council of Jewish Women.

To understand how this individual growth occurs, we must examine the history of the Greater Miami Section: its projects, programs, and interconnectedness to the national organization. The NCJW was founded in Chicago in 1893 by Hannah Greenebaum Solomon, a social activist searching for a new woman. She asked, "Who is this new woman? . . . She is the woman who dares to go into the world and do what her convictions demand." The NCJW's national pamphlet, "The NCJW Story: Daring to Make a Difference" (published in 2001), provides a decade-by-decade timeline, enumerating the NCJW's groundbreaking impact on American society.

In the late nineteenth and early twentieth centuries, the NCJW pioneered the settlement-house movement (working with Jane Addams's Hull House in Chicago), provided vocational training for girls and women, developed school health programs, fought to bring about low-income housing, child labor laws, and public health programs, worked for women's suffrage, and championed Margaret Sanger's National Birth Control League. When the federal government turned to the NCJW to assist with the processing and absorption of new immigrants, the NCJW provided a permanent immigrant aid station on Ellis Island and helped to settle sixty-five thousand immigrants in port cities nationwide.

In 1918, a group of twelve women in Miami met in the living room of Ida Cohen (Mrs. Isidor; wife of Dade County's first Jewish settler and founder of Beth David

Congregation) and formed the Daughters of Israel, which was chartered in 1921 as the Greater Miami Section (GMS) of the National Council of Jewish Women, when its membership reached fifty women. From its earliest days, the GMS followed the lead of the national organization in its work with immigrants, and lent assistance to Russian and Polish refugees living in Cuba. The women organized food drives for the needy at Passover, distributing food locally and sending packages of food and clothing to Cuba and to settlers in Palestine. The GMS also provided assistance to the victims of the devastating hurricane of 1926. During the years prior to World War II, GMS volunteers organized English lessons for new Americans, assisted immigrants in job placement, became the local cooperating agency of the Hebrew Immigrant Aid Society (HIAS), were responsible for port and dock reception of German refugees, assisted in the naturalization process of new immigrants and were instrumental in the organization and establishment of the Greater Miami Jewish Federation in 1937. During the war, these programs continued, but the section was also involved in all levels of the war effort.

Additionally, study groups were formed on legislative issues and consumer welfare education. According to Myra Farr, past president of the Greater Miami Section and an honorary national vice president, these groups were very detailed, with tables for each subject moderated by an expert. Reports to the entire group were provided at the end of the day. "We were watchdogs of the legislative process, early precursors of the Tallahassee Institute," said Farr. Public forums, debates and educational programs, sponsored by the NCJW, often in coalition with other like-minded women's groups, have remained an important service to members and the community at large to this day. Additionally, advocacy training and face-to-face meetings with legislators at the state and national level continue to be a major focus of the NCJW's efforts to effect societal change (figures 1 and 2). The organization is well known on Capitol Hill in Washington, D.C., where many of its leaders have testified at congressional hearings on a variety of topics ranging from education to aging. In 1991, Representative William Lehman of South Florida read Greater Miami Section into the Congressional Record for its history of community service (figure 3).

FIGURE 1. *Members of greater Miami Section meeting with Representative Claude Pepper in Washington, D.C., at the NCJW's 1971 Joint Program Institute. Courtesy National Council of Jewish Women, Greater Miami Section.*

FIGURE 2. *Senator Lawton Chiles of Florida is hosted by members of the Dade delegation (Greater Miami Section, NCJW) at a congressional reception.* Left to right: *Betsy Singer, Senator Chiles, Arlene Pritcher, Nanci Goldstein, Evelyn Cohan. Courtesy National Council of Jewish Women, Greater Miami Section.*

FIGURE 3. *Greater Miami Section, NCJW, is entered in the Congressional Record, 1991.* Left to right: *Annette Zipper, Myra Farr, Representative William Lehman, Nancy Luria Cohen, Theodora Skolnick. Courtesy National Council of Jewish Women, Greater Miami Section.*

The postwar era brought new issues to the forefront of the NCJW's local, national, and international agenda. The Ship-a-Box program, established to provide toys, books, and educational materials to children abroad, primarily in Palestine and war-torn communities of Europe, struck a chord in the women of the GMS. Events were organized to raise funds specifically for this program and volunteers spent countless hours purchasing, organizing, and packing materials that were shipped to Hungary, France, and the newly born State of Israel. Children in synagogue and day schools were encouraged to fill the *Tzedakah* boxes distributed by the section throughout the city. For more than fifty years, the NCJW's Ship-a-Box provided generations of Israeli children, as well as soldiers in rehabilitation centers, with materials that improved their physical and intellectual skills (figure 4).

This concern for the needs of children led to the Greater Miami Section's leadership in providing the youth of South Florida, particularly physically and mentally challenged youth, with the resources to participate more equitably in the educational process. In 1947, following a survey of educational needs for the hearing impaired, the NCJW funded a pilot project for hearing-impaired children of preschool age. The impetus for this survey came when the mother of a deaf child, a close friend of an active NCJW member, approached the section with her concern about the lack of services for her child in the Miami area. A similar survey of sight-impaired children in the early 1950s led to the establishment of a program at Miramar School, for which the GMS provided financial and volunteer assistance. Originally, the NCJW offered to fund the cost of a teacher, but when the county paid the salary for one staff person, the NCJW purchased talking books, Braille typewriters, Braille slates, stylus, paper and textbooks, and play equipment. Both programs were eventually adopted by Dade County Schools, following massive efforts on the part of NCJW's social services and legislative departments to have laws enacted allowing these children admission to public schools.

This pattern of providing seed money and volunteers for needs in the community and then passing on the continued development of the program to established agencies allows NCJW to refocus its energies and resources as new needs arise. The GMS maintained its involvement with the sight- impaired community, however, for many years. Beginning in 1954, NCJW organized Braille classes for volunteers

FIGURE 4. *Ship-a-Box container, 1991. Courtesy National Council of Jewish Women, Greater Miami Section.*

willing to transcribe printed texts. In 1956, the section founded its Braille Bindery Library Project, a model for similar projects in other communities around the country. Twenty-seven volunteers assisted more than one hundred sight-impaired children, adults, and their teachers. In addition to binding Braille books, these volunteers staffed a lending library for these individuals. The *Miami Herald* twice recognized the NCJW, GMS with its Club of the Year Award: in 1956 for its Sight-Handicapped Program and in 1961 for the Braille Bindery Library Project.

In 1949, neither educational nor custodial care for the mentally retarded was available in the county. The single facility in Central Florida had a waiting list of several years. The Haven School for the Retarded was established and the NCJW, in partnership with other women's clubs, among them the Jaycee Auxiliary, Navy Fleet Reserve Auxiliary, Homestead Women's Club, South Florida and West End Garden Clubs, Coral Gables Women's Club, and Miami Music Club, provided furnishings for the new institution.

Throughout its history, the Greater Miami Section has maintained its emphasis on projects and programs concerned with the welfare and support of children in the community: funding of child care centers in public-housing developments such as Larchmont Gardens in 1973, as well as at the South Dade Jewish Community Center; involvement in Tay-Sachs screening programs (initiated once again by a member whose child suffered from the disease); establishing South Florida's first crisis intervention nursery in 1980; helping to develop and fund religious school programs for physically and mentally challenged Jewish children, KESHER; establishing the Guardian ad Litem Program, protecting the rights of dependent children in court proceedings, CHARLEE (Children Have All Rights, Legal, Educational, Emotional), and HIPPY (Home Instruction Program for Pre-school Youngsters), a home-based program for the educational enrichment of disadvantaged preschool children; providing holiday gifts for children in foster care; purchasing equipment and supplies for Resourcemobile, a mobile resource unit for family day care providers (figure 5); introducing the Safe Child Project to the community; funding legal interns for Voices for Children; sponsoring the Teen Dating Violence and Intervention project in Dade County Middle Schools; providing seed money for GAP (Girls' Advocacy Project) Girls' Club; funding materials for the Bully-Proofing Your School project in several Dade County Public Schools; and advocating locally, statewide, and nationally for issues promoting the health and well-being of all children, particularly in the legislative arena.

According to the timeline published by the national NCJW, the decade of the 1970s was a time when the national organization focused particularly on children and childcare. In 1972, the NCJW published "Windows on Day Care," a landmark nationwide study that was the first to raise awareness of the growing crisis in childcare. It also published "Children Without Justice," setting up services for children in shelters, group homes, and the courts. A comprehensive manual on child abuse detection and prevention, "Innocent Victims," followed soon after. The NCJW received four major awards for work with CASA (Court Appointed Special Advocates), and played a leading role in the first White House Conference on Families. Sections around the country followed National's lead, using the data from these

FIGURE 5. *Resourcemobile dedication, 1990.* Left to Right: *Annette Zipper, Greater Miami Section president; Nan Rich, founding president of Resourcemobile. Courtesy National Council of Jewish Women, Greater Miami Section.*

FIGURE 6. *Child care luncheon, 1973.* Seated, left to right: *Janet Reno, Elaine Bloom, Mona Lighte.* Standing, left to right: *Doris Rich, Bea Kazan, Sophie Thaw, Nanci Goldstein, Florence Tamarkin, Mitzi Garfield, Anna Singer. Courtesy National Council of Jewish Women, Greater Miami Section.*

publications to set up programs and projects addressing these priority issues. The Greater Miami Section seized the opportunity to improve the lives of abused, abandoned, and neglected children of all ages (figure 6).

South Florida's first crisis nursery, located in Coconut Grove, came into being largely through the combined lobbying efforts over a two-year period of the NCJW, The Dade County Federation of Jr. Women's Clubs, and the Parent Resource Center. Its goal was to provide a cost-free, all-night nursery where parents who felt that they were on the verge of abusing their children could leave them in a safe environment. The lobbying efforts resulted in the crisis nursery receiving a portion of the $440,000 grant given by the state to the Department of Health and Rehabilitative Services for child abuse treatment. The NCJW provided additional funding and volunteers.

Once again networking with other women's organizations, this time with the Junior League, the Greater Miami Section was instrumental in bringing the CASA project to Florida, where it became known as the Guardian ad Litem program. Over the past twenty years, abused, abandoned, and neglected children who find themselves adjudicated as dependents of the court have been represented by volunteers, whose sole responsibility is to see that these children receive the treatment and services they deserve and are ordered to receive by the court. Many of the volunteers have been NCJW members, and some of those involved in the Guardian program as professionals have joined the organization because of its substantial efforts on behalf of children.

One of those professionals, Cindy Lerner, who was a lawyer for the Guardian ad Litem program for several years, not only joined the NCJW (Greater Miami and Kendall Sections), but became state public affairs chair of the organization, helping to guide NCJW advocacy efforts statewide on a wide range of issues. She recently served a term as state representative in the Florida Legislature from South Dade and shared these thoughts: "NCJW taught me how to translate my passion for children's issues into effective legislative advocacy. On my first NCJW trip to Tallahassee, meeting other women legislators with an NCJW background, I realized that I could one day be the one changing the policies, being an advocate from the inside."

Many other South Florida NCJW leaders have moved into the political arena. Broward County Commissioner Sue Gunzberger, State Representative Eleanor Sobel (a former NCJW state public affairs co-chair), and Mayor Mara Giulianti of Hollywood (former national board member) are among them. Two of the Greater Miami Section's past presidents, Elaine Bloom and Nan Rich, have gone on to serve in the Florida State Legislature. Bloom is often heard to claim that her first experience in public speaking was at an NCJW event, and when she introduced the speaker, she was so nervous her knees were knocking. Her experiences in leadership positions in NCJW, however, gave her the skills, knowledge, and confidence to run for public office. Rich began her campaign for state office shortly after completing her three-year term as national president of NCJW, 1996–99. She stated, "It was an easy transition from the volunteer world to political office because of the public policy issues. I was approached to run for the legislature because I knew all the issues." Two of the projects mentioned earlier, CHARLEE and HIPPY, were established under Rich's section presidency and her term as state public affairs chair.

It became apparent after publication of the NCJW's national survey, "Girls in the Juvenile Justice System," that there was a need in this area for long-term residential placement facilities for girls. The NCJW joined forces once again with the Junior League and the Episcopal Diocese of South Florida to lobby the state legislature for funding. Three Miami legislators, Elaine Gordon, Gwen Margolis, and Jack Gordon, fought for a separate line item in the budget for CHARLEE, amounting to several hundred thousand dollars. The first CHARLEE House on Biscayne Boulevard and 73rd Street was purchased and renovated. Broward County soon followed suit, led by Barbara Miller, who later became Rich's NCJW co–state public affairs chair. CHARLEE in Dade County grew to five houses, despite major zoning fights in which the NCJW advocated publicly and vocally; it is at present providing supportive foster care for eight hundred children. The Greater Miami Section maintains a tie to CHARLEE with a representative on its board, as well as individual participation by NCJW members in supporting CHARLEE's work, including Nan Rich, who served as its second president.

As a member of the NCJW's national board (following her section presidency in 1981–83), Nan Rich traveled to Israel for visits to the NCJW's Research Institute for Innovation in Education (RIFIE), founded in 1968 at Hebrew University to study education techniques for at-risk children from all segments of Israeli society. During field trips to HIPPY projects, where parents with limited formal schooling are helped to provide educational enrichment at home for their preschool children, it was obvious to Nan and other board members that this program would work in the United States. In 1984, a Ford Foundation grant was used to bring American educators to Israel to study HIPPY and its possible application in this country. Tulsa, Oklahoma, became the first city to offer HIPPY and the NCJW section there was among the initial supporters. In 1985, the Greater Miami Section moved to bring HIPPY to this community. Paul Bell, the assistant superintendent of schools, applied $25,000 from a state grant for prekindergarten education, along with $10,000 from the Greater Miami Section, to start HIPPY in Dade County.

By a fortunate coincidence, in 1985 Hillary Clinton, then first lady of Arkansas, was in Miami for the Southern Governors' Conference at the same time as HIPPY's debut. Reading about the project in the local newspaper, Clinton had her aide contact Nan Rich and invited her to an early childhood conference in Arkansas. HIPPY Arkansas opened in 1986 after five educators from that state flew to Israel to learn about the program. HIPPY outgrew the NCJW, so HIPPY USA was created with Miriam Westheimer as its first director. Westheimer had been with the NCJW's Center for the Child, an institute established to apply research to children's issues and to effect public policy. Today, HIPPY USA has 120 programs in twenty-six states, plus the District of Columbia and Guam, serving more than fifteen thousand families. Florida HIPPY programs serve sixteen thousand children in sixteen counties. Funding continues to be a battle that Nan Rich fights in Tallahassee (figure 7). Is it any wonder that she says of NCJW:

> It is a thinking woman's organization. The kind of women who get involved are progressive women. The organization gave me the opportunity to express my commitment to social justice and *Tikkun Olam* (repairing the world). It gave me the ability to fulfill the Jewish expression of my life; to work with all kinds of people and women from across the country and Israel who are dedicated to raising the consciousness of others to unmet needs and correcting societal problems. We are dedicated to making a difference in people's lives.

In 1992, the Greater Miami Section brought an innovative program to Dade County that taught children assertiveness, independence, and communication skills, called Safe Child. Alarmed over rising child abuse statistics, the group, led by co-chair Nancy Kipnis (also co-chair of state public affairs at the time and at present a national vice president), searched for an educational tool that would provide children, particularly preschoolers, with the skills to protect themselves. Aided

by the NCJW's Center for the Child, the committee established Sherryll Kraizer's program, a combination of videotapes, role-playing exercises, and scripted explanations by classroom teachers. Safe Child was piloted at three synagogue preschools and, after several years, was incorporated by Dade County Schools into their curriculum.

Over the last several decades, social issues confronting our nation such as poverty, civil rights, the aging of our population, women's equality and reproductive rights, domestic violence and gun control have echoed in the meeting rooms and homes of NCJW members around the country. Speakers, study groups, and surveys have recommended solutions at every level of the organization, from national to district to area to section to branch. Resolutions have been passed at national conventions, providing a framework for the work done by sections under the aegis of the national organization. Following World War II, the NCJW launched a "Speak Up for Freedom" campaign to protect civil liberties during the McCarthy era and started an interethnic coalition, "Freedom to Read," to combat censorship. It was the first Jewish organization to develop Meals on Wheels programs around the country.

In the 1960s the NCJW helped organize the first White House Conference on Aging; began the Senior Service Corps, which later became the government's Retired Senior Volunteer Program (RSVP); helped launch Women in Community Service (WICS), an interfaith effort to help low-income young women find jobs and other assistance (Martha Myers, past Greater Miami Section president and national board member became national WICS president in 1969); promoted voter education and registration following passage of the Voting Rights Act; joined civil rights coalitions to fight segregation; and helped train teachers for the Head Start Program. During the 1980s the NCJW, in coalition with other groups, conducted silent vigils at the Soviet Embassy in Washington, D.C., to free Soviet Jewry; published "Domestic Violence—An NCJW Response"; and continued the post–Roe v. Wade fight for women's reproductive choice.

As the 1990s brought us closer to the new millennium, the NCJW continued to turn its beliefs into action. It held a National Day of the Working Parent to focus attention on the needs of working families; launched Strategies to Prevent (StoP) Domestic Violence (a national initiative, including hundreds of education and action projects); participated in White House conferences on race relations, hate crimes, child care, and early childhood development; reissued an updated "Windows on Child Care" and advocated making quality, accessible, affordable child care a key issue in national elections; began providing financial support to Israeli programs for at-risk women, children, and families through Yad b'Yad (Hand in Hand). The NCJW's Promote the Vote campaign in 2000 was supported by sections nationwide and BenchMark: the NCJW's Campaign to Save Roe (whose national chair is GMS member and national vice president Nancy Kipnis) has used the advantages of computer technology to create the electronic ability for members and nonmembers alike to voice their opposition to federal court appointees unwilling to uphold women's right to choose (figure 8).

This overwhelming array of opportunities to make a difference in the future of our nation is only matched by the multiplicity of programs on the section level that complement all of the above. Following World War II, the GMS assisted immigrants from displaced persons camps and also created the United Restitution Office to help expedite the paperwork for Holocaust survivors applying for restitution from the German government. South Florida was home to a large population of survivors who were able to receive economic assistance as a result of this project. Soviet immigrants were assisted in the late 1970s by a coalition of NCJW volun-

FIGURE 8. *Washington Institute, 2001. Left to right: Penny Pensack, co-vice chair of the event, Marsha Atkind, chair; Jan Schneiderman, NCJW national president; Nancy Swerdlow Kipnis (GMS), co-vice chair. Courtesy National Council of Jewish Women, Greater Miami Section.*

teers and Federation funds. Judy Levin, recipient of the NCJW's 1979 Hannah G. Solomon Award for her work in this field, said, "Volunteerism is an act of loving kindness at the core of Jewish values."

According to an article by Martha Ingle in the July 16, 1968, issue of the *Miami Herald*, in the wake of the 1968 publication of the report of the National Advisory Commission on Civil Disorders (also known as the Kerner Report), the GMS, Greater Miami YWCA, and the Tropical Council of Girl Scouts responded with discussion groups and seminars, hoping to bring out personal feelings about racial tensions. In the late 1960s, the Greater Miami Section became involved in building a nonprofit, low-cost, urban-renewal housing project, Larchmont Gardens. They joined the Greater Miami Coalition, an interracial group of civic, business, and city government leaders that was part of the National Urban Coalition. According to the *Miami Herald* of September 5, 1968, Section President Reva Wexler stated, "I'm very happy it passed. Council has always been in the forefront of meeting human needs . . . and decent housing is among the first and most basic of these needs today." Five years later, the GMS funded the creation of the Larchmont Gardens Child Care Center on the site of the housing project.

During Wexler's second term of office as president of the section, an incident occurred related to race relations in South Florida. The NCJW was the only Jewish organization at the time to be a member of the Dade County Federation of Women's Clubs. According to Wexler, this membership was seen as a crowning achievement for the group. In a forgotten context, Wexler saw that the constitution of the umbrella organization read that "white women only" were permitted membership in the federation. As the NCJW was in the forefront of support for civil rights and affirmative action, Wexler was outraged: "I was an activist. I was passionate about my job and told them that in today's world such a clause didn't belong there. Their response to this objection was, 'If you don't like it, you are free to leave.'" When the issue was brought to the section board's attention, they voted to withdraw from the Federation of Women's Clubs. Reva Wexler went on to become president of Greater Miami Jewish Federation's Women's Division, as well as a professional with the Jewish Federation of South Broward as a trainer for their volunteer solicitors.

Services for the aging of the community were also a priority for the Greater Miami Section. Section members were involved as volunteers at the Miami Jewish Home for the Aged, not as part of the home's auxiliary, but as NCJW members. In 1964, the section initiated a senior citizens' program, offering recreational programming at senior day centers throughout Dade County. In 1974, the section instituted Telecare, a project that paired members with elderly citizens living on their own. The seniors received daily phone calls from their "buddies," ensuring that they were well and safe in their homes.

As the issue of domestic violence and spousal abuse gained awareness, the GMS joined the community coalition of Jewish women's groups, Shalom Bayit, cosponsoring events such as candlelight vigils and educational seminars. In addition, in 1997, the section became the caretakers for the Silent Witness Initiative, a project to create greater public awareness and elimination of domestic violence. Public displays of life-sized silhouettes honor and memorialize women and girls who have died in Florida from domestic violence. These silhouettes are made available to schools and other groups to use in the context of education and consciousness-raising.

Over the last ten to fifteen years, the nature of the volunteer has changed, not just in the Jewish community, but in the secular nonprofit world, as well. More women are in the workforce, dividing their time at home between family responsibilities and community obligations. Young women, especially, are looking for opportunities to improve the lives of women, children, and families with a time commitment that fits into the rest of their lives. The National Council of Jewish Women continues to offer a broad spectrum of projects and programs to attract, as Nan Rich said, "the thinking woman who wants to make a difference." A member of the NCJW, Greater Miami Section's new generation of leadership, Nancy Kipnis, credits the NCJW with providing opportunities for her to apply her legal experience to issues that resonate with her: "Collaborating with like-souled women across the country who share the same commitment to activism and progressive ideals has enabled me to truly integrate my professional skills, my Jewish values, and my core beliefs." She also believes that her experience in the NCJW has given her the opportunity to transform her beliefs into social activism.

"I am currently president of my temple," Kipnis continues, "a very large Reform congregation on Miami Beach. I am the second woman in the sixty-year history of this congregation to hold this position. I am certain the extraordinary leadership opportunities I enjoy as an NCJW national leader prepared me to undertake this position in my congregation and greatly influenced my actions, vision, and courage in all aspects of my life."

The Greater Miami Section of the National Council of Jewish Women has had a powerful influence in its eighty-two-year history, both on the community it has served and continues to serve, and on the women who have nurtured and been nurtured by it. Many of them, as we have seen, have used their NCJW experience as a springboard to positions of local and national leadership, as well as political office. In the process, they have worked to fulfill Hannah G. Solomon's call for the new woman "who dares to go into the world and do what her convictions demand."

Andrea Greenbaum

Yizkor

Not to remember means to side with the executioners against its victims; not to remember means to kill the victims a second time; not to remember means to become an accomplice of the enemy.
—Elie Wiesel, Holocaust Memorial Dedication, February 4, 1990

For Jews, the fundamental concept of *yizkor* is simple: recall the souls of the dead and contribute to charity in their honor and memory. The belief is that when physical life ends, the soul can no longer perform good deeds; thus the obligation falls to the living to give *tzedakah*, so that the departed can derive new sources of merit. So too might we view the erection of a Holocaust Memorial as an opportunity for the descendants of the dead to remember those whom they lost, pay tribute to the good deeds of those who perished, and for "the children of Holocaust survivors [a chance], to remember a world they never knew, an act of recovery whereby they locate themselves in a continuous past" (Young 285).

The difficulty, however, in creating a physical space, a metonymic substitution that stands for the Holocaust, far removed from the "topography of terror" (Young 283) of European memorials, is that the builders, no matter their good intentions, risk creating a narrative that either sensationalizes or inadvertently trivializes and packages the experiences of survivors. As Geoffrey Hartman asks in *The Longest Shadow: In the Aftermath of the Holocaust*, "Will our Holocaust museums become a series of macabre theme parks?" (12). Or can the construction of memory offer a genuine experience of history?

At the Miami Holocaust Memorial, like many memorials throughout the country, it is the Holocaust survivors themselves who offer that experience of history, giving life to the unavoidably inanimate structure. It is their testimony that "keeps the events before our eyes. The volume of testimonies is remarkable; it not only contradicts the notion of the Holocaust as an inexpressible experience (though that retains an emotional truth) but creates an internally complex field of study" (Hartman, *Holocaust* 6).

Currently, there are twenty-five active Holocaust survivor volunteers, and it is their constant presence at the memorial, whether working the information window or walking through the memorial with visitors, their narratives, that transforms the experience from one of removed intellectual encounter to visceral experience.

The Miami Holocaust Memorial

On April 5, 1985, Kenneth Treister was commissioned by a group of Holocaust survivors to create a sculpture dedicated to the memory of the Six Million. The group was called the Holocaust Memorial Committee, and it was composed of Norman

Braman, chairman, Jack Chester, Dr. Helen Fagin, George Goldbloom, Abe Resnick, and David Schaecter (figure 1). An experienced sculptor, Treister's daunting task was to create a memorial that, in his words, paid tribute to a "lost civilization," a culture that was systemically decimated, a culture that had inhabited Europe for thousands of years. Treister researched several memorials and traveled to Jerusalem to study the archives at Yad Vashem, Israel's Holocaust memorial museum.

The Miami Holocaust Memorial project took five years to develop. Treister went to Mexico to do the bulk of his sculpture work at a foundry: Fundición Artística. Working at the foundry, it took Treister three years to cast the memorial's bronze sculpture (figure 2). It took another year and half to enlarge the marquette to full size in plaster and then cast in bronze.

In constructing the memorial, Treister decided not to use barbed wire and twisted steel ("The materials of war and destruction") but, rather, to incorporate more organic elements by creating a garden with a reflection pool that contains blooming white water lilies, and a colonnade resplendent with white bougainvillea. He also used Jerusalem stone and a forest of palms (Triester 13) (figure 3). Like the survivors' narratives, Treister's memorial tells a story, and its circular architecture, with its seven distinct "chapters," allows for the unfolding of events, beginning, as all compelling stories do, with characters.

THE BEGINNING SCULPTURE

The first sculpture a visitor encounters depicts a nameless mother shielding her two children. In back of her, on the wall, an inscription from Anne Frank: "Then, in spite of everything, I believe that people are really good at heart." It is the irony of that inscription that sets the tone for the rest of the memorial; by the time the

FIGURE 1. *Holocaust Memorial Committee, Miami, April 5, 1985.* Left to right: *Jack Chester, Helen Fagin, Abe Resnick, Kenneth Treister, Norman Braman, Harry Smith, George Goldblum, and David Schaecter. Ezra Katz and Rabbi Soloman Schiff (not pictured). Photo by Charles Treister. Courtesy of the Holocaust Memorial Committee Inc., Kenneth Treister, FAIA, Al Barg and Jeff Weisberg.*

visitor journeys through to the gruesome end, Frank's words ring painfully naive and hollow.

The Beginning Sculpture also has special meaning for Holocaust Memorial volunteer and survivor, Ann Rosenheck. Born 1931, in the Carpathian Mountains of Czechoslovakia, in a small town called Rachov that one of her great-great-grandfathers had started in the 1700s, she was sent to Hungary in March 1944.

"German troops came in and said we had twenty minutes to pack," she recounts. She was thirteen at the time, and was with both her parents, and her sister with her two children. A kind family had let them stay in a stable, but four weeks later she was taken to Auschwitz. She recalls getting onto the cattle cars. "Poppa and myself pushed Mama up. It was unreal," Ann remembers. There were one hundred and

FIGURE 2. *The Foundary, Mexico City, 1988. Courtesy of the Holocaust Memorial Committee Inc., Kenneth Treister, FAIA, Al Barg and Jeff Weisberg.*

FIGURE 3. *The Great Hand of the Memorial reaches toward the sky. Like many survivors, its forearm is tattooed with a number. Photographed by Al Barg and Jeff Weisberg. Courtesy of the Holocaust Memorial Committee Inc., Kenneth Treister, FAIA, Al Barg and Jeff Weisberg.*

FIGURE 4. *The Beginning Statue reminds Holocaust survivor Ann Rosenheck of the sacrifices her mother made for her survival. Photographed October 21, 2002, by Andrea Greenbaum.*

nine people in a single cattle car. She recalls that they brought in two buckets: one for water and one for human waste. "We had an advantage," Rosenheck explains. She and her family stood by a hole in the cattle car, which allowed them to "stick our fingers out to get water, but at night we were cool."

It took four and a half days to arrive at Auschwitz. Men and women were separated. "Mama didn't come down. The S.S. is chasing us with guns and dogs." She also notes that her mother was "never bare-headed." And when her mother finally emerged from the train, another inmate told her, "Nobody is younger than seventeen—nobody is older than thirty-eight." A little girl at the time, Ann tells me, she was wearing a braid, and so in order to make her look older, her mother had a plan.

"My mama took off her kerchief and put it on me. 'Now remember,' her mother told her, 'you are seventeen, say you were born in 1927, use the same birthday.'"

And so it was her mother's sacrifice, handing over her kerchief, that Rosenheck credits with saving her life. It was also the last time she saw her father. Her Mama, sister, and her two children came before the notorious Dr. Mengele and he had Ann alone go to the left side—right meant you went straight to the crematorium. She finds that even today she can't stomach the smell of barbeque. "Today if a barbeque is on . . . it has the same smell." In 1945 she was liberated from Dachau.

She says that the Beginning Sculpture has particular meaning for her: the mother figure of the sculpture, clinging to her two children, reminds her so poignantly of her own mother (figure 4).

FIGURE 5. *Young men liberated by American forces at Buchenwald, April 1945. Memorial volunteer Josek (Joe) Dziubak is one of the boys. Yad Vashem Archives. Courtesy of the Holocaust Memorial Committee Inc., Kenneth Treister, FAIA, Al Barg and Jeff Weisberg.*

FIGURE 6. *Holocaust volunteers. From Left to Right: Herbert Karliner, Joe Dziubak, and Arnie Erban stand in front of the Memorial. Photographed on October 21, 2002, by Andrea Greenbaum.*

THE ARBOR OF HISTORY

Passing from the first sculpture, the visitor encounters black granite panels etched with photographic history of the Holocaust. One of the panels displays a photograph of American forces liberating young men at Buchenwald in April 1945 (figure 5). Josek Dziubak (or "Joe," as he prefers to be called) is one of those young men in the photograph. A Holocaust survivor and one of the first volunteers at the memorial, Dziubak points out the photograph to those who visit the memorial (figure 6). Dziubak was born in Lodz, Poland, September 6, 1925. His mother was widowed at an early age, and in order to make a living, Dziubak and his five siblings worked with leather, making soles for shoes. "It was a rough life," he admits. But it was about to get worse.

In 1939, the German army had moved in, and as Dziubak recalls, "We already had knowledge of what Hitler was doing." Hitler made his way into Lodz, and on September 2, the lights went out. In the ghetto, Dziubak worked at a leather factory making harnesses and saddles. But when the Germans liquidated the ghetto, he and his family were taken in cattle cars to Birkanau. When they got off the train, he recalls that the grim selection was made: "Men on this side, women on this side. My mother was holding my hand . . . a trustee, a capo that was there before, a Jewish guy, said [to my mother] let him go, just let him go to the other side. My mother let go of my hand. Nobody knew that there were gas chambers. Who ever heard of gas chambers? Nobody knew."

Dziubak also recalls another incident when he stepped off the train; he overheard two capos talking. One said to the other, " 'Look at the smoke; they're burning yesterday's transport.' " He was taken to a barracks where an S.S. officer picked out a hundred and twenty-one boys. These boys had numbers tattooed on their forearms. "The Poles told us, 'now you're going to live.' " The numbers meant they were to be used for the labor force. Alone, already separated from his family, along with thirty other boys, Dzuibak went to Auschwitz and did an assortment of jobs ranging from working on a farm, to picking up garbage and ashes from the crematorium.

In an attempt to dismantle the camps, the Germans sent the prisoners from Auschwitz to Buchenwald. Ultimately, as the photograph in the Arbor shows, he was liberated from Buchenwald. Afterward, he recounts, "We were sent to France, to an orphanage home, an organization called OSE." At the orphanage, Dziubak says Elie Wiesel was "three bunks away from me." Dziubak eventually made his way to the United States, where he worked as a busboy at Grossinger's Hotel in the Catskills. Today his focus, like the other survivors at the memorial, is singular: "I'm here to teach the kids."

THE DOME OF CONTEMPLATION

Moving from the Arbor of History, the visitor encounters the Dome of Contemplation, an area enclosed by a dome. Above, an eternal memorial flame, and the inscription from the twenty-third Psalm: "Yea, though I walk through the valley of the Shadow of Death, I will fear no evil, for thou art with me." For the first time, the visitor encounters music, a haunting Hebrew melody sung by children.

THE LONELY PATH

From there, a visitor moves down the Lonely Path (figure 7), where on the wall, engraved in stone, are the names of the concentration camps. A skylight projects a yellow Star of David.

Another Holocaust survivor volunteer, Nathan Glass, remembers when the order came to wear that Star of David. On September 1, 1939, Hitler invaded Poland, and Glass recalls that the "One thing we learned very fast. If you want to live, you obey the order." Born in Poland in Pabianice in 1922, Glass remembers,

"Anti-Semitism was every day. . . . We knew we were Jewish at every step. We went to a movie, a bunch of hooligans would beat you up. They knew from a Jew, they could take." Like most Jewish boys, Glass attended a *chedar* (a Hebrew school) and belonged to a Zionist organization.

When the Germans invaded, they took over Glass's father's textile factory. And like all the Jews, Glass was sent to live in the Lodz ghetto, where they were systematically starved. "The worst thing a human being can observe is hunger," Glass says. Nevertheless, Glass argues, in the midst of this starvation, madness, and murder, Jews continued to resist. "People said we went to the slaughter house like sheep. It's a lie. We did things. . . . It was not allowed to gather, so we created a young adults group. [We] said we would do everything in our power to educate the younger generation." It was their goal to keep Jewish values alive. Glass remembers that at the meetings they would sing Yiddish Zionist songs, and he sings a song for me, his voice strong and resonant. He translates the Yiddish for me: "I want to go home, I want to go home to Zion."

Glass maintains that the Jews attempted, as best they could, to construct a life within the confines of the ghetto, having a Jewish theater, and even playing soccer games where they took in a German policeman to referee. "We lived a 'normal life'—one thing you had to see to it that you don't get sick." Hospitals didn't have medications, and when the Germans went into the hospitals, they would remove the patients.

In the ghetto, Glass remembers, "we lived six people in a three-room apartment. We had to share our apartment with two other families. Twelve people in three rooms." Every now and then, in the ghettos, the Germans came in and took which-ever people they needed. "When you left the house, you never knew if you came back. They needed people to build the concentration camps. The Jews built the camps." When they liquidated the ghetto, Jews lined up in front of their apartment buildings, and the Germans marched them to a sports field. "The irony was that the Poles were standing as we walked, applauding, 'Bravo, there would be no Jews in our cities.' They took all the kids away." Glass notes, however, that his family was still together, and the Germans had them go back and clean up the ghetto.

Eventually, like the others, he was put on a cattle car; when the train doors opened, he found himself at Auschwitz. His first thought, when he smelled the smoke, was, "What is it? A bakery? A chimney? When I got off the train was the last time I saw my mother and my sisters, Esther, Rachel, and Florence." At the camp, Glass saw his father and brother, "and I was happy." In the barracks, Glass remembers that a man walked in and told him, "Guess what happened? They just removed one of my testicles."

At Auschwitz Glass worked in the crematorium and received extra rations. At the crematorium someone remarked to him, "I just burned my father and mother." This was life at Auschwitz. Glass was liberated by Americans, the Eighty-second Di-vision, and was sent to a displaced persons camp. He eventually found his brother, Morris, and he came to the United States to live with his uncle in Paterson, New Jersey.

As painful as the memories were, Glass knew he had to speak about the Holo-caust, and so, in the 1960s, he joined the New Jersey Speakers Bureau. "Somebody had to preach the gospel about the Holocaust." And Glass continues to do just that. Not only does he work at the memorial, he also volunteers at the Jewish Federation, visiting the lonely and sick. When he lectures at schools, he talks about tolerance. "We survivors don't hate, because we saw what hate can do" (figure 8).

THE SCULPTURE OF LOVE AND HATE

From the Lonely Path, a visitor moves to the ultimate sculpture, a giant out-stretched hand, marked by a number. "The sculpture represents my portrayal of a scene from hell ... frozen in bronze" (Treister 18). The grotesque sculptures that surround the hand are eerie in the accuracy of their depiction of human misery, and they are a frightening reflection of the photographs the visitor has earlier glimpsed in the Arbor of History: naked, human skeletons, barely clinging to life; dead bodies littering the ground (figure 9). The sculpture forces a visitor to react to its brutality. This is not a Steven Spielberg, Roberto Benigni version of the

Holocaust; rather, it is a horrific, brutal, confrontation with the visitor, challenging him or her to ask, as Elie Wiesel imagined a visitor might, "Was the killer really that cruel? Were the victims that hopeless, that lonely, that abandoned? How was it possible for an entire people, the Jewish people, to be singled out for humiliation and annihilation?" (Treister 9).

While to trace the origins of that cruelty is an impossibility, one Holocaust survivor and memorial volunteer, Herbert Karliner, remembers the experience of *Kristallnacht* ("the night of broken glass") as the beginning of the end. In Germany, on the night of November 9, 1938, Herbert Karliner remembers his father's store being ransacked, and the synagogues burning to the ground. "A Brown Shirt made a bonfire with books and a Torah," Karlinger recalls. "My father tried to retrieve it. He was kicked."

The Cuban Council in Hamburg was selling permits to go to Cuba, and the German government gave a luxury liner for the Jews: the S.S. *St. Louis* (Figure 10). On May 13, 1939, Karliner recalls the exhilaration he felt as they boarded the ship. "For us children it was very exciting, a big adventure. We had a wonderful trip. The weather was beautiful, the food was good. The German captain was fantastic" (figure 11).

The ship arrived in Havana, and this is where Karliner says that he learned his first Spanish word: *mañana*. "But *mañana* never came." After seven days the ship was ordered to leave Havana. "Outside Miami, I remember well," Karliner reflects. "I saw beautiful homes. I was 12½ years old, 'This place, I'm going to come back some day.'" The ship returned to Germany, and Karliner and his brother made their way to France to the Jewish Children's home, where he was sent to work at a

FIGURE 9. *The Hand. The tattoo number was chosen at random. Courtesy of the Holocaust Memorial Committee Inc., Kenneth Treister, FAIA, Al Barg and Jeff Weisberg.*

FIGURE 10. *Passengers on the S.S. St. Louis, 1939. Courtesy Jewish Museum of Florida.*

FIGURE 11. *Herbert Karliner as a child with his father aboard the S.S. St. Louis, 1939. Courtesy Jewish Museum of Florida.*

bakery in a small village. "One morning the French police came and arrested me and took me to a camp where all the Jews were taken. They took boys over sixteen and it was one week from my sixteenth birthday. Those boys were taken and they never came back."

Karliner's uncle sent a visa for him to come to the United States and in 1947 he went to Hartford, Connecticut, and then to Florida. He takes solace in his work at the Holocaust Memorial and believes, frighteningly, that "It can happen again—even here in the United States," even as he maintains that "America is a wonderful country."

THE MEMORIAL WALL

From the horror of the Sculpture of Love and Anguish, the visitor comes upon the Memorial Wall, a black granite wall etched with the names of victims. The names were submitted to the memorial by the families of Holocaust survivors.

It is here that the executive director of the memorial, Avi Mizrachi, bends to point out his own relative's name etched onto the granite (figure 12). Mizrachi's association with the memorial goes back to 1987, when he was involved with the construction company that built the Memorial. Working with the Holocaust Committee and Treister, Mizrachi became more involved in the memorial project, moving from a construction position to that of executive director. "In the past six or seven years," Mizrachi remarks, "we really started to establish this memorial as a focus for Holocaust education."

Mizrachi's direction has helped the memorial develop a lecture series with al-

FIGURE 12. *Holocaust Memorial Executive Director Avi Mizrachi points out his relative's name on the black granite walls of the memorial. Photographed October 21, 2002, by Andrea Greenbaum.*

liances with different organizations, including Florida International University, various synagogues, and March of the Living. The memorial also publishes a newsletter and was even used as a site for a recent Rally for Israel on Yom HaShoah. The memorial survives on private donations and grants.

THE FINAL SCULPTURE

The visitor arrives at the end of the memorial: the mother and her two children we saw at the beginning of the journey now lie crumbled in death. Above their heads, etched into the wall, a more somber, less idealistic quote from Anne Frank: "Ideals, dreams, and cherished hopes rise within us only to meet the horrible truths and be shattered."

We are coming to a historical end of firsthand Holocaust narratives: all that will remain will be Holocaust museums and memorials. It is inevitable, as Geoffrey Hartman notes, that "education will have to replace all eyewitness transmission of those experiences" (*Longest* 5). But what a loss it will be: not to hear their Eastern European accents, not to see the blue dye of their numbered tattoos on their tired skin, not to hear them say, "I was there, I saw, I know."

REFERENCES

Hartman, Geoffrey H, ed. *Holocaust Remembrance: The Shapes of Memory*. Oxford: Blackwell, 1994.

———. *The Longest Shadow: In the Aftermath of the Holocaust*. Bloomington: Indiana University Press, 1996.

Holocaust Memorial: A Sculpture of Love and Anguish. Video. Kenneth Treister, sculptor. Narration by Chaim Topol. Introduction by Elie Wiesel. N.d.

Interviews conducted with Nathan Glass, Herbert Karliner, Ann Rosenheck, and Joe Dzuibek. September 2002–May 2003.

Treister, Kenneth. *A Sculpture of Love and Anguish: The Holocaust Memorial, Miami Beach, Florida*. New York: S.p.i. Books, 1993.

Young, James E. *The Texture of Memory: Holocaust Memorials and Meaning*. New Haven: Yale University Press, 1993.

David Weintraub

Behind the Pastel Facade

*Yiddish is the secret language my parents spoke when they didn't want me to hear.
Now that I've unlocked the door to Yiddish, I realize how much I've missed!"*
—A current Yiddish student

YIDDISH

CULTURAL

REVIVAL

IN MIAMI

There is a town I know whose streets were filled with *yiddishkeit*, where Yiddish culture and *bubbe mayses* flowed like wine. A place where Yiddish folksingers lined up along the ocean singing *Bay Mir Bistu Sheyn, Mine Yiddishe Mame, Yidl Mitn Fidl*, and *Oyfn Pripitchek*. They performed for all who cared to listen, singing their *yiddishe lider* from the heart.

Yiddish shows ran several times per day at several local theaters, packed with audiences lined up for blocks, paying twenty-five or fifty cents to watch the best of Molly Picon and to see Yiddish vaudeville and theater. Long before Dr. Ruth and Dr. Laura, Howard Stern or Imus in the morning, Yiddish radio streamed through the airways providing advice to greenhorns, playing Yiddish swing, Klezmer, and, of course, the notorious radio dramas—Yiddish matzo operas.

This town blossomed with lectures from Yiddish literary figures, political activity, and cultural performances conducted in Yiddish, under the auspices of the Arbeter Ring/Workmen's Circle, the YIVO Institute for Jewish Research, the Miami Beach Jewish Cultural Center, and other groups. Before Joe's Stone Crabs came to Washington Avenue, there was a Yiddish *shule* teaching the *mameloshen* to young people. Before it became the land of the "beautiful people," the *yiddisher filosopher* broadcast on Yiddish radio.

Where is this town? Like the ancient Scottish folktale about a place that vanishes, only to reappear once every one hundred years to celebrate its history and culture, Miami Beach of the 1920s to mid-1980s relives the story of Brigadoon. Arising from the ashes of the Holocaust, Yiddish culture picked up the pieces, creating a tropical oasis suffused in *yiddishkeit* in what is now called South Beach. It blossomed for years, taking its precious legacy from the uncertain future of czarist pogroms to the sweatshops of the Lower East Side to the azure skies and turquoise waters of South Beach.

Its passing was not subtle. An embarrassment to the tourist-hungry Art Deco crowd, buildings were allowed to decay and neon lights and pastel latex replaced the Yiddish communal scene to further the Art Deco revival and the corporatization of Miami Beach. Yet Isaac Bashevis Singer, who spent his final days here, was right when he declared that Yiddish culture has not seen its final days. It may not come from the *shtetlekh* of Eastern Europe, or be varnished with the taste and smells of *di alte heym*, the old country. But as long as there are people to enjoy and continue playing Klezmer, as long as Yiddish is still being learned by young people,

and long as people understand that the best way to move forward as a people is to grasp firmly on one's roots, one's heritage, and one's culture, Yiddish culture has a future. It is this belief that led to the founding of the Dora Teitelboim Center for Yiddish Culture in Miami.

The center was founded by the internationally renowned Yiddish poet Dora Teitelboim. Ms. Teitelboim was the author of a dozen highly acclaimed volumes of poetry that were translated into more than a dozen languages. Her fiery social motifs sang and wept joys and sorrows, hope and disappointment, and above all, the love of humankind. And she practiced what she advocated by constantly giving of herself through worldwide lectures on Yiddish poetry and Jewish culture, and by establishing a reputation as the poet for whom "the wind itself speaks Yiddish." Ms. Teitelboim's dream was to promote Yiddish poetry and prose to a new generation of Americans by making Yiddish works more accessible to the American public, thereby cultivating a new harvest of Yiddish educators, writers, speakers, and performers. And where else to establish ourselves, but on the tropical shores of Yiddish's American Mecca?

The center's mission is fourfold: First, to translate and publish the best of Yiddish literature written by Yiddish writers, scholars, and poets the world over and circulate them at reduced costs to Jewish cultural institutions, schools, and organizations. Because the traditions, history, and wisdom of Jewish literature are often lost on the younger generations, many of whom no longer speak or write Yiddish, the explicit goal of the center is to open a new world to children by heightening their awareness of the rich cultural legacy of their forefathers and contemporaries.

Second, to create new Yiddish *and* English fiction, the center runs an Annual International Jewish Cultural Writing Contest, awarding cash prizes to winners, while also providing rising stars in the literary world with their first international exposure by publishing their pieces in leading Jewish periodicals.

Third, to promote Jewish culture in all its rich texture and beauty by holding lectures and seminars, using its published educational and cultural works to further the understanding of Jewish history and tradition. Additionally, the center produces documentary films. The first documentary currently in production focuses on the surviving remnants of Eastern Europe Jews, who remained in their homeland throughout the Holocaust and continue to live there today.

And finally, to keep the Yiddish lights burning, the center teaches Yiddish—live and online—on both a conversational and college level.

Since formally establishing its base of operations in South Florida, the center has carried on the dream of its namesake through the publishing of seven highly acclaimed books of Yiddish poetry and prose in translation including *All My Yester-days Were Steps, The Last Lullaby, The Little House, The Four Butterflies, The Witness Trees, The New Country,* and *The Jewish Book of Fables.* Additionally, seven books are planned for the coming years, including two children's bilingual Yiddish-English picture books (the first to be printed in America in fifty years), a book of short stories, a volume of Yiddish poetry for children, a historical novel, a collection of poetry by America's Yiddish rebel poets, and more.

Additionally, to carry out its mission of bringing Jewish culture to younger generations, the center runs a myriad of cultural programs. Annually the center presents the Winter Evening of the Arts, a celebration of Yiddish culture through a mélange of visual art, music, poetry, and drama in Yiddish and English at a prominent South Beach venue. Moreover major cultural events are produced, such as the nationally acclaimed "Creative Defiance and the Holocaust," a commemoration of the artists, writers, and poets who challenged Nazi tyranny through performances of a Terezin opera, poetry readings, children's educational events, art exhibits, and performance art. The Center also runs "Common Threads, Stories from Many Cultures," a children's program that celebrates all the cultures that live in South Florida with performance art, storytelling, dancing, and music demonstrating the

FIGURE 2. *Professor Mindelle Wajsman teaching Yiddish II at Florida International University, simultaneously live and online. Courtesy Dora Teitelboim Center for Yiddish Culture.*

FIGURE 3. *Cover of record album celebrating Miami's Yiddish theater scene, depicting the long-running Yiddish theater on Miami Beach's Washington Avenue, the Cinema Theatre. Courtesy Jewish Museum of Florida.*

FIGURE 4. *Fourth Annual Winter Evening of the Yiddish Arts featuring a Klezmer performance by Henry Sapoznik, Mark Rubin, and Cookie Segelstein at Temple Beth Sholom. Courtesy Dora Teitelboim Center for Yiddish Culture.*

beauty of the multicultural landscape and the universal themes and connecting strands that link us all through the lens of a Yiddish fable, a Haitian folktale, and a Ciboney (native Cuban) tale.

For more than one thousand years Yiddish was the language of the Jewish troubadour, poet, sweatshop toiler, revolutionary, and dreamer. For Jews coming to America, it was the Yiddish writers with the noise of the sweatshop in their ears, and the stench of the tenements in their nostrils, who became the new American poets, writers of tales, journalists, and pamphleteers. Writers like the great Sholem Aleichem (whose epitaph declared that his "tales in Yiddish were written for the common man and women") wrote about social wrongs, the fight against injustice, and the betterment of life, with poignancy, tenderness, humor, and love, weaving a living web of Jewish culture from city to city across America.

Yiddish became the vehicle of secular Jewish life giving solid footing to a people without their own territory. The Yiddish language and Yiddish literature became the common ground by which an increasingly secularized Jewishness could achieve a cohesion that had seemed anomalous to the non-Jewish world. Jews could travel the world over, with nothing but the *mameloshen* on their tongue and get along quite well. As the group Bnoth Agudath Israel stated so eloquently in 1937, Yiddish is a language created by Jews in the Diaspora that became the expression of the Jewish soul, of Jewish longing and aspiration, of Jewish joy and suffering.

Of course, fewer and fewer Yiddish readers and writers remain because the language, as Nobel Laureate Isaac Bashevis Singer once explained, was itself a victim; it did not die a natural death, but was murdered. Many of the best and brightest Yiddish writers and poets perished in the concentration camps, and most of those who died in the Holocaust spoke Yiddish.

But Yiddish did not die. In fact, in the opening years of the twenty-first century, Yiddish literature and teaching is experiencing a new renaissance: Universities are establishing Yiddish programs and postgraduate Yiddish chairs in increasing numbers, and Yiddish scholarship is being taken up by new generations of students. Yiddish festivals are popping up internationally and growing numbers of young people are interested in learning about Yiddish culture. This growing thirst for Yiddish programming is being driven by younger people who are seriously reflecting on the significance of Yiddish in their lives in an effort to recapture a vital aspect of what it means to be a Jew.

The Dora Teitelboim Center has a multifaceted role to play in this revitalization of the Yiddish language. An important aspect of the center's work is Yiddish education through classes, as well as utilizing the tremendous wealth of Yiddish speakers in South Florida to act as mentors for the next generation, connecting the older population and snowbirds with fledgling Yiddishists. Furthermore, by expanding book publishing to include more academically useful books for Yiddish

FIGURE 5. Der Yiddisher Mikado at Temple Sinai of North Dade. Courtesy Dora Teitelboim Center for Yiddish Culture.

FIGURE 6. *Avi Hoffman performing Menasha Skolnick, the famous Yiddish comic, at Winter Evening of the Yiddish Arts. Courtesy Dora Teitelboim Center for Yiddish Culture.*

FIGURE 7. *Performance of the* Emperor of Atlantis, *an opera written in Terezin, as part of the Center's Creative Defiance and the Holocaust program. Courtesy Dora Teitelboim Center for Yiddish Culture*

educational programs and by producing more bilingual Yiddish/English books, the center hopes to aid in fostering a balanced Jewish education in important works of Yiddish fiction.

The center's lecture series on the history and culture of Judaism in general and Yiddish in particular has featured some of the leading scholars and performers in the world including Itche Goldberg on Itzik Manger, Miriam Hoffman on Yiddish theater, Henry Sapoznik on Yiddish radio, Michael Wex on Yiddish humor, Troim Handler on Yiddish poetry, Curt Leviant on Sholem Aleichem and many more.

The center's cultural activities, from musical events to sponsoring theatrical performances has invigorated and reaffirmed South Florida's connection with *yiddishkeit*. Programs have included such internationally acclaimed performances and performers as Adrienne Cooper and the Klezmatics, the Southeast debut of the powerful Holocaust opera *Emperor of Atlantis* in conjunction with the Florida International University School of Music, Jerry Silverman performing rare Holocaust songs in sixteen different languages, Henry Sapoznik and his band performing the best in Klezmer music, the Gilbert and Sullivan Yiddish Opera performing *Der Yiddisher Mikado* and a variety of local readers reading the hidden gems of Yiddish poetry.

The Center's Major Projects

Rather than focus on the preservation of Yiddish as an artifact, the center works to keep Yiddish alive and thriving by attracting new generations of Americans to discover the value of Yiddish literature, both in the original mother tongue and in translation, to inspire new Yiddish scholarship, and to help foster a revival of Jewish culture through everything we do. For what makes a culture sacred and eternal is its language, customs, and traditions carried forward by its practitioners. By learning the songs and poems of our ancestors in *their* language, we learn who we are as a people, in all our diversity and beauty, while finding direction for our culture into the future.

YIDDISH TRANSLATION AND BOOK PRODUCTION

One of the most important missions that the center undertakes is translating the works of Yiddish writers, scholars, and poets into English, producing English and bilingual English/Yiddish books. The goal is to make accessible to both children and adults important pieces of literature heretofore lost on American readers, while encouraging young people to learn Yiddish and appreciate Jewish literature in the original *mameloshen*. And toward this end, children's publishing is the most important focus. A treasure chest exists of Yiddish poems, fables, and lullabies that have mostly remained unread because they were published in just a handful of copies, in Yiddish, and have long since gone out of print. Some of the titles currently in production include a book of children's short stories, a collection of Yiddish poetry, *A Children's Garden of Yiddish Verse* and several picture books — many in Yiddish and English with Yiddish lessons and CDs.

Historical novels have also played an important role in Yiddish literature and the renowned author, Joseph Opatochu, was the reigning *zeyde* of historical fiction. The center is currently translating his *Bar Kokhba* (The last revolt).

MAJOR CULTURAL EVENTS

From time to time, the center launches major events, exhibits, and festivals that provide multisensory appreciation of Jewish history, culture, philosophy, and Jewish secular movements in America. Currently being planned is an exhibit that begins in Miami and is expected to tour the country, "Celebrating Miami's Yiddish Past," which will re-create the various living spaces of Yiddish culture in Miami from the beach to the hotels along Ocean Drive in what is now South Beach to the delis where Yiddish readings and *koffeeklotching* took place, through photography, video, music, and more.

YIDDISH FOR YOUTH INITIATIVE

The goal of establishing the Yiddish for Youth Initiative is to foster a rebirth of Yiddish culture, not as a step backward to the shtetl days, but as a step forward by bringing all Jewish traditions, songs, and poetry to students to rekindle the lamp of *Yiddishkeit*. The mission of the project is to reinspire younger Jews to learn the Yiddish language, its literature, traditions, and music through specially targeted educational programs, cultural activities, and initiatives to help foster Yiddish home learning once again. The key to Yiddish's continuance is that it once again becomes a language spoken in the home and the depth of its cultural reach is available in a growing number of accessible mediums.

For more than seventy years, the United States and Canada have had active Yiddish Schools that ran anywhere from once a week to five days a week. The *shules*, as they were called, taught the Yiddish language, held history and culture classes, developed Yiddish choruses, and inspired Jewish continuance on a visceral level. The Yiddish *shule* movement and curriculum are helpful models to promote well-rounded educational initiatives as well as continuing education for young adults.

The center plans on launching Yiddish classes and clubs at various Hebrew day schools to create an environment for Yiddish learning. The goal is to establish cultural programs, such as Klezmer workshops, as well as exposure to poetry and literature, to inspire an interest in Yiddish culture. The center will create a Yiddish survival kit of books, flashcards, video, children's stories, practice lessons, and exercises to create a Yiddish-language environment in the home. Coupled with this package is planned a ten-week intensive Yiddish educational program for families to use the materials to teach basic Yiddish lessons, learn Yiddish songs, poetry, and celebrate the holidays.

Yiddish culture will never be what it once was, but for tens of thousands of people wishing to connect with a dimension of their heritage without equivalent, Yiddish is increasingly becoming part of the journey. They understand that if efforts to sustain and restore Yiddish culture are not taken now, an important part of the Jewish cultural spectrum will be lost forever. Whether to tap into an important corridor of Jewish history or connect with the language of their *bubbes* and *zeydes*, a growing number of South Florida's Jewish population are utilizing the technology of the present to create a future for a culture that was once thought to be long dead. And as interest grows among our youth, Yiddish culture is being reborn for new generations.

CONTRIBUTOR BIOGRAPHIES

HENRY ABRAMSON is associate professor of history and Judaic Studies at Florida Atlantic University. He is the curator of the critically acclaimed exhibit at the Jewish Museum of Florida, "The Art of Hatred: Images of Intolerance in Florida Culture" (catalogue published under the same title in 2001). He is also the author of a monograph on the history of the Jews of Ukraine (Harvard University Press, 1999) and several scholarly articles on the history of anti-Semitism.

ZEV BEN BEITCHMAN has a Psy.D. in clinical psychology. He is a graduate of the WUJS Institute in Arad, Israel. Dr. Beitchman also has a certificate in Jewish Studies from the Florence Melton School. He has traveled extensively to Jewish sites throughout the world.

STEPHEN BENZ is the author of *Guatemalan Journey* (University of Texas Press, 1996), *Teaching and Testimony / Rigoberta Menchu* (State University of New York Press, 1996), and *Green Dreams* (Lonely Planet, 1998). He has also written articles for several magazines and journals. He is especially interested in cross-cultural and environmental issues. Formerly a professor of English, Dr. Benz has twice been awarded Fulbright fellowships, first in Guatemala (1988–90) and later in Moldova (1999).

LINDA BROCKMAN is a former reporter/writer for the *Jewish Star Times* and *Miami Herald*. She has been writing about the South Florida Jewish community for fourteen years.

ANNETTE B. FROMM is a folklorist and museum specialist. Her doctoral dissertation is on the Jewish community of Ioannina, Greece. Over the past twenty-five years she has worked in a number of museums. Dr. Fromm has published articles on immigrant-ethnic groups in America, Jews in Greece, Greek folklore, Native Americans in museums, multicultural museums, and folk art. She has taught many workshops on folklore and folklife, Sephardic Jewry, American ethnicity, and multiculturalism in museums. She is currently manager of the Deering Estate at Cutler.

JOANIE GLICKSTEIN has been a proud and active member of the National Council of Jewish Women (NCJW) for the past twenty-five years. Ms. Glickstein's involvement in the organization began in Worcester, Massachusetts, where she joined the local section to meet women her age soon after moving to the area. She served as co-president of the Worcester Section from 1982 to 1985, moved to Miami Beach in 1985 and helped to found the Beach/Bayside Branch of Greater Miami Section. She served as president of the Greater Miami Section from 2000 to 2003 and has recently been appointed as a national commissioner by NCJW National President Marsha Atkind.

HENRY A. GREEN, professor of religious studies and sociology in Miami, is the founding director of the Jewish Museum of Florida, and the former director of Judaic and Sephardic Studies Programs at the University of Miami in Coral Gables, Florida. He has published extensively on Florida and American Jewry. A frequent visitor to Israel, he serves as a consultant to national Jewish and Israeli organizations and leads academic missions. Dr. Green has been a visiting fellow at the Hebrew University of Jerusalem, Oxford University, and the University of Toronto. He also serves as the U.S. national chair of the Home Instruction for Parents of Preschool Youngsters Program (HIPPY), a literacy and school readiness program for at-risk children and families.

ANDREA GREENBAUM is assistant professor of English at Barry University. She is the author of *Insurrections: Approaches to Resistance in Composition Studies* (State University of New York Press, 2001) and *The Emancipatory Movements: The Rhetoric of Possibility* (State University of New York Press, 2002). Her articles and reviews have appeared in *Humor: The International Journal of Humor, American Studies, Composition Studies, Writing on the Edge, JAC, The Journal of Men's Studies, Composition Forum, Studies in American Jewish Fiction, Teaching English in the Two-Year College, Hypatia, Femspec,* and *Film and History.* She is currently working on a book with Deborah Holdstein, *Judaic Perspectives in Composition* (Hampton Press).

GARY MONROE is professor of art at Daytona Beach Community College. He is a native of Miami Beach and received a master's degree in the fine arts from the University of Colorado at Boulder in 1977. Since then he has documented the old-world culture of Miami's South Beach, traveled throughout Haiti, and looked at tourism across Florida. Mr. Monroe has photographed at Cassadaga; this work resulted in *Cassadaga: The South's Oldest Spiritualist Community* (University Press of Florida, 2000). Mr. Monroe has received grants from the National Endowment for the Arts, Florida Department of State's Division of Cultural Affairs, Florida Humanities Council, and the Fulbright Foundation to support his photography. His longtime interest in "outsider" and vernacular art resulted in his books *The Highwaymen / Florida's African-American Landscape Painters* (University Press of Florida, 2001) and *Extraordinary Interpretations: Florida's Self-taught Artists* (University Press of Florida, 2003). He is a lecturer for the Florida Humanities Council's Speakers Bureau. He lives in DeLand, Florida.

JACK MOORE was emeritus professor of English at the University of South Florida, where he chaired the American Studies department and was graduate director of English. Among his books on aspects of American culture are *Skinheads: Shaved for Battle* (Bowling Green State University Press, 1993) and *Joe DiMaggio: The Yankee Clipper* (Greenwood Press, 1987). His fiction has appeared in *Esquire* and *The Long Story.* He has twice been a Fulbright Scholar and was a Fulbright Senior Specialist in American Studies when he passed away in July 2003.

SUSAN NEIMAND is the Director of Beth David Gordon Day School. She has a doctorate in curriculum and instruction and a master's degree in elementary education from Florida International University. Dr. Neimand has been an outstanding educator involved in Jewish education for more than twenty years in South Florida.

JOEL SAXE, a South Florida native, has been documenting Yiddish culture and Jewish immigrant radicalism on Miami Beach and in New York. Saxe produced a series of documentaries from this work while also writing his doctoral dissertation, an ethnography of Yiddish culture on South Beach. Saxe teaches video and oral history at various colleges in Western Massachusetts including Hampshire College, the University of Massachusetts–Amherst, and Mount Holyoke College.

IRA SHESKIN is associate professor of geography and regional studies and a fellow in the Sue and Leonard Miller Center for Contemporary Judaic Studies at the University of Miami. He has completed major demographic studies for more than twenty-five Jewish Federations throughout the country. He is currently working on demographic studies for the Jewish Federation in Tucson, Arizona; Bergen, New Jersey; Rhode Island; Jacksonville; and Washington, D.C. His numerous publications include *Survey Research for Geographers* and *How Jewish Communities Differ.*

DAVID WEINTRAUB is the executive director of the Dora Teitelboim Center for Yiddish Culture. Mr. Weintraub has had a multifaceted career as a labor organizer, a civil rights attorney, and Jewish cultural organizer. As the cofounder of the Center for Yiddish Culture he has produced cultural and arts programming from coast to coast, edited nearly a dozen books on Yiddish culture and literature, and is currently finishing a screenplay about the Holocaust. He is also a freelance writer and political activist and is completing work on a collection of political essays, several children's books, and his own short stories.

STEVEN J. WHITFIELD holds the Max Richter Chair in American Civilization at Brandeis University, where he has also served as chairperson of the Department of American Studies. He has taught as a Fulbright visiting professor at the Hebrew University of Jerusalem and at the Catholic University of Leuven, Belgium, and has twice served as visiting professor at the Sorbonne. Professor Whitfield is the author of eight books, of which the most recent is *In Search of American Jewish Culture* (University Press of New England, 1999; paperback edition, 2001).

MARCIA KERSTEIN ZERIVITZ is founding executive director of the Jewish Museum of Florida and has been a leader in the organized Florida Jewish community for more than forty years; she has specifically been involved with Florida Jewish history for the past seventeen years. Beginning in 1985, Marcia traveled around Florida to research and retrieve the state's Jewish history. Working with volunteers in thirteen communities, she created a collection and a storyline of Jewish life in Florida and helped develop the MOSAIC exhibit that traveled to thirteen cities from 1990 to 1994. Under her direction, this project evolved into a permanent Jewish museum on South Beach.

INDEX

Illustrations are indicated by page numbers in boldface.